Gabon
São Tomé and Príncipe
THE BRADT TRAVEL GUIDE

THE BRADT STORY

The first Bradt travel guide was written in 1974 by George and Hilary Bradt on a river barge floating down a tributary of the Amazon. In the 1980s and '90s the focus shifted away from hiking to broader-based guides covering new destinations – usually the first to be published on those places. In the 21st century Bradt continues to publish these ground-breaking guides, along with guides to established holiday destinations, incorporating in-depth information on culture and natural history alongside the nuts and bolts of where to stay and what to see.

Bradt authors support responsible travel, with advice not only on minimum impact but also on how to give something back through local charities. Thus a true synergy is achieved between the traveller and local communities.

* * *

Gabon jumped into my consciousness in the late 1990s when a tour operator friend telephoned in a state of euphoria. 'I've just done a recce to Gabon,' he said, 'and it's fabulous! You must do a guidebook!' Derek is a keen birdwatcher and was particularly impressed with the number of West African rarities he was able to spot, but he also enthused about the wildlife in general, the untouched rainforest coming right down to the beach, the lack of tourist hordes, and the welcoming people. All we needed was an author...

Happy travelling!

Hilary Bradt

23 High Street, Chalfont St Peter, Bucks SL9 9QE, England
Tel: 01753 893444; fax: 01753 892333
Email: info@bradtguides.com
www.bradtguides.com

Gabon
São Tomé and Príncipe
THE BRADT TRAVEL GUIDE

Sophie Warne

Bradt Travel Guides Ltd, UK
The Globe Pequot Press Inc, USA

First published in 2003, Reprinted with amendments January 2007
Bradt Travel Guides Ltd
23 High Street, Chalfont St Peter, Bucks SL9 9QE, England
www.bradt-travelguides.com
Published in the USA by The Globe Pequot Press Inc, 246 Goose Lane,
PO Box 480, Guilford, Connecticut 06437-0480

Text copyright © 2003 Sophie Warne
Maps copyright © 2003 Bradt Travel Guides Ltd
Photographs copyright © 2003 Individual photographers

The author and publishers have made every effort to ensure the accuracy of the
information in this book at the time of going to press. However, they cannot accept any
responsibility for any loss, injury or inconvenience resulting from the use of information
contained in this guide.

All rights reserved. No part of this publication may be reproduced, stored in a retrieval
system, or transmitted in any form or by any means, electronic, mechanical, photocopying,
recording or otherwise without the prior consent of the publishers.
Requests for permission should be addressed to Bradt Travel Guides Ltd,
23 High Street, Chalfont St Peter, Bucks SL9 9QE in the UK;
or to The Globe Pequot Press Inc,
246 Goose Lane, PO Box 480, Guilford, Connecticut 06437-0480
in North and South America.

British Library Cataloguing in Publication Data
A catalogue record for this book is available from the British Library

ISBN 1 84162 073 4

Photographs
Front cover Male mandrill, *Papio sphinx* (NHPA/Kevin Schafer)
Text David Harwood (DH), Troy Inman (TI), Paul Miles (PM), Martine Papin (MP),
Jean Trolez (JT), Dr Lee White (LW)

Illustrations Annabel Milne, Carole Vincer
Maps Steve Munns

Typeset from the author's disc by Wakewing
Printed and bound in Italy by Legoprint SpA, Trento

Author

Sophie Warne has written guidebooks and travel pieces on a number of different destinations, including Thailand, Iceland, Athens and Istanbul, but when she is travelling purely for pleasure her destination is more often than not in Africa. Her work has been published in newspapers and magazines including *The Times* and *Wanderlust*.

FEEDBACK REQUEST

Every effort has been made to ensure that the details contained within this book are as accurate and up to date as possible. Inevitably, however, things move on. Any information regarding such changes, or relating to your experiences in Gabon – good or bad – would be very gratefully received. Such feedback is priceless when compiling further editions, and in ensuring pleasant stays for future visitors.
Happy holidays!

Bradt Travel Guides Ltd, 23 High St, Chalfont St Peter, Bucks, SL9 9QE
Tel: 01753 893444; fax: 01753 892333
Email: info@bradtguides.com
www.bradtguides.com

Contents

Acknowledgements

I've been really looking forward to writing the acknowledgements for this guide. I'm indebted to so many people who have helped me with research and been so welcoming at the same time. Special thanks go to Bryan Curran (for his role as consultant and his good company) and Patrice Pasquier at Mistral Voyages (for tirelessly helping with my questions). I am enormously grateful to Patrice Christy and Lee White (WCS) for generously sharing their knowledge. The same goes for the rest of the friendly WCS crew, including Kate, Steve, Chris, Malcolm and Peter Ragg – and Muriel Vives (ECOFAC).

I would like to thank my cousin, Simon Trépanier, for excellent preparatory advice and for putting me in touch with Marc Ona Essangui, whom I always look forward to seeing in Libreville. It was also a pleasure spending time with my Libreville neighbours, Martine and Jacky Papin, both in and out of the water. The Mikongo-Ololo team – Nerissa, Julian, Jonathan, Donald, Guy, Troy Inman and James – have been great, from start to finish. Thanks to Ahab, Mireille, Piet and Isabelle for good laughs at Ye Tsanou, and Rombout Swanbourne of Operation Loango for making my visit possible. I am indebted to Julian and Justin at Discovery Initiatives; Nick Anstead and Mike J Fox at Explore Worldwide; and Air Gabon. Thanks also to the efforts of Emmanuel de la Barthe, Dianne Reilly and Tricia Hayne; without their generous assistance, the guide wouldn't have been possible.

Other invaluable friends and helping hands along the way include Jean-Pierre Bayé, Jean Bourgeais, Frederic Jeammes, Martin Fanguinoveny, Olivier Dosimont, Jean Philippe Biteau, Brigitte Tripodi, Vincent Deschaumes and Patrick Menesson. Olivier Bourry and Kara Gaye kindly sent me update emails after I'd returned home. Hello and thanks to my impromptu guides, Leo Nguema and Pacôme Boucka, whom I met on the road to Mayumba. Cheers to all the friendly faces at ASF, especially Christian Mbinda, Guy-Philippe Sounguet and François Lamoo Boussamba. I would also like to say thanks to Christian at the Lopé Hotel and to all the staff at the Tropicana, especially Eric. Thanks must also go to Justin, who cheerfully took me wherever I needed to go in Libreville.

As for the photographs, David Harwood gallantly came to my rescue hours before I left Libreville, and Troy has enthusiastically shown his support from the word go. Mr Trolez was also very generous with his photos.

Last but not least, STP. Luis and Bibi are exemplary travel agents and guides. Thank you also to Pedro Nobre, Luis Mario and Stefan Coco at

ECOFAC for some amazing walking, and to Paul Miles, who graciously allowed himself to be badgered into handing over his pics! Thanks must also go to Carlos Villa Nova at Mistral Voyages, to the team at Bom Bom Island, and to Tjerk Hagemeijer, who kindly lent me his linguistic expertise.

Finally, it's only right that I finish with those special people on the home front – who've allowed me to talk of little else for the past nine months – especially Mins, Elle, Jo, Harriet, Sarah, Will, Mum and Dad (for their unqualified support again), and, above all, Stephen, my inspiration.

LIST OF MAPS

Introduction

When I told people I was going to be writing a guide to Gabon and STP, the most common reaction was one of surprise. Almost nobody knew where either country was, and even fewer could think of a reason for going. (Later, I was gobsmacked to hear through the family grapevine that my French Canadian cousin – whom I'd met twice, before the age of 12 – had just spent two years in Libreville working for the UN.) It is both comforting and irresistible to know that there are still places stable enough to avoid coverage in the world press, yet (almost) unknown to tourists. Mary Kingsley was probably the first tourist in Gabon, albeit one motivated by keen scientific interests. In recent times tour operators have brought a trickle of international tourists wildlife-watching at Lopé, and rainforest trekking on the islands of STP. This has largely been the extent of the tourist trail. Foreign appreciation of Gabon and STP has been predominantly confined to expats. Independent travellers – not counting the American Peace Corps volunteers who travel around the region in their time off – are a rarity. Certainly I never met one, and the reaction of many people I met on the road suggested they hadn't either.

Central Africa has over 80% of the total rainforests on the African continent and 25% of the world's rainforests in a region often referred to as the Congo Basin. This Basin extends into Gabon, Cameroon, Equatorial Guinea, Republic of Congo, Central African Republic, Democratic Republic of Congo, Rwanda, and Burundi. Over 70% of Gabon is covered in dense rainforest, and the remainder is savanna and coastline, and for each of these habitats Gabon has the wildlife to match. This is a country where gorillas and elephants can be caught on camera on the same stretch of beach.

Just before this guide went to press, President Bongo announced the creation of a national park network in Gabon, so now 10% of the country is protected. This is fantastic news, not just for the future of Central Africa but for the future of tourism. With national parks in place, tourist infrastructures will follow, enabling visitors to reach places of enormous environmental value that were previously virtually inaccessible. The involvement of environmental organisations WCS, ECOFAC and WWF means that wildlife tourism – from gorilla and elephant trekking to whale watching and turtle observation – will be conducted alongside precious research. The money generated by tourism will feed back into conservation and research.

It's the same story in STP. An estimated 74% of the country is covered by rainforest, the boundaries of which more or less correspond to those of Obo

National Park. Once again, ECOFAC are active here, clearing trekking trails in the forest interior and promoting turtle protection on its beaches, all good stuff for ecotourism.

True, getting to both Gabon and STP is expensive, and getting understood and getting around can be hard work, but the rewards are great. The Saotomeans are very welcoming and communicative with visitors, even ones who don't speak Portuguese, and there's always a cheap way of getting where you want to go if you have the time to travel as the locals do. Similarly, as my cousin enthused about Gabon, the uncertainty and dust that comes from travel by taxis-brousse is part of appreciating the country as it is, with and not separate from its people. The Gabonese travel around a lot to see friends and family, particularly in the holidays, and the atmosphere is invariably fun and friendly. Plus, the time and effort of getting around is an incentive to spend sufficient time in each place, which is, of course, infinitely more rewarding than darting about, ticking places off some imaginary list.

get closer

As the world's leading specialist in small-group adventure travel, we offer the most diverse range of trips to more than 100 countries around the world, including 32 countries in Africa.

Africa offers some of the best game viewing on earth, including a rare opportunity to track the Lowland Gorillas of Gabon. Our unique safari ventures deep into Gabon centered for 6 nights in the Lopé Wildlife Reserve, where we track on foot, through pristine equatorial rainforest, in search of Western Lowland Gorillas.

We also offer other trips in Africa - from the majestic Basotho people of the Southern Highlands, to the gentle Nubians of Sudan; from the snows of 'Kili' to the historic wonders of Ethiopia.

Call for a brochure on 01252 760 100
or visit www.exploreworldwide.com

EXPLORE
worldwide

Part One

Gabon:
General Information

GABON AT A GLANCE

Location West coast of Central Africa
Capital Libreville
Size 267,670km^2 (103,347 square miles)
Population 1.2 million
President Omar Bongo
Languages French (official language) and 40 living African languages
Religion Christian (60%), Animist and Muslim
Currency CFA franc
Time GMT +1
Climate Tropical; always hot, humid
Border countries Republic of the Congo, Cameroon and Equatorial Guinea
Flag Horizontally striped green-yellow-blue
Main towns Franceville and Port Gentil
Ethnic divisions Gabon has some 40 or so Bantu tribes, including the Fang, Eshira, Bapounou and Bateké. Other Africans and Europeans (154,000, including 10,700 French).
Type of government Republic; multiparty presidential regime
Independence August 17 1960 (from France)
International telephone code 241
GDP purchasing power parity 6.7 billion dollars (2001 est)
Inflation 1.5%
Internet country code .ga
Electrical voltage 220v

Background and History

FACTS AND FIGURES
Location
Gabon straddles the Equator on the west coast of Central Africa. Its capital, Libreville, has a latitude of 0°25' north. Bordering Gabon to the north are Equatorial Guinea and Cameroon, to the east and south is the Congo, and to the west is the Atlantic Ocean.

Size
Gabon covers an area of 267,670km^2 (103,347 square miles). To put this in context, Gabon could fit into the USA 35 times, into France twice and into Zimbabwe once.

Population
The estimated population of Gabon is 1.2 million. The population density equals 4.5 people per km^2. Gabon is one of Africa's most urbanised countries. Almost 80% of the population is urban. The capital, Libreville, is home to some 450,000 people. Other areas of dense population are Port Gentil, Franceville and Woleu-Ntem. By comparison, the country's interior is little populated. Within Africa in particular, Gabon enjoys its image as a country of peace, economic growth and underpopulation, which explains why it attracts so many immigrants from Equatorial Guinea, Benin, Cameroon, Senegal and Mali. There are also some 10,700 French expats living in Gabon. Gabon has a very young population. More than 45% of the total population is under 16 years old, and life expectancy at birth is 53 years. Gabon has a low birth rate, and infant mortality is high, at 95 deaths per 1,000 live births (2001 estimate).

Government
Since Gabon achieved independence from France in 1960, it has, for the most part, enjoyed political stability. From the death of the first president in 1967 up until 1990, Gabon was a one-party state under the rule of Omar Bongo and his Parti Démocratique Gabonaise (PDG). The first multi-party elections were held in 1991, and Bongo and the PDG were returned to power with an overwhelming majority. Bongo remains president to this day. Beneath him there is a highly decentralised administrative system with many levels of authority. The country is divided into nine provinces, or administrative districts: Estuaire, Middle Ogooué, Ngounié, Coastal Ogooué, Nyanga,

3

Woleu-Ntem, Ogooué-Ivindo, Haut-Ogooué and Ogooué-Lolo. Each province is split into departments, each department into districts and communes, each district into cantons, and finally at the lowest level there is a multitude of villages.

Economy

A comparatively small population, abundant natural resources (oil, timber, manganese) and foreign private investment have combined to make Gabon the envy of its neighbours. Gabon holds the third place in Africa in terms of average annual revenue per inhabitant (US$4,170), which stands at about three times that of most nations in sub-Saharan Africa. Gabon even has the world's highest per capita consumption of champagne. But the picture is not rosy for everyone. In spite of its seemingly enviable combination of riches and manageable population growth, Gabon's economy is not without its problems. Libreville is as expensive as any leading city in the West, yet only a tiny proportion of the population can afford the inflated prices. With a third of its Gross Domestic Product coming from oil, Gabon is at the mercy of fluctuations in oil prices, and is now faced with the reality of oil supplies running out.

The resulting paradox is that a relatively wealthy country is saddled with an enormous debt that it finds itself unable to shift. According to the World Bank, Gabon's foreign debt stood at US$3.3 million, or US$2,750 per inhabitant, in 2002. Gabon's revenues and resources mean it does not qualify for the international aid granted to its poorer neighbours. As a result 40–45% of revenue that should be channeled into education and health is instead immediately swallowed in debt repayment. Poor fiscal management, government overspending on off-budget items, delayed privatisation and administrative reform are all on the government agenda. Similarly, the crucial task of generating non-oil-related revenue and reducing the reliance on imported produce means other areas – such as agriculture, fishing, forestry and tourism – are being reassessed.

Languages and peoples

The official language in Gabon is French – this is the language used by the government, the media and between different tribes. Even people speaking in an African language use some French words, such as the days of the week. There are over 40 living African languages listed for Gabon, although the number of people speaking some of these languages is not always very large. The vast majority of Gabon's different ethnic groups is of Bantu origin, and includes the following major groupings: the Fang, the Eshira, the Mbede, the Myéné and the Okandé. The Fang – numerically the largest – are mostly concentrated in Woleu-Ntem, but are also found in Ogooué-Ivindo, Middle Ogooué and the estuary. For the most part, the Eshira are found in the south of Gabon, the Mbede in the southeast, the Myéné in the Coastal Ogooué, and the Okandé in the country's interior. The most important of the remaining Bantu groups are the Bandjabi, the Bapounou, the Batéké and the Mérié.

Gabon is becoming an increasingly integrated population, but set apart by their appearance and their customs are the Pygmies (see box page 7).

Religion
Roughly 60% of the population is Christian, and of those most are Roman Catholics. The rest of the population is Animist or Muslim.

Currency
The unit of currency in Gabon is the CFA franc, which originally stood for Colonies Francais d'Afrique but has long since been changed to Communauté Financiaire Africaine. The CFA franc is issued by the Banque des Etats de l'Afrique Centrale (Bank of Central African States) and is the currency in the following countries: Gabon, Cameroon, Chad, Equatorial Guinea, Congo and the Central African Republic. One CFA divides into 100 centimes. Notes come in denominations of 10,000, 5,000, 2,000, 1,000 and 500CFA. The CFA has been tied to the French franc at a guaranteed rate since the 1940s, and is now fixed to the euro at a rate of 1 euro to 655.957CFA. The tie is still guaranteed by the French Treasury, but since France converted to the new European currency changes now have to be approved by the European Central Bank in Brussels. As at March 2002, the rate of exchange for 1US$ was 739.98CFA.

Time zone
The time in Gabon is one hour ahead of GMT.

Topography
Gabon's coast stretches for 855km (531 miles), so it is hardly surprising that it is not uniform. Just by looking at a map, you can see how craggy it is to the north of Cape Lopez, while to the south the coastline becomes much smoother, straighter and sandier. At its deepest, the coastal region encroaches some 200km (125 miles) inland. In parts it is very swampy and the only way to get around is by *pirogue*.

Inland from the low-lying coastal plain lie elevated plateaus of up to 500m in height. Rising above these plateaus is the occasional mountain range reaching around 1,000m, notably the Cristal mountains and the Chaillu range, which is the location of the highest point in Gabon, Mount Oboundji (1,575m).

Of Gabon's many rivers, the largest is the Ogooué River, which flows between Cape Lopez on the Atlantic to its source in the Congo 1,200km (745 miles) away, fed by many tributaries on the way. Just beyond Lambaréné, the absence of mountains enables it to open out into an enormous delta of lakes.

Over 80% of Gabon is covered in dense tropical forest. Ancient forest dominates the mountain ranges and remote areas, while post-agricultural forest grows in areas that once were cultivated. Compared to the forest, savannahs represent a minute proportion of the landscape in parts of Coastal Ogooué, Ngounié, Nyanga and Haut-Ogooué.

Climate

Like all equatorial regions, Gabon's is a tropical climate. It's hot and humid all year round, averaging 26°C and 85% humidity, with a typical annual rainfall of 2.51m. The climate does of course vary slightly depending on where you are. Thanks to the trade winds, the humidity on the coast is less intense, and there is less rain the further south you head. Broadly speaking, Gabon has two main seasons: a long rainy season between February and May, followed by a long dry season from late May to mid September. The rest of the year is made up of two shorter seasons, a rainy season from October to November (the month with the highest average rainfall of the year) and a dry season from December to January.

HISTORY
Gabon's early history

Archaeological research has uncovered a handful of artefacts in the Ogooué valley, particularly around Lopé, testifying that human life here dates as far back as 7000BC. These prehistoric peoples probably came to the area from the Congo, or from Cameroon. Of the people living in Gabon today, the earliest inhabitants are the Pygmies, who can be traced back to AD1100. The Pygmies came from Central Africa, driven by the spread of Bantu tribes to find alternative areas to support their nomadic forest existence. Unfortunately for the Pygmies, the Bantu kept on coming. In fact, the Bantu migration into western Africa was to continue for several centuries. As late as the 19th century, massive instability and intertribal fighting were caused when the Fang invaded southwestern Gabon from the northeast.

The arrival of the Europeans: traders, explorers, missionaries

Little is know about Gabon before the Europeans arrived and started making notes. These sources tell us just as much about European attitudes – invariably exploitative, patronising and prejudiced – as they do about the damage they wreaked. European attempts to replace traditional societies and their practices (see box on pages 96–7) with European models of civilisation and spiritual fulfilment have since been well documented.

Gabon's European history starts with a Portuguese sailor, Lopez Gonzalvez, who trawled Africa's west coast in 1474 and entered the Gabon estuary. There is a story that he named the estuary *gabâo* because its shape reminded him of a *gabâo*, or sailor's cloak, and that later *gabâo* was transformed to become Gabon. It's not a very popular story, because the estuary's shape doesn't, in fact, look much like a cloak. An alternative idea is that the name Gabon was derived from the name of an important local ruler.

What we know of the history of Africa's west coast, from the arrival of the first Europeans up to the 18th century, is all trade-related. The Portuguese struggled to fend off the Dutch but by the mid 17th century had effectively lost the fight for trading supremacy, leaving the Dutch traders happily plying the coast buying gold, ivory and enough slaves to supply their country's sugar

PYGMIES

The Pygmies of Gabon – whether the Baka of Woleu-Ntem, the Babongo of Ngounié, or the Bakoya around Mékambo – traditionally keep themselves to themselves. The number of Pygmies is not known, but as a rough estimate there are certainly no more than a few thousand left, a tiny minority of Gabon's total population. Although their nomadic hunter-gatherer lifestyle has given way to a more sedentary way of life in modern times, they still choose to live deep in the forest to a degree unparalleled by any other peoples in the interior, who for the most part have moved their villages to the roadside. This is not so surprising when you consider that the Pygmies were the first people known to inhabit the Gabonese forests.

To call someone a Pygmy is considered an insult, and yet however small (in height and in number), these forest people possess skills far superior to their Bantu neighbours, notably in hunting, healing, polyphonic music and collecting honey. Their traditional weapon for small game is the bow and poisoned arrow, and for larger game traps and harpoons. Nowadays they are just as likely to hunt with rifles. Despite these skills, the Pygmies are ignored rather than respected by Bantu peoples, until they have need of a Pygmy tracker or a Pygmy healer that is. Pygmies are often treated with derision and contempt, and are often cheated and exploited. More often than not they are paid in kind rather than money for their services, which only reinforces their marginalised position. Pygmy children often miss out on school as their parents cannot afford it. The Pygmy children that do make it are taunted and ostracised by their peers.

Traditionally politicians have taken no account of Pygmies either, until perhaps elections are on the horizon. Tourism and the perceived need for 'authentic cultures' seems to have sparked new interest in the Pygmies, but isn't this just another form of exploitation? In early 2002 there was an exhibition at the CCF (see pages 97–8) about the Pygmies and their way of life. The exhibition was accompanied by talks and meetings, in which it was decided that a comprehensive record of all things Pygmy should be made by the year 2004, including brochures on their history and languages, and CDs of Pygmy songs and rhymes.

plantations in South America. A century later much of the Dutch-controlled coast had passed into the hands of the English and French.

Slavery was banned in Britain in 1792, in France in 1792 and in the United States in 1865, but trade continued illegally well into the 19th century. The slave trade was to make a serious dent in the population of Gabon. There were known slave depots at Lopé and at Cape Lopez. Men were chained together in sixes by their necks before being ruthlessly herded on to ships bound for Brazil and Cuba. Prices for slaves tended to be more expensive on the coast than in the interior, where according to Albert Schweitzer (see pages 110–11) men might be sold into slavery by their fellow tribesmen for bad behaviour, or children might be sold by parents who wanted them to live in a country where there was enough food to eat. From the late 1820s French anti-slavery naval patrols were operating – with the underlying agenda of finding suitable areas to establish trading posts – but the coast was too large and the number of vessels too small for their efforts to definitively halt trade. In 1839 the French naval lieutenant Bouët-Willaumez obtained territory on the Gabon estuary from the local king Rapontchombo. (The French called him Denis as Rapontchombo was too much of an effort.) The French now had a base from which to combat slave-traders and spread French control. In return, Rapontchombo was given a few goods, including two sacks of tobacco, ten white hats and 20 guns. This was the first of many such treaties the French were to sign over the years with local chiefs.

Not long after, the first missionaries descended on the estuary. The year was 1842 and the missionaries were American Protestants. They chose to build their mission at Glass, immediately to the south of the spot that would be chosen for Libreville seven years later (see page 81). Before too long these first missionaries were joined by Roman Catholics from France, and the race was on to save African souls.

Gradually the great trading firms of Europe built factories in Glass and then further inland. A firsthand, if exaggerated, account of life for one European trader is the book *Trader Horn*, which is a record of tales Aloysius 'Trader' Horn told to a South African writer in 1926. **Trader Horn** arrived in Africa around 1871 as an employee of the British trading company Hatton and Cookson, of Liverpool. He was based at the first factory in Lambaréné, on Adolinanongo, and made frequent forages into the unexplored interior in search of new trading routes and treaties. Trade at that time consisted of exchanging cloth, cooking pots, brandy, guns, gunpowder and salt, for ivory, rubber, ebony and padouk wood.

Hot on the heels of the traders were the European explorers. While the traders were keen to exploit Africa's riches as cheaply as possible, the explorers were motivated predominantly by curiosity and the desire for glory. Their accounts are peppered to varying degrees with tales of tribal skirmishes, light-fingered porters, and reports of the constant haggling and bribing necessary to progress peacefully further into the interior. A large number of the crates on any expedition were crammed with the necessary bribes, above all cloth and alcohol.

Paul Belloni du Chaillu undertook an expedition in 1855 with the intention of finding animals and tribes never before seen by the white man, as well as to locate any healthy places in the interior where missionaries could do their work without dying in such great numbers as they were on the coast. An ambitious agenda by anyone's standards, but he was better equipped than most for the task in hand. Having lived for several years on the coast, where his father had owned a trading post, du Chaillu was fluent in the languages and customs of the coastal tribes at least. There can be no doubt that this knowledge, coupled with an iron constitution, was a decisive factor in his return alive. He journeyed 'always on foot, and unaccompanied by other white men' across 12,000km (8,000 miles) of jungle, withstanding the relentless tropical rains, the unrelenting insect bites and the 50 attacks of fever, on an uncertain diet and masses of quinine.

Unfortunately for du Chaillu, when his books were published in England – most famously his *Explorations and Adventures in Equatorial Africa* in 1861 – they were heavily criticised as being far-fetched and unscientific, little more than flights of fancy. He had shot, stuffed and carted home 2,000 birds and 200 quadrupeds, of which 60 and 20 respectively were identified as new species. He was probably the first white man to have come face-to-face with a gorilla, to have met Pygmies, and to have eaten with (and not been eaten by) the Fang, and yet his encounters were dismissed as overblown story-telling. An angry du Chaillu undertook a second expedition, in 1863. His account of that trip – *A Journey to Ashango-Land* – was more kindly received, but none the less he vowed never to do another.

Du Chaillu's stories struck a chord with a naturalised Frenchman born in Italy. **Savorgnan de Brazza** obtained sponsorship from the French Navy and threw himself into exploring Gabon's forest interior in 1875. Three years later he re-emerged, barefoot, a feverish, starving wreck. He had got as far as the Poubara Falls (see page 169), and was able to report that the Ogooué River was neither a tributary of the Congo nor a suitable trading river, on account of its numerous rapids. Believing that with trade would come 'civilisation', he suggested that a railroad be built into the interior along the river instead.

By this time the American **Henry Morton Stanley** had just succeeded in crossing Africa east to west, and had written up his achievement in a book entitled *Through the Dark Continent* (1878). Brazza immediately set about preparing another trip. In 1879, they were both setting off again. The race for territory was on between Brazza (for the French team) and Stanley (for the Belgian). Brazza came up trumps. He founded Franceville and Brazzaville, and in-between made a treaty with the King of the Bateké, who agreed to place his land west of the River Congo under French protection.

Of all the explorers, Brazza was probably the least aggressive but the most dissembling. (His protagonists claim he conquered an empire without firing a single shot, which is not quite true, but he was certainly a tireless campaigner against slavery.) He won the trust of local peoples with patience and artful persuasion. He waxed lyrical about the benefits of free trade in order to extract treaties from the chiefs in which they committed their kingdoms to French protection. It is because of his efforts that the land between the coast and the River Congo was recognised as being under French control, firstly by the Congress of Berlin in 1885, and in 1888 with the creation of the **Congo Français**, with Libreville as its capital and Brazza as its governor.

French rule

Thus when the formidable Victorian spinster **Mary Kingsley** set off on her travels in 1893, the area known as modern-day Gabon was an administrative district within the Congo that Français referred to as the Gaboon. By this time

MARY KINGSLEY

At the end of the 19th century, West Africa was a surprising, even alarming, choice of destination for an English lady from Cambridge to travel around alone. Mary Kingsley, of course, was not altogether ordinary. Her father, a doctor, spent virtually Mary's entire childhood travelling the world. Mary was left at home without any formal education, and with no companions except for her depressive mother and sickly younger brother. When her father finally retired and came home, it was to spend virtually all his time in his study researching sacrificial rites. Later, Mary was to nurse both parents for almost two years, until they died within weeks of one another in 1892. Mary may have been grief-stricken, but she was also free. As Mary herself put it, 'for the first time in my life, I found myself in possession of five or six months that were not heavily forestalled, and feeling like a boy with a new half-crown, I lay about in my mind ... as to what to do with them'.

What she did with them was to go to West Africa. Little is known about that first trip in 1893, but for her second trip made the following year we know she was looking for fish for the British Museum of Natural History and a greater understanding of African 'fetish'. Plus, of course, the sort of adventure that couldn't be found in upper-middle-class England (like Brazza, she too had read du Chaillu). She found plenty of all three and wrote an entertaining account of it all on her return. When *Travels in West Africa* was published in 1897, it was a runaway success. Immediately pounced upon as an authority on all things African, Mary Kingsley was plunged into a whirlwind of speeches and social events, and urged to write more. The results were *West African Studies* (1899), *The Story of West Africa* (1899) and, finally, an overwhelming desire to escape. She had not wanted the fame – right from the start she had asked her publishers to be published anonymously – and it did not agree with her. In 1900 she once more set out for Africa; she was never to return. She fell ill and died whilst nursing typhoid patients in a military hospital in South Africa.

The tone of Mary Kingsley's writing is often ironic, funny and blasé. She is a formidable woman of her time, taking whatever is thrown at her without compromising her quintessential Englishness. She made huge efforts to learn to row, and to get to grips with the languages and customs she encountered, but steadfastly refused to wear anything other than the clothes befitting an English lady, whether she was crossing mountains or valleys, forests or swamps. Mary Kingsley had occasion to defend this

there was quite a lively expat community, not just on the coast but strung along the Ogooué River into the interior. There were government posts (French), trading posts (mostly British) and mission houses (American Protestants and French Catholics).

By the turn of the century Brazza had been fired from his position as governor for being difficult. When he saw the reality of colonisation, Brazza seemingly ridiculous get-up when she fell into a game pit. 'It is at these times you realise the blessing of a good thick skirt ... here I was with the fullness of my skirt tucked under me, sitting on nine ebony spikes some twelve inches long, in comparative comfort, howling lustily to be hauled out.' Despite her efforts to maintain this feminine wardrobe, she was continually called 'Sir' by the Africans. She felt sure the reason for this was not due to any wish to show disrespect on the part of the Africans (quite the contrary), but from the annoying absence of gender in their languages.

While today the Fang are the most important tribe in Gabon, at the time of Mary Kingsley they were still in the throes of migrating into the Ogooué region from the north, scattering terrified tribes before them. Famed for their aggressive, cannibalistic natures, they were greatly feared by both Europeans and other Africans. In an incident that might have ruffled a lesser character, Mary Kingsley is loaned a Fang chief's hut for the night. Disturbed by a strong, putrid smell in the night, she investigates a bag hanging from the roof poles, and empties the contents into her hat. 'They were a human hand, three big toes, four eyes, two ears, and other portions of the human frame. The hand was fresh, the others only so-so, and shrivelled.' Mary Kingsley took great care to investigate and explain Fang cannibalism in a reasoned, non-alarmist way: human flesh being a good and tasty source of food, a Fang will sell his dead relatives to his neighbours, and buy theirs in return, the odd body part having first been removed to be kept as a memento.

One of the rites Mary Kingsley noted among certain tribes was the stipulation of a prohibition upon a child: something the child cannot do, eat or see for fear of certain death. She believed adhering to these prohibitions, or taboos, functions as a form of sacrifice through abstinence. Her approach was surprisingly non-judgemental (elsewhere she identifies drinking unboiled water as her own taboo). In this her reactions are quite different to those expressed by the eminent Dr Albert Schweitzer years later (see box on pages 110–11). Unlike Schweitzer, Mary Kingsley tried not to judge or interfere. She saw her role as that of an impartial observer, and as such her responsibility was to try to understand and record African rites and customs, not change or undo them.

All Mary Kingsley's quotes are taken from *Travels in West Africa* (London, 1897).

seriously regretted the role he had played, but by then it was too late. French attempts to monopolise trade and levy taxes had naturally been fiercely resented by the local peoples. Direct attacks on Europeans became much more frequent and there were violent rebellions in numerous different areas. The French government invested nothing in its newly acquired colony, but simply sold large concessions to rubber companies. They used forced labour to meet

EL HADJ OMAR ALBERT-BERNARD BONGO

Albert-Bernard Bongo was born in Lewai (now Bongoville), in the High Ogooué, on December 30 1935. His childhood was a humble one. He has said, 'I do not forget my peasant origins. I was not born in a hospital bed or a cradle and never had a nanny. I was born in the grass. Despite honours, power and all its attendant advantages, that is a fact I have never forgotten.' He was ten years old when he attended school for the first time, but quickly made up for this late start with his ambition. He defied his guardian (his father had died when he was just seven years old) to attend technical school in Brazzaville. He started work there as a civil servant in the post office and was a supporter of the Mouvement Socialiste Africain (MSA). Before independence he had worked his way up to the French rank of lieutenant in the air force.

After independence, his political rise was speedy. In the 1961 elections for the National Assembly, Bongo took an active role in the campaign in his home province, Haut-Ogooué. A year later he became assistant director of the Cabinet that supported the president, and just months after that appointment he was promoted to director of the Cabinet. Léon Mba, the president, nominated him vice-president in 1966. Another year on and Bongo was the official president.

Bongo was motivated by ambitions that upped the country's international profile in conjunction with his own. He wanted to build a country that looked modern and wealthy, and a people that were superior to their African neighbours. For him the *Transgabonais* railway was a symbol of Gabon the modern, progressive state. Bongo was not the first man to visualise a railway that would transport raw materials from Gabon's interior to the coast – Savorgnan de Brazza drew up plans for a railway back in 1885

punishing quotas, and then punished the labourers severely when they failed to meet them. Death and disease were rife, as was hatred for the white man. But hatred alone could not overcome the superior training and equipment of the French, and within a couple of decades the French had quashed all opposition.

In 1910, the Congo Français was replaced by the **Federation of French Equatorial Africa**, which united Gabon, Chad, the Central African Republic and Congo under a governor general based in Brazzaville. In 1913 another formidable European arrived on the scene for the first time. Doctor Albert Schweitzer was overflowing with the usual paternalistic attitudes of his time, but he did at least put his energies into doing something of practical importance (see page 108). He was still there in 1958, when the Federation of French Equatorial Africa broke down and a **Gabon Republic** within the French Community was proclaimed. With legal and government systems based on the French model, Gabon was finally granted **independence** from France on August 17 1960.

– but he was the most determined. The stories about how he financed it smack of political opportunism. Supposedly, having been turned down for financing by the World Bank and the West, Bongo turned his attentions elsewhere. He is reported as saying about the *Transgabonais*: 'It will be built by one means or another with the help of this country or that country...' In the end the money came from Abu Dhabi. Bongo ditched Catholicism as a poor investment and made a calculated conversion to Islam. On his way back from Mecca he dropped in on Sheikh Zayd of Abu Dhabi. When his plane left the following morning it was full to bursting with French francs.

Work on the railway started at Owendo, 20km (12 miles) south of Libreville, in December 1973. The final section was finished in December 1987, not at the iron deposits in the northeast as had originally been planned, but in the southeast, at Franceville. The official reason why Bongo had changed the route was to transport the High Ogooué's manganese and uranium to the coast. To many it looked more like a thinly veiled attempt to contain the power of the Fang, the prominent tribe in the north, while favouring the Bateké, Bongo's own tribe in the southeast. The *Transgabonais* stretches from west to east for 660km (410 miles) through the forest. It far surpassed the original budget, costing approximately 20 million French francs a kilometre. Gabon was left teetering on the brink of bankruptcy.

In the early 1990s Bongo married the daughter of Denis Sassov-Nguesso, thereby becoming son-in-law to the Congo (his first wife was the singer and drummer Patience Dabany, a Bateké from the Central African Republic). As for the future, the general feeling amongst the Gabonese seems to be a desire for change. The question on everybody's minds is, what lies in store for Gabon after Bongo?

From independence to neo-colonialism

The first President of the Gabonese Republic, Léon Mba, presided over a multi-party system, but not without some difficulty. In early 1964 the tension culminated in an attempt by the opposition to seize power. The attempt was quashed by French troops, and Mba was reinstated, only to lose the election in April 1964. He made a comeback in the election of March 1967, when he took 99% of the vote, but wasn't destined to enjoy his success for very long.

The man who is now known as **El Hadj Omar Albert-Bernard Bongo** was appointed vice-president on November 12 1966. As a result of Mba's illness, Bongo was acting as president weeks before Mba actually died on November 28 1967. Bongo was officially confirmed president on December 2, and wasted no time in founding the Parti Démocratique Gabonais, or Gabonese Democratic Party (PDG), believing that one-party rule meant national unity while a multi-party system could only foster divisions. Bongo's one-party state was to survive unchallenged for 22 years, with Bongo being re-elected president in 1977, 1979 and 1986 to seven-year terms. In April 1975, the office of vice-president was abolished and replaced by the office of prime minister, with no provision for automatic succession.

Bongo's arguments in support of his one-party state in Gabon were clear and convincing. He maintained that while not opposed to the multi-party system in principle (the West was living proof that it could work well), it was 'ill-suited' to Gabon. He described Gabon as a country where voters always chose the man from their province, irrespective of ideas or issues. Bongo's avowed primary concern was to suppress old tribal divisions in the move towards national unity, a necessary precursor of the stable, successful Gabonese nation he envisaged. From the start, Bongo's single-party system met with criticism, and not just from the Western democracies. The Mouvement de Redressement National (MORENA) – an opposition group made up of nationalist intellectuals and students – claimed that the interests of several ethnic groups were not being addressed. Other opponents, some in voluntary exile, made allegations of electoral rigging and corruption. Some even accused the president of being involved in drug trafficking.

With the discovery of oil offshore in the early 1970s, Gabon was catapulted into the limelight as the smallest country to be a member of OPEC and the country with the highest per capita earning of any in Africa. With 'les petrodollars' came change. Many exchanged a life of rural subsistence for an urban existence dependent on imports. More than 80% of the food and goods required by Gabon's urban populations are imported – mangoes from Mali, pineapples from Cameroon and so on – a costly reflection of the underdeveloped state of the country's farming, fishing and manufacturing resources. Agricultural projects existed – cultivating manioc, tomatoes, taro, cucumbers and coffee – but yields were insufficient and transport unreliable.

Already in the late 1970s the country was in financial difficulties. The renovation of the presidential palace in Libreville had severely dented the country's coffers. What little was left, plus some, was devoured by the massive cost of the *Transgabonais* railway (see box on Bongo). The 1980s saw a fall in the price of oil paralleled by a drastic drop in worldwide demand for timber. To make matters worse, by 1991 the production of both manganese and uranium would also have sharply declined. Alongside all this the cost of imported goods rose, while predictably salaries did not. These economic problems came at a time when resentment at the way Bongo squandered Gabon's income could no longer be contained. Violent protests in the early 1980s led to MORENA leaders being imprisoned, but violence in 1989 was to force Bongo to amend the constitution and legalise opposition parties.

However, in May 1990 Joseph Redjambe, President of the opposition Gabonese Progressive Party, was killed in a fire in a Libreville hotel. Anti-governmental feeling reached new heights in a ten-day demonstration that was the most violent yet, to the extent that 5,000 French residents were evacuated. In June 1990 it was agreed that presidential elections would be held in 1992, but Bongo then brought the date forward to the end of the year. In doing so, he was safeguarding his own success by depriving the opposition of any fair chance of gathering support.

A new constitution was founded in March 1991 confirming a multi-party system and stipulating that the president, to be elected for a seven-year term, would appoint a Council of Ministers headed by a prime minister. The constitution also granted real power to the National Assembly and the Senate, both of which are directly elected for five and six terms respectively. In the event of the president's death, the prime minister, the National Assembly president, and defence minister should share powers until new elections are held.

Bongo once again won the elections of 1993, but the word on the street was that he had shuffled the figures. Protests broke out and were quashed, leaving 30 people dead. The 'Paris Accords' negotiated in Paris in 1994 between majority and government representatives agreed to a more transparent electoral process and reforms of government institutions. In the parliamentary elections of December 1996 Bongo's GDP gained a clear majority, but in many towns the opposition carried away the municipal elections. This was the case in Libreville, where Paul Mba Abessole of the opposition party the Rassemblement des Bûcherons, or the Association of Woodcutters, stormed to victory and became Mayor of Libreville. Abessole immediately requested the UN to supervise the presidential elections to be held later that year. Once again the elections confirmed Bongo as president, with a landslide victory, for another seven years. In early 1999 there were more protests. Bongo retaliated by closing schools and universities, which he identified as hotbeds for demonstrators.

Gabon into the 21st century

The parliamentary elections of December 2001 looked as if they were going to be a replay of the same, tired old story. The ruling GDP retained a convincing majority. Once again there were murmurs of electoral fraud and accusations that multi-party elections were nothing but a sham in what was to all intents and purposes a single-party state. The public made their feelings clear by abstaining in large numbers, up to 80% in the larger towns. The story started to get interesting when Bongo seemed to respond positively to that public feeling by appointing four opposition members as ministers in his new government, including Paul Mba Abessole and Pierre Claver Maganga Moussavou, President of the Parti Social Démocrate or Social Democratic Party (PSD). Also, for the first time, the government looks determined to make the fight against corruption a priority, coupled with the fight against poverty. Not everything has changed – the defence minister is still Ali Bongo, the president's son – but even so, some would like to interpret these moves as a turning point in Gabon's government.

The winds of change look as if they might finally blow when it comes to French–Gabonese relations. Of all the Western powers, the French have proved the most reluctant to withdraw from the affairs of their former colonies. French politicians seem to have believed that their country's continued involvement in Africa somehow enhanced France's credibility on the world stage. Irrespective of the leftness or rightness of their politics on the home front, French presidents from François Mitterrand through to Jacques Chirac have been equally committed to safeguarding their hegemony in French Africa. Their motives have been three-fold: strategic, linguistic and cultural, and, most important of all, economic. A neo-colonialist system was sealed at independence with a military treaty signed between Libreville and Paris. In return for French military support, Gabon would serve as a military base for France in Africa.

In economic terms, not only are former French African colonies an invaluable source of cheap raw materials, but they also serve as a very useful market for surplus French goods. French attempts to line its own pockets under the guise of establishing mutually beneficial trade relations have fooled nobody, least of all the Africans themselves. Of course, no relationship is entirely one-sided. There has to be an element of collusion for any relationship, however exploitative, to work. For Gabon's political leaders the trade-offs of French patronage have been regime stability and financial aid. Both Presidents Léon Mba and Omar Bongo have needed the threat of a French military presence to sustain their regimes. However, there is a growing feeling within sections of the French government that French commercial interests (notably oil) and French foreign policy are too interdependent. There are those who would love to see French aid spread wider than the former French colonies, and there are others who would like to stop all aid to Gabon. This is paralleled by the desire for a less dependent attitude on behalf of the Gabonese government, as seen in the way Bongo boycotted the Franco-African summit in Paris in 1998.

Subtle shifts in attitude have been taking place much more widely across Africa. The formation of the African Union (AU) in July 2002 was in part born from the feeling in Africa that neo-colonialism must finally be rooted out. Neo-colonialism stunts political and economic development and fosters a resentful, angry people who lack real pride in their country. The AU is determined to address and overcome African problems as a unit, while moving towards the twin goals of economic progress and good governance. These goals may be reached with the help of foreign aid, but not with the kind of foreign aid that has strings attached. It is hoped that such talk means the world can look forward to a day in the near future when a strong Africa stands on the world stage.

Natural History and Conservation

HABITATS AND VEGETATION
Forest

Most of Gabon – nearly 75% in fact – is covered in dense, tropical rainforest. Gabon forms part of the most heavily forested area in Africa, an area that also includes Cameroon, Equatorial Guinea, Congo, and Central African Republic. Parts of these Central African rainforests are among the oldest in the world, possibly between 60 and 100 million years old. About one million years ago, with the onslaught of the last Ice Age, only patches of rainforest survived in Equatorial Guinea, northeast Democratic Republic of the Congo (DRC) and Gabon. It is generally recognised that rainforests need upwards of 2,000mm of rain a year to survive. The forest zones that managed to survive amidst the savannah – and it is thought that there were three in Gabon – were regions at altitude or alongside rivers, where the levels of rainfall had been less affected. The most likely zones in Gabon have been identified as the Crystal Mountains, the du Chaillu Mountains and the Doudou Mountains. Areas such as Lopé National Park, where patches of savannah still survive, give us an idea of what the majority of the Central African landscape must have looked like between 18,000 and 12,000 years ago.

Effectively serving as safehouses for the plants and animals of the rainforest, these forest strongholds were to become the key in the relentless process of recolonising the savannah of Central Africa, a process that began with the return of the warmth and the rain about 12,000 years ago. It's thanks to the survival of this ancient rainforest that Gabon boasts such a rich and varied vegetation. There are between 6,000 and 10,000 species of plants in Gabon, including some important endemic species that are still being discovered, such as the *Cola lizae*. This tree is found in abundance in the Lopé region (in places there are an estimated 6,000 trees per km^2), but was only recorded as a separate species in 1987.

Rainforest is characterised by very tall, very straight hardwood trees, whose branches and trunks are often entwined with vines and covered with epiphytes that take root in crevices in the bark. The average height of the trees varies between 90ft and 150ft (30–45m). The emergents rising above this canopy can reach heights of up to 190ft (60m). Little light penetrates past the canopy, so there's not much on the ground in the way of bushes and foliage. Younger, post-agricultural forest is found in areas that were once cleared for cultivation, often in valleys and on the edges of large blocks of impenetrable forest. In comparison with the ancient forest, it is lighter and less dense. It has a higher concentration of faster growing trees and softwoods, such as okoumé and ozigo, and sometimes the forest floor is covered in dense vegetation.

Savannah
As a general rule in Gabon, where there's no forest, there's savannah – wide, open areas of high grass, shrubs and isolated trees. Gabon's savannah is mostly found in the Coastal Ogooué region and in the southern half of the country, for example in the Ngounié region around Mouila. The Bateké Plateaux in the far southeast – known as the 'Highlands of Gabon' – are characterised by open grasslands and valleys, and Lopé is renowned for its unique mosaic of forest and savannah.

Wetlands
There are mangrove swamps at Mondah Bay near Libreville, in the briny lagoons near the coast and along the banks of the Ogooué. These strange trees have tangled roots above the ground. They delighted Mary Kingsley when she saw them for the first time in 1894. She described them in *Travels in West Africa*: 'At high water you do not see the mangroves displaying their ankles in the way that shocked Captain Lugard. They look most respectable.' The Ogooué delta is the second largest freshwater delta of the African continent. In addition to mangroves, it is also known for its marsh forests, papyrus, reedbeds and floating grasses.

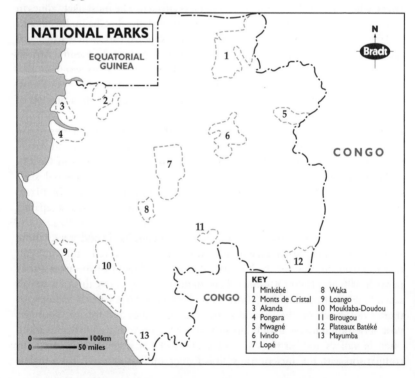

NATIONAL PARKS

EQUATORIAL GUINEA

N

Bradt

CONGO

CONGO

KEY
1 Minkébé
2 Monts de Cristal
3 Akanda
4 Pongara
5 Mwagné
6 Ivindo
7 Lopé
8 Waka
9 Loango
10 Mouklaba-Doudou
11 Birougou
12 Plateaux Batéké
13 Mayumba

0 ——— 100km
0 ——— 50 miles

RAINFORESTS

Derek Schuurman

Rainforests are arguably the most important of the world's hotspots of biodiversity. Although they account for only 2% of the earth's surface, they hold the majority of the world's species. Almost half the world's rainforests are concentrated in just three countries – Brazil, Indonesia and the Democratic Republic of Congo (DRC). Africa's rainforests belong either to the Guinean Forests of West Africa, or to the Central African Congo Basin. The latter block includes the rainforests of Gabon.

Conservation International estimates that the DRC alone has 1.2 million square kilometres of rainforest. Add to that the rainforests of Gabon, Cameroon, Equatorial Guinea and Central African Republic and the figure shoots up to 1.9 million square kilometres.

Remarkably, today 74% of Gabon is still covered in rainforest. The so-called Gabonese Jungle Belt is not only the biggest intact forest area in all of Africa, but it is one of the largest worldwide, and it holds the highest tree and bird diversity for a given area anywhere in Africa. Of the 8,000+ plants, an estimated 20% are endemic, and there are also over 670 bird species. In such rainforests, a warm, even climate of around 25°C is maintained year round and annual rainfall averages around the 2,000mm mark – significantly lower than say, the rainforests in parts of Indonesia where rainfall can easily double that. So, the rainforests of Gabon and CAR experience a dry season and even feature some deciduous trees.

At every level of the forest – from canopy to the dark, damp forest floor, live a myriad life forms. These include many of Africa's most fascinating, enigmatic and poorly understood creatures. (Aside from the high bird species count, Gabon's 17–20 million hectares of rainforest also hold 190 species of mammal and an unknown number of reptiles and amphibians.)

WILDLIFE
Mammals

The vast majority of Gabon's tourists to this date have come to see Gabon's wildlife, and specifically the gorillas, of which there are an estimated 35,000. Gorillas have been identified as having mainstream appeal and gorilla trekking has therefore been the focus of the few tour operators and travel agencies who have shown any interest in Gabon. In actual fact, gorillas are just one of many reasons why a wildlife enthusiast should visit. Gabon has been identified as having very important populations of large mammals, including an estimated 60,000 elephants and 64,000 chimpanzees. There is also a large number and variety of monkeys, including the black colobus monkey, the moustached monkey and the sun-tailed monkey (an endemic species). Other mammals include the Congo sitatunga, mongoose, forest buffalo, civet, hippopotamus,

NATURE HIGHLIGHTS
Derek Schuurman

- Gabon is one of the few countries where vast, pristine rainforests are not just a memory. Botanists are in for a treat, with some 20% of the country's flora being endemic.
- Where else can you see forest elephants on a deserted beach, while humpback whales cavort offshore? And not only that, but lowland gorillas are also known to hit the beach and, strangest of all, hippos often frequent the surf (Loango).
- At 'bais' (meadow-like clearings in the forest with nutrient rich sedges and salt licks), you can take in wonderful sightings of forest elephants, forest buffalos, the timid Congo sitatunga and of course, western lowland gorillas which can appear in large numbers.
- Mandrill troops – in the dry season, Lope's mandrill troops are enormous – up to 1,000+ baboons may be seen together, one of the largest primate gatherings on earth (the other is Ethiopia's gelada baboon).
- Smaller mammals: monkeys galore inhabit the forests, as do small forest-dependent antelope including various duikers. These are all important seed distributors. Other noteworthy animals include Congo clawless otter, the tiny water chevrotain and the African golden cat.

leopard, porcupine, and numerous different species of pangolin and squirrel, including flying squirrels.

Primates

Gorilla (*Gorilla gorilla gorilla*) There are three separate subspecies of gorilla whose morphological differences are primarily due to their different habitats. In comparison to the mountain gorilla, for example, the western lowland gorilla that inhabits Gabon's rainforests has wider, shorter body hair, longer arms and a wider, larger skull. The western lowland gorilla can be up to 6ft (1.8m) tall when standing and can weigh up to 450lb (204kg). The western lowland gorilla is a herbivore, feeding on leaves, fruit, shoots, bulbs, even tree bark. A silverback can eat up to 3kg (6.6lb) of vegetation a day. The silverback is the leader of the family group, deciding when the group plays, sleeps, eats and moves on. He is the only fully adult male amongst several females. The western lowland gorilla is a peaceful, non-aggressive animal, who never attacks unless provoked. However, if he fears for the safety of his family group, an adult male will attempt to intimidate his aggressor by standing on

Mountain gorilla

his legs, roaring and slapping his chest with cupped hands. As a last resort, he will charge toward the intruder, but his intention is not to crash into him. At the final second he will aim to veer slightly to the side. The western lowland gorilla's only known enemy is man.

Chimpanzee (*Pan troglodytes*) The common chimpanzee has a long, black coat covering all its body except the face, hands and feet. Chimpanzees have long digits, large ears and small beards in the adults of both sexes. (Unlike gorillas, their sexual organs protude.) The chimpanzee is equally at home on the ground or in the trees, although invariably this animal will build its night nest above ground. Most of its diet is made up of fruits, but it will eat leaves, flowers, seeds, insects and birds' eggs and even monkeys. Chimpanzees live in groups of between 20 and 100 animals, within which there are smaller sub-groups. The chimpanzee lives in ancient and post-agricultural rainforests in Gabon, up to altitudes of 3,000m (9,840ft).

Chimpanzee

Baboon (*Papio cynocephalus*) There are three commonly recognised species of baboon inhabiting semi-arid, wooded savannah areas in Africa. The species most common to lowland areas of Central Africa is the yellow baboon, so-called because of its yellowish coat. Baboons are easily recognisable – they have extended muzzles, long hair and short tails. They tend to live in large groups (up to 150 animals), and group members are part of a complex social structure where rank is all-important. Often they are not shy to approach human settlements, stealing accessible food stores for example.

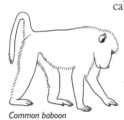
Common baboon

Mandrill (*Mandrillus sphinx*) The mandrill and its close relative, the drill (*Mandrillus leucophaeus*), are two large and very distinctive primates confined to West Africa's rainforests. Until recently, they were thought to be baboons, but genetic studies revealed closer affinities to the mangabeys, making them the largest of the monkeys.

The mandrill is found in Cameroon, Equatorial Guinea and Gabon, where it is locally common. The drill is found only in Cameroon, Bioko and Nigeria, where it is heavily persecuted for bushmeat.

The mandrill is best known for the unmistakable, bright red and blue facial markings sported by males: the more dominant the male, the brighter his facial colours will be and the more offspring he will sire. Both species also feature strikingly coloured rumps, which besides probably being used for social and sexual signals, are thought to aid navigating of troops through the dark rainforests.

While the mandrill is known to occasionally leave the rainforest and enter savannah, the drill has never been seen outside rainforest. (Today, the drill is

MONKEY BUSINESS
Derek Schuurman

Gabon's marvellous assemblage of primates includes a large variety of monkeys. Among these conspicuous and animated characters are several of the guenons. Africa's 17 guenons are generally regarded as the most colourful group of monkeys in the world. Just as the Tamarins of South America's rainforests often do, the African rainforest monkeys regularly travel through the forest in loosely knit multi-species troops. The various species then forage at the specific levels of the forest, where each of their favourite foods are found. The advantage of the different species travelling together is that there are then many pairs of eyes to watch for predators at all different levels of the forest (visibility is generally not the best in the dark, densely foliaged closed canopy setting). It has been found that these monkeys have predator-specific alarm vocalisations, and that the different species understand each-others' specific alarm calls. So, if for instance an arboreal colobus monkey spots a crowned eagle low overhead, it will sound the 'eagle' alarm and all the other monkeys, regardless of species and at which level in the forest they are, will react in the same way, i.e. they will drop down and scramble for cover. In the same way, if one of the more terrestrial monkeys spots a leopard, it will give the 'leopard' alarm call and all the monkeys will hang around at a safe distance above the cat, creating a cacophonic din until the foiled predator has had enough and slinks away (they know the leopard is an ambush predator).

regarded by many experts as Africa's most endangered primate, with its population on the African mainland being estimated at 3,000 and declining.)

Both species are diurnal and omnivorous quadrupeds and they tend to forage widely by day. In the dry season (July–October), mandrills congregate in impressive numbers with such 'super groups' sometimes numbering hundreds of individuals.

Sun-tailed monkey (*Cercopithecus solatus*) Not surprisingly, this monkey takes its name from the bright orange colour at the tip of its tail. It is also characterised by its reddish back and blue scrotum. This monkey is known to inhabit a very small area of about 12,000km² (4,630 square miles) centring on the Foret des Abeilles to the east of the Lopé Reserve. These monkeys normally live in groups, averaging fewer than 20 animals, but solitary males are also common. They are curious animals, and might be spotted either in the trees or on the ground.

Black colobus monkey (*Colobus satanas*) Of the five species in the colobus genus, three are found in Central Africa. Of these the one most likely to be seen in Gabon is the black colobus. As its name suggests, this monkey is entirely black. Other characteristics to note are its long, thin tail and its small, wide-set eyes. More often than not this monkey will be spotted high up in the forest canopy in groups of 10–20 animals. Its food of choice is seeds, and failing that young leaves.

Moustached monkey (*Cercopithecus cephus*) This monkey's preferred habitat is post-agricultural forests in Gabon, because of their dense, low vegetation. It is usually seen on branches lower than 15m (50ft) or sometimes on the ground, in groups of 5–20 animals. Its identifying features are its white moustache, blue face, bluish-grey stomach and red tail. The largest part of its diet is made up of fleshy fruits. The females and young are much noisier than the males.

Putty-nosed monkey (*Cercopithecus nictitans*) This monkey lives in rainforest, relatively high up in the trees. It is entirely black apart from a white splodge at the end of its nose. On the male the tail may reach as much as 1m (3ft) in length. This monkey is a popular target with hunters as it is the largest and heaviest of the tree monkeys and the easiest to track down, mostly because of the distinctiveness and regularity of the male's call. Its diet is fruit-based.

Crowned monkey (*Cercopithecus pogonias*) Crowned monkeys take their name from the white headband beneath a crest of fur, flanked by tufts of yellow fur protruding from the ears. These medium-sized monkeys tend to be found in groups of about 20, often of different species. Given the chance this monkey will eat mostly fruit, but when fruits are not available it will make do with seeds and young leaves. It is found high up in the canopy (never on the ground) of ancient forests on the left bank of the River Ogooué and on the islands of São Tomé and Príncipe (probably making it the islands' largest mammal).

De Brazza's monkey (*Cercocebus neglectus*) The young De Brazza's monkey is pale, but its coat darkens and it acquires a red crown as it gets older. It is one of the heavier monkeys, the male's weight being up to twice that of the female. The De Brazza's monkey is found along the Atlantic coast all the way to western Kenya. The enormity of its range can be explained by its ability to swim. For this reason it is often spotted in forest alongside rivers or on river islands, however small. This monkey lives in small groups of about five animals. It eats seeds, leaves, mushrooms and caterpillars, amongst other things.

Red-capped mangabey (*Cercocebus torquatus*) This mangabey's coat has just a splash of identifying colour – its body is grey on top and white underneath, its black face is fringed with white and crowned by a red skullcap. It lives in mixed-sex groups of 10–60 animals. The mangabey eats fruits, leaves, roots and insects, amongst other things. The red-capped mangabey is found in Gabon's coastal region, in swampy forests beside water and in mangroves.

Agile mangabey (*Cercocebus agilis*) This monkey is lighter and less distinctive in colour than the red-capped mangabey. It is grey with a white underbelly and a darker, blackish face with a single white spot on its crown. It lives in groups averaging 15 animals, led by a dominant male. The agile mangabey frequents the area inland north of the River Ogooué. Like its relative the red-capped mangabey, it inhabits swampy, flooded forests bordering water.

Grey-cheeked mangabey (*Lophocebus albigena*) This slim, agile monkey is noted for the long, grey hair on its large cheeks, which spreads over its shoulders. The rest of its body is black-flecked with dark-grey hairs. It lives in groups of about 15 animals – including several males – which sometimes divide into smaller groups that keep within sight or sound of one another as they climb in the treetops. This monkey, especially the female, spends a lot more time than most other monkeys searching for insects. It also eats seeds and, to a lesser extent, fruit. It is found all over Gabon, in ancient forests, favouring the higher canopy and rarely being seen on the ground.

Antelopes

Duikers (*Cephalophus*) are small forest-dwelling antelopes. They are most widespread of all African forest antelopes and are separated into some 17 species. They have low-slung bodies on slender legs, and regularly run through areas of dense vegetation and when disturbed tend to plunge into thick cover to hide – the name duiker means 'diver' in Dutch and Afrikaans. Gabon's duikers include the large yellow-backed duiker, the attractive bay duiker and the Peters duiker, as well as the much more widely distributed common (grey) duiker.

Common duiker

The **common duiker** (*Sylvicapra grimmia*) is small and greyish in colour, with a white underbelly and a short, black tail. Its identifying feature is the small tuft of black hair between its horns, which are V-shaped in males and very small, almost non-existent, in females. Both the bay and yellow-backed duiker are heavily persecuted for bushmeat and also, regrettably, by certain European hunting tour operators (notably the largest, the yellow-backed duiker).

The attractive reddish-brown **bay duiker** is strictly nocturnal and by day hides in hollow trees or in dense vegetation. They tend to use tunnel-like paths through thick vegetation on a regular basis. While vegetable matter constitutes their main diet, they will stalk, kill and eat small animals and birds on rare occasions. Population densities are very low, with 12–20 hectares of habitat holding only two to three individuals.

The **yellow-backed duiker** is predominantly nocturnal, also lying up singly during the day in 'forms', which are regularly used places under fallen tree trunks or in dense, tangled vegetation. They have been seen resting on termite mounds, possibly to survey their surroundings. They mark their territory with maxillary glands and communicate by means of shrill bleats and grunts. When alarmed, they erect their bright dorsal crests and emit a shrill whistle, before fleeing into the dense undergrowth.

The **bushbuck** (*Tragelaphus scriptus*) is found in forests, in particular those bordering rivers, throughout Africa. The male tends to be dark brown in colour with short, straight horns; the female lighter in colour. The bushbuck is shy and any sightings are likely only to be fleeting. Larger than the common duiker and the bushbuck is the **reedbuck** (*Redunca arundinum*), which is fawn or grey in colour and known for its bounding gallop. Antelope populations have suffered from over-hunting, resulting in several – including both the common duiker and the reedbuck – meriting inclusion on Gabon's protected list. Less vulnerable to hunters is the **sitatunga** (*Tragelaphus spekei*), which inhabits swamp forests and marshes. Its skittishness means it is rarely seen by humans, but keep an eye out for it in boggy papyrus beds. Its excellent swimming ability means it can flee to safety through deep water, sometimes keeping only its nostrils above the water. Another antelope resident in Gabon is the **bongo** (*Tragelaphus eurycerus*), found in dense tropical forests below 4,000m (12,800ft). This is the largest forest antelope in the world. Its coat is a rich red colour, with vertical white torso stripes and a black muzzle. It is immediately recognisable for its spiral horns, in both sexes. It is extremely shy and not seen very often. When startled, it darts off into the surrounding forest.

Reedbuck

Bushbuck

Water chevrotain (*Hyemoschus aquaticus*) This unusual animal superficially resembles a small duiker and is the most primitive of ruminants, sharing certain taxonomic features with pigs. Although the chevrotains are also called 'mouse deer', they are not closely related to true deer and are placed in their own family. The smallest of the hoofed mammals, they stand 8–14in (20–35cm) high at the shoulder. The body is rabbit-like, with an arched back; the slender legs end in small feet; the snout is tapered and somewhat pig-like. The reddish-brown coat is spotted with white in most species. Chevrotains lack antlers but have tusk-like upper canine teeth, used by the males for fighting. Solitary, nocturnal denizens of dense, humid forest, they browse on leaves and fruit. The water chevrotain of tropical Africa lives, as its name implies, near water. It has been seen feeding underwater and will readily take to water to escape predators such as snakes, eagles and cats. The three other chevrotains (*Tragulus* species) are found from India to Indonesia and the Philippines.

Other medium and large mammals

Hippopotamus (*Hippopotamus amphibious*) Hippos are most commonly found in still pools or slow-running water. Observers are more likely to see hippo tracks on the river bank than a hippo itself. Hippos normally spend all day in the water, often totally submerged, or with just their eyes, ears and upper nose showing. Hippos are noisy and sociable, and are often found in groups of about ten. They are highly territorial, and are known for capsizing boats that drift too close or charging people that cross their path on land. When they defecate they rotate their stubby tails, thereby spraying their dung around in a good 2m radius. This habit probably functions as a territorial display for the benefit of hippos from other groups.

Forest elephant (*Loxodonta africana cyclotis*) Much less is known about the forest elephant than about its relative the savannah elephant. Forest elephants tend to be smaller and darker in colour, with smaller and rounder ears and a different skull shape. Another difference is their tusks, which on forest elephants are straighter and aimed to the ground. The elephants use them to eat the saline soil and tree bark. Research is currently being undertaken on the forest elephants at Langoué Bai (see pages 161–2). The researchers are building up a database of animals, noting the frequency of their visits to the *bai* and their social habits. Individual elephants are recognised by a combination of factors: their age, size, tusks, tails, and any identifying scars, tears, holes or notches they may have sustained on their ears while playing or fighting.

Forest buffalo (*Syncerus caffer nanus*) is a reddish-coloured buffalo that is smaller than its savannah cousin, weighing no more than 700lb (320kg). The forest buffalo lives in lowland rainforest areas, where it tends to remain close to water and grassy glades, where it can graze. Social groups usually comprise no more than ten to 12 animals, with several females and their offspring accompanied by one or more males. Males often form bachelor groups. Forest buffalo can be seen in *bais* in Gabon and CAR.

Leopard (*Panthera pardus*) The leopard is a large, spotted cat. It is a solitary animal, a natural tree-climber and a nocturnal hunter. It eats antelopes, monkeys and baboons, birds, snakes and fish. Its preferred habitats are wooded grassland and forest, and it tends to rest in large rocks or large trees alongside rivers. It is difficult to spot, being both easily camouflaged and wary of humans. It is territorial, and will charge in defence of its home range. A charge is indicated by a series of short coughs followed by a chilling scream. Leopards in Gabon tend to have very dark fur. Melanistic examples are known to occur.

Leopard

Jackal (*Canus*) There are different types of jackal, but most live in long-term pairs or families. They are also scavengers, emerging at night or at dusk and dawn. Their diet consists of insects, small reptiles, birds and vegetation. Their movements are very similar to those of domestic dogs. The jackal lives in Gabon's grassy savannah areas, for example in the Batéké Plateau, finding shade in the heat of the day under shrubs or long grass.

Red river hog (*Potomochoerus porcus*) The red river hog is usually a striking reddish colour, with white markings on its large head and long black-and-white tassels hanging from its ears. It has a long, thin tail (up to 45cm or 1.5ft) and short, pointy tusks, and weighs 65–100kg (143–220lb). Its preferred habitats are thickets, forests, savannas and swamps throughout western and central Africa. This pig is happy wallowing in water, hence its name. Bushpigs live in noisy groups of 6–20 animals, led by a large male. They are nocturnal, staying hidden during the day. It eats anything from reptiles to fruits. Their main predators are panthers and man. As a defence the red river hog makes itself look much larger, by fluffing out its ear tassels and the erectile mane that runs along its spine. Until recently, the red river hog and its eastern African counterpart the bushpig (*Potomochoerus larvatus*) were considered to be a single species, classified under *P. porcus*.

Manatee (*Trichechus senegalensis*) The manatee is a large, grey, cylindrical mammal that lives in coastal areas, brackish lagoons and large rivers. It can be up to 4m (13ft) long and weigh 500kg (1,100lb). It has a bristly upper lip, front flippers and a flattish paddle-shaped rear end. A manatee may travel up to 40km a day (25 miles) through lagoons and rivers. Actual sightings of manatees in Gabon are rare, but sometimes they are heard splashing. The manatee is on Gabon's list of protected animal species. The population decline has been attributed largely to hunting and accidents with boat propellers or fishing nets.

Small mammals

If you are lucky you might spot **genets**, **mongooses** or **civets** in the forest. With few exceptions these are small, nocturnal mammals with large eyes

African civet

and long tails. They are deft and lively animals with excellent speed and night vision. During the day they hide under bushes and in abandoned termite mounds. The marsh mongoose is more diurnal. It is most likely to be glimpsed weaving through the bush, occasionally stopping to look around on their hind legs. Rare and rarely seen are **pangolins**, including the tree pangolin and the giant pangolin. They are distinctive because of their unique protective scales. Pangolins are insectivores, equipped with a long, thin tongue specially adapted for catching ants and termites. The tongue on a giant pangolin can be up to 70cm (28in) long, and it can eat up to 200,000 or 700g (25oz) of ants a night. Also

Pangolin

nocturnal, but this time protected by spikes rather than scales, is the **porcupine**. Also living in the forest, largely out of sight, are bushbabies (small nocturnal primates) and squirrels. The squirrel species include the flying squirrel, which is able to glide thanks to a membrane of skin joining its legs.

Reptiles

There are **crocodiles** in many of Gabon's lagoons and rivers. They are difficult to spot during the day. Looking for crocodiles along riverbanks at night is easier as their eyes shine red. Also keep an eye out for **monitor lizards** on branches overhanging rivers. Gabon's most famous snake is the **Gabon viper**, which is light brown in colour with detailed markings on its back. It eats rodents, hares, small monkeys, birds and toads. This adder reaches up to 1.2m (4ft) long and can weigh up to 8kg (18lb).

Marine life
Sea turtles

Gabon's beaches are world-renowned nesting grounds for turtles, in particular the **leatherback** turtle (*Dermochelys coriacea*). It has a supple 'leathery' shell without plates or scales. It is the largest turtle, measuring up to 190cm (6.2ft) and weighing more than 600kg (0.54 tons). On average 300 leatherbacks lay their eggs at Pongara Point each year between mid November and mid January.

There are three other species of sea turtle known to frequent the Atlantic waters near Gabon and São Tome and Príncipe. The **loggerhead** (*Caretta caretta*), which has a large head and a long shell coloured orange or brown, can weigh up to 200kg (0.18 tons). The two smallest sea turtles, at less than 45kg (99lb), are the dark green **olive ridley** (*Lepidochelys olivacea*) and **Kemp's ridley** (*Lepidochelys kempii*), which has a roundish shell with four shields on the bridge.

Whales

Gabon's coast is a very important breeding ground for humpback whales – an estimated 800–1,500 of them can be seen from July to October each year. They work their way up the coast as far as Cape Lopez before heading towards São Tomé and Príncipe. These whales are spectacular to watch and easy to identify, both from the way they look and the way they behave. The females average about 15m (50ft), and the males 12m (40ft). Both have knobbly heads and long flippers, black topsides and white or mottled undersides. The undersides of their flukes is speckled black and white. Each animal's pigmentation is as unique as a human fingerprint making identification of individual animals quite straightforward. Humpbacks sing long and complex songs, and enjoy breaching, lobtailing and flipper slapping. Killer whales, (otherwise known as orca whales), sperm whales and dolphins are also seen.

Research is now being conducted annually to build up a database of individual animals and their particular characteristics, with a view to building a more accurate picture of their migratory patterns.

Birding in Gabon and the islands
with Derek Schuurman

In terms of the diversity of bird species rainforests are the richest environments on earth, and the rainforests in Gabon are no exception. There are 680 species recorded for the country, most of them forest birds and some of them endemic or regionally endemic. Recognising the sounds of the different birds is an important factor in successful identification in the forest. Some species are rarely seen, only heard, such as the cuckoos that live in the forest canopy. Other birds with very distinctive calls are various orioles, bush shrikes and the spot-breasted ibis, and the black-wattled hornbill makes a whistling sound when it flies.

Gabon is a very under-birded country (ie: with few birdwatching visitors) so many visiting enthusiasts may still find themselves making a significant discovery. With a species list in excess of 670, a fabulous, intact habitat, and a stable political climate, Gabon is fast becoming one of Africa's top birding destinations. It is certainly *the* place to go to see many of the species local to Central and West Africa. Those at the top of many visitors' lists include the likes of the spot-breasted ibis, Hartlaub's duck, Congo serpent-eagle, black guineafowl, the remarkable red-headed picathartes (grey-necked rockfowl), African river martin, Congo moor chat, the lovely Rachel's malimbe and the highly localised Dja River warbler. There are more than 430 bird species in the Ivindo Basin, mostly forest dwellers. The Lopé region boasts more than 400 species, including forest, savannah and river birds. On a river trip birdwatchers will usually spot kingfishers, various sunbirds, white-crowned lapwings and, if lucky, the African finfoot.

The standard birding circuit for Gabon can be covered in two weeks and takes in the following sites:

Lopé National Park With its mosaic of rainforest and savannah, the Lopé holds somewhere around 400 species and is usually the first major stop on the birding itinerary. A bonus is the comfortable lodge overlooking the scenic Ogooué River. A minimum of two nights is needed here, but four is more realistic if one is to scratch beneath the surface as it were (forest birding is far more demanding and time consuming than that in other, more open habitats). There is actually a birding field guide devoted just to the Lopé, written by Gabon's premier field ornithologist, Patrice Christy, see *Further reading*, page 238.

Key species include various hornbills (always an indicator of a forest in good condition) such as black casqued, white-crested and piping hornbills; sunbirds, including Reichenbach's, green-headed, green-throated and violet-tailed; and blue-breasted and black bee-eaters. Weavers include the enigmatic yellow-mantled weaver and several of the gorgeous malimbes (Cassin's, blue-billed, blue-bellied and red-headed). The Dja River warbler (discovered here by Patrice Christy in 1994), and the sought-after lyre-tailed honeyguide, the bizarre display flights of which are more often heard than seen.

Ipassa Reserve A four- to six-night stay in this 10,000ha reserve with its grid of paths and species list of about 430 is bound to deliver impressive results. Many rate it as Africa's single best forest birding site.

Key species include: blue-headed dove, bare-cheeked trogon, yellow-throated cuckoo, the tiny African piculet, Rachel's malimbe, the lovely blue cuckoo-shrike, yellow longbill, a huge selection of greenbuls, rufous-sided broadbill, a cluster of barbets, including bristle-nosed and hairy-breasted; tiny and little green sunbirds; Gosling's and black-capped apalises, and Maxwell's black and yellow-capped weavers. On the forest floor – especially at ant columns – keep a lookout for various ant-thrushes, alethes and the shy forest robin.

The 'Highlands' of southeast Gabon Between Franceville and the Congo border, altitude rises and rainforest gives way to Brachystegia copses, open grassveld and heathland, the latter being rather unexpected in the tropics. Birders come here to look for Finch's francolin, Congo moor chat and black-chinned weaver, among others. Other 'megaticks' include the distinctive black-collared bulbul, Petit's cuckoo-shrike, Salvadori's eremomela, yellow-bellied hyliota, Joanna's sunbird, the sought-after black-headed bee-eater and Luhder's bush shrike. This is the one region of Gabon where one will see many species that enjoy a much broader distribution across the continent, so birders would do well to stay only a night or two.

Almost every Gabon birding tour – and indeed many other Gabon itineraries – ends with a spell on the sublime Gulf of Guinea islands of São Tomé and Príncipe. There are regular flights to the islands from Libreville.

São Tomé Ticking off the endemics of this large and rugged island is very demanding and walks involved can be a lot more challenging than on mainland Gabon. In the drier northeast, look for 'São Tomé' prinia and spinetail as well as golden-backed bishop and Newton's sunbird. But the bulk of the endemics, including some of the world's rarest, are hidden in the humid rainforests of the southeast. There you can look for 'São Tomé' kingfisher, weaver, speirops and paradise flycatcher (all quite common), and then try for 'São Tomé' olive pigeon, oriole, scops owl, giant sunbird and giant weaver. Very lucky visitors may see the dwarf olive ibis, but only a tiny handful of birders have ever seen a São Tomé fiscal and São Tomé grosbeak, both of which are critically endangered. (The grosbeak has been seen a few times since 1992 after having 'vanished' for 100 years.)

Príncipe A relaxing few days on this lovely island with its upscale resort make for a great end to any Gabon holiday. And all the Príncipe endemic birds are easily seen. They include the 'Príncipe' glossy starling, speirops, kingfisher, golden weaver and the strange Dohrn's thrush-babbler.

ECOFAC

The Ecosystèmes Forestiers d'Afrique Centrale (ECOFAC) – in English the Programme for Conservation and Rational Utilization of Forest Ecosystems in Central Africa – was set up in 1992. It is funded by the European Union and works in conjunction with government bodies. Its founding objective was to protect the equatorial rainforests of Central Africa in the six following countries: Cameroon, Congo, Central African Republic, Equatorial Guinea, Gabon, and São Tomé and Príncipe. The scope of its conservation interest has now broadened beyond the forest, for example to include turtles, but all initiatives conform to ECOFAC's founding principle that the protection of the environment and economic development are linked. Any activities should not only take into account the needs of local populations but also, wherever possible, involve them in the management of projects. ECOFAC is keen to promote carefully managed tourism as an alternative way for local communities to capitalise on their natural resources. ECOFAC also has a research arm – for example at the Lopé Wildlife Reserve there is a research station – which furthers our understanding of different ecosystems.

Further information
Birding field guides
Birds of Western Africa, the long-awaited masterpiece by Nik Borrow and Ron Demey (London: Helm Identification Guides, 2001) is the definitive and indispensable guide for Gabon, the Gulf of Guinea islands and all of West Africa.

Bird checklist for Gabon
You can find a checklist for Gabon at www.bsc-eoc.org. Look under the African section for Gabon.

Gabon birding tours
Nik Borrow leads annual tours to Gabon for Birdquest (see information on *Tour operators*, page 39). The tours tend to run in August–September (dry season). Vanga Tours (see *Tour operators*, page 40) have also been arranging tours to Gabon and the islands for years.

Birding trip reports on the web
An informative and evocative trip report with photos and sketches by Don Robertson – who visited with Vanga Tours and Patrice Christy in July 1996 – is at http://montereybay.com/creagrus/Gabon1996.html. Robertson was one of a few lucky birders to see the enigmatic grey-necked rockfowl (picathartes), most probably *the* most sought after bird in Gabon. On his special 'Rockfowl page' http://montereybay.com/creagrus/rockfowl.html,

he provides a marvellous description of the rockfowl and highlights the logistics involved just to enjoy a few seconds of observing these elusive 'wraiths' of the forest.

CONSERVATION

The big news is that in September 2002 at the World Summit in Johannesburg, President Bongo announced the establishment of a network of 13 national parks: Akanda, Bateké Plateau, Birougou, Crystal Mountains, Ivindo, Loango, Lopé, Mayumba, Minkébé, Moukalaba-Doudou, Mwagné, Pongara, Waka. Altogether the national parks will cover 10% of the country's land mass, protecting some 25,900km² (10,000 square miles) of vital wildlife habitats. National park protection is vital for the future of conservation in Central Africa, as is better management of the resources outside the national parks. In addition to the national parks, there are plans to create other protected areas, such as nature reserves and sanctuaries. For example, the Ogooué Delta is under consideration as a biosphere reserve.

Previously Gabon had no national-park system and so-called 'protected areas' were in actual fact not well protected at all. To illustrate this point, look at the Lopé National Park, which had been a reserve since 1946. Under laws passed in 1960 and 1982 'rational exploitation' was allowed in protected areas. This officially meant controlled hunting and logging, but inevitably logging roads reaching previously inaccessible parts of the forest also opened the forest up to poachers. In 1996 the permissible exploitation was confined to a peripheral area of the Lopé Reserve, while a core zone of about 2,400km² (167,000 hectares) was designated out of bounds. Selective logging and mineral exploitation were thus permitted in all but a meagre area totalling less than 1% of the country. (The meagre area legally protected from logging was the small Ipassa Reserve and this core part of the Lopé Reserve.)

The future of the Central African rainforest depends on the healthy interdependency between its plants and animals. One cannot survive without the other. Many forest trees depend on large mammals – notably elephants, gorillas and chimpanzees – to disperse their seeds. Where hunting is greatly reducing their numbers then the whole dynamics of the forest are threatened. Similarly, the loss of trees by logging represents a direct blow to the botanical composition of the forest on which the animals rely for their food. So the battle for conservation is really the battle against logging and poaching. As an economic alternative to logging, many of the new parks will be developed for ecotourism. Some of the funding necessary has been pledged by the US Secretary of State, Colin Powell.

The decision to create the national park network represents the successful culmination of years of hard work by environmental organisations and the Direction de la Faune et de la Chasse (DFC), the government department in charge of protected areas. The most prominent international environmental organisations are ECOFAC (see box, page 31), the Worldwide Fund for Nature (WWF) and the Wildlife Conservation Society (WCS). In a recent high-profile bid to raise awareness and funds for the precious habitats of

Central Africa, WCS biologist Mike Fay trekked through 2,000km (1,200 miles) of dense forest to the Atlantic coast. The Megatransect took 15 months, during which Fay and his team tirelessly made notes and took photographs (for more details on the Megatransect see the National Geographic website, www.nationalgeographic.com). Working alongside these international organisations to protect the turtles and whales of Gabon's coast is the local NGO, Aventures sans Frontières (ASF). For an overview of Gabon's network of national parks, you can also see www.gabonnationalparks.com.

Logging

The reasons for logging in Gabon, as elsewhere in Central Africa, are economic. After oil, timber has traditionally been the most important export product and, according to the government, the logging industry is the country's main employer, providing 60,000 people either directly or indirectly with their means of living. Okoumé and ozigo are the most heavily exploited woods, but other important trees are moabi, padouk, bilinga and sipo.

Gabon's logging industry operates on a system of 'selective logging', which is supposed to ensure that only trees fitting certain criteria can be cut down. The criteria for okoumé, for example, stipulate that cut trees must be over a certain size – their trunks must have reached a diameter of 70cm at ground level – and not more than 3–4 trees per hectare can be felled. In reality, getting to a tree that fits the criteria can sometimes mean the loss of up to 200 trees in logging roads.

Under the new national park network, a large number of logging concessions will be cancelled or scaled back – the surest way to prevent further deforestation.

Poaching

Hunting for subsistence living has traditionally been a way of life in Gabon, and is still permissible under certain criteria. All hunting is illegal between September 15 and March 15, and at any time of year inside any of Gabon's newly created national parks. Outside this period and areas, hunting the adult males of non-protected species is allowed (gorillas, chimpanzees, hippos, manatees, giant pangolins and leopard are all protected). The limit is three mammals of the same species and up to four mammals of different species per day per hunter with a hunting permit. Any hunting that does not fit into these criteria is illegal poaching.

Poaching may be an informal sector of the economy, but it's a highly important one, and worryingly it is not confined to subsistence levels. The threat of large-scale poaching is very real. Growing urbanisation has increased the market for bushmeat in the last generation, and economic recession has meant unemployment for a lot of young men for whom commercial hunting is one way, perhaps the only way, to earn a bit of money. Arms from the Soviet Union, China and the West are easily available, and when an AK47 assault rifle can be bought for under US$100 it can seem like an invitation to potential 'large-scale' poachers. Poachers have normally grown up with the forest and know and understand its animals. A common hunting trick to attract prey is to imitate the animal's call, for example that of an injured monkey.

Logging roads have facilitated the job of poachers by providing a means of reaching previously isolated forest and a route to market. What's more, logging trucks are a readily available means of transport. To make things even easier, the logging camps in the middle of the forest are themselves an immediate market. Sometimes hunting on logging concessions is limited to subsistence levels, but even that's worrying. A study by the Ministère des Eaux et Forets in a single logging camp recorded that 1,037 animals (including three gorillas and 424 monkeys) were killed in a two-month period in 1994, just for local consumption. Added to that, a 1999 report (French) estimated that a single logging camp in central Gabon consumes up to 80 tonnes of bushmeat in just one year. This is unsustainable. Hopes are high that the national park network will secure the future of local primate populations.

Bringing poaching down to sustainable levels is a conservation priority. Under pressure from environmental organisations, logging companies have recently agreed to do their bit, introducing roadblocks to confiscate any bushmeat found in logging trucks, and providing alternative sources of protein to logging camps, such as fish, chicken and beef. But half the battle is in re-educating the local communities and in providing them with some workable alternative. Ecotourism may well be the answer.

The same is true for turtle poaching. Turtles are under threat as they and their eggs represent a traditional source of nutrition to fishing communities. In a bid to raise awareness and appreciation of turtles in Central Africa, ECOFAC has produced educational materials, such as comics that show how tourism can more than replace the money made from turtle meat and eggs. Even more important in the battle is the research work of ASF, at Pongara Point, Mayumba and Iguela.

Oil

Gabon's principal natural resource, oil, is running out. This may have played a role in President Bongo's decision to create the national park network, with the purpose of encouraging new revenues from ecotourism. Extensive oil production in Gabon – whereby special dispensations were given to the oil companies by the Gabonese government, enabling them to operate in protected areas – looks as it is a thing of the past. So what have the environmental consequences been? A lot of research has been carried out looking at the effects of oil exploration and exploitation around Gamba (see page 132). The vast majority of experts agree that certainly with the big multi-nationals like Shell, who have strict internal guidelines relating to the environment, the direct negative effects of oil-related activities are limited. That said, they also agree that indirectly oil companies are placing enormous pressure on a sensitive environment. The greater demands of larger local populations and improved access to remote areas have given poachers an enormous helping hand and animal populations are under severe threat. Environmental organisations and oil companies in Gamba are working together to change attitudes towards poaching by holding environmental training programmes that emphasise the

RAINFOREST AFRICA

Sarah Monaghan www.gabonmagazine.com

It's early days yet but Gabon is set to become the world's premier destination for African equatorial tourism if its government has its way. President Bongo's bold decision to create 13 national parks and protect 11% of his biodiversity-rich country was announced to worldwide acclaim at the World Summit on Sustainable Development in 2002.

Since then, the Wildlife Conservation Society (WCS) has worked with the government to develop its blueprint for ecotourism development. Entitled *The Vision*, this ambitious plan puts tourism at the heart of the country's development agenda.

The rainforest 'that has it all' is Gabon's big sell. 'Going to Gabon is like going to Antarctica,' says John Gwynne, WCS vice-president. 'It's that rare. What Gabon has just doesn't exist elsewhere. Sure, the Amazon has fantastic biodiversity, but let's face it, it's mostly birds and beetles. Gabon's rainforest has them but it has mega-vertebrates too: great apes and bongos, elephants and more...'

Gabon is to follow the lead of Costa Rica and Australia whose marketing slogans *No Artificial Ingredients* and *Life in a Different Light* helped ignite their tourism sectors. 'Rainforest Africa' is the new motto being used to promote Gabon's wildlife wealth and dispel the negative associations of unrest experienced elsewhere in Central Africa but not stable Gabon.

With investment, high-end tourist lodges will be opened, national infrastructure improved and a new international airport built. In the next few years, Gabon's tourism scene is going to change fast. My advice? Go now, get there first ...

For more information visit www.wcsgabon.org.

importance of conserving environment and the possible dangers of consuming bushmeat. Overturning traditional attitudes is still a long way off, but at least steps are being taken in the right direction.

GEOGRAPHICAL EXPEDITIONS

LOGISTICS, WALKING SAFARIS & EXPEDITIONS

www.geographicalexpeditions.com

mistral VOYAGES

GABON
SAO TOME & PRINCIPE

Ecotourism specialist in the heart of Central Africa's tropical forest – one of the earth's most pristine rainforests.

Come and see the last paradise of chimps, gorillas, forest elephants, sitatungas, humpback whales, turtles, rare birds and endemic orchids.

**Mistral Voyages, BP 2106, Libreville, Gabon
Tel 241/74 77 79, Fax 241/74 77 80
e-mail Mistral.lbv@internetgabon.com**

Previous page Western lowland gorilla, Lopé National Park (TI)

Above Curtain of greenery, Ogooué (DH)

Right Forest elephants (JT)

Below Baby squirrel, Lopé National Park (TI)

Below Splashes of colour brighten up the deep greens of the rainforest (JT)

Planning Your Trip

TOURIST INFORMATION

Given that tourism in Gabon is still in its infancy, it is hardly surprising that at the time of writing there were virtually no Tourist Boards outside Gabon. In 2002 one opened next door to the old Air Gabon office in Paris, although there is very little information there. Offices are planned for Washington and South Africa next.

The closest thing to a tourist office in Gabon is the Centre Gabonais de Promotion Touristique, who advertise themselves as **Gabontour**. This is the information arm of the Ministry of Tourism. Their main office is in the centre of Libreville, and they also have a satellite office at Libreville airport (BP 2085, Libeville; tel: 72 85 04; fax: 72 85 03; Comptoir Aeroport Leon M'Ba, international arrivals hall; tel: 73 47 61; web: www.internetgabon.com/tourisme; email: gabontour@internetgabon.com or men@internetgabon.com). You might also want to surf the following websites – www.mbolo.com and www.assala.com – which will then direct you to further sites (mostly in French), or talk to the Gabon representative at a travel agency (see under *Tour operators* later in this chapter).

GETTING THERE
By air

Libreville is serviced by most of the usual international airlines, which between them run regular flights to the following cities: Abidjan, Bata, Brazzaville, Bruxelles, Casablanca, Cotonou, Dakar, Douala, Dubai, Johannesburg, Lagos, Lomé, London, Luanda, Kinshasa, Malabo, Marseille, Paris, Pointe-Noire, Port Harcourt, Rome, São Tomé and Zurich. Details of the Libreville offices you are most likely to need are listed below.

Air Afrique The Air Afrique building in the town centre; BP 311; tel: 76 44 00
Air France Bd de l'independence; tel: 77 36 77. Airport office; tel: 73 20 88
Air São Tomé Via Mistral Voyages; BP 2969; tel: 76 04 21 or 76 12 22
Cameroon Airlines Opposite the Renovation building, second floor; BP 2191; tel: 76 46 22 or 72 41 38
Lina Congo Near to SDV Voyages Mbolo; BP 4176; tel: 74 31 28/29
Nigeria Airways Ltd On the second floor of the Air Afrique building; BP 1964; tel: 72 48 30 or 76 45 20
Royal Air Maroc Hotel Inter-Continental; tel: 73 10 25

SN Brussels Tel: 0870 735 2345; www.flysn.com
Swiss International Airlines The Frangipaniers building; BP 1125; tel: 74 34
51/52/53. The airline no longer flies to Libreville, but flights to Douala in Cameroon
are still in operation.

If you are leaving from Europe, your choice is essentially Air France or
Swiss International Airlines. Between them there are flights several times a
week from Paris and Geneva, and every Saturday from London. The direct
flight time to Paris is about seven hours and for London would be about an
hour longer, but more often than not there is a stopover that usually adds
another couple of hours' journey time. When leaving Libreville airlines
advise passengers to check in as much as seven hours before the plane is due
to leave. For example, for a flight leaving at 23.00, passengers check their
bags in at 16.00, then leave the airport and return at 21.00. This system in
theory ensures that your seat is secure, although of course it's no guarantee
that when you return to the airport there won't be delays, and at this end
you're more likely to be spending the night in the waiting lounge than in a
hotel.

From Europe
Swiss International Airlines There are counters at Heathrow (terminal 2) and
London City airport, or contact Reservations (tel: 0845 601 0956; fax: 020 8762 7199).
Swiss International Airlines There is a counter at Charles de Gaulle airport
(terminal 2B, Gate 3; tel: 01 48 16 50 00), or contact Reservations (tel: 08 20 04 05 06).

From North America
There are no direct flights to Libreville from any North American cities.
Passengers must first fly to Europe and then take a connecting flight.

Getting to/from Libreville's aiport
The Aeroport de Libreville (ADL) is 12km (7 miles) from the centre of
Libreville. For airport information call 73 62 44/46/47 or fax: 73 61 28. Taxis
charge 2,000CFA to take you into town or 4,000CFA after 21.00.

Tour operators
The number of tour operators offering organised trips to Gabon is not
extensive, but there are a few European-based options. Some of them combine
trips to Gabon with São Tomé island or the wildlife reserves of Odzala and
Nouabalé Ndoki in northern Congo. **Explore Worldwide** currently offer a
seven-day package to Gabon (the highlight of which is forest trekking at
Lopé), with an optional seven-day extension to São Tomé island. Trips have a
maximum of 12 participants. **Discovery Initiatives** run trips to Lopé, Iguela
and parks elsewhere in Central Africa, as well as offering tailor-made trips. A
specialist birdwatching trip to Gabon and São Tomé and Príncipe is run by
Birdquest Limited most years, leaving in early August. It's about 24 days

long and on the Gabon part takes in not only Lopé, but also the Mpassa Reserve and southeastern High Ogooué around Léconi. **Geographical Expeditions** run 15-day tours to Lopé, Langoué Bai, Iguela and Petit Loango. The enthusiastic company director, Charlie Rapoport, is committed to leading small groups with a maximum of six people, with an emphasis on camping in remote places of extreme beauty.

French historical links explain why certain French tour operators have had a Gabon interest. **Club Faune** specialises in fishing trips to camps on Gabon's coast between September and April, and **Terra Incognita** run ten-day trips to Lopé. **Mistral Voyages** in Marseilles is an excellent point of contact. They also have a branch in Libreville, and can give you up-to-date details of the different trips on offer. Mistral Voyages in Libreville act as the ground agents for a number of tour operators, including **Vie Sauvage**, who offer an expensive tailor-made programme to Lopé and Nyonié, with an optional extension to Petit Loango.

If visitors ask the tour operator at the time of booking, it is normally possible to delay their return flight after the official end of an organised tour. This way travellers can be introduced to a new country in the security of a group, but have the thrill and freedom of continuing their trip independently.

Given the difficulties of getting around Gabon, organised excursions can save a lot of time and effort. For more flexibility, you can book excursions in Libreville. In my experience the local travel agencies are very helpful and reliable. There is a list of reputable agencies in Libreville under *Tourist information* in *Chapter 6*.

Birdquest Ltd Two Jays, Kemple End, Stonyhurst, Clitheroe, Lancs BB7 9QY, UK; tel: 01254 826 317; fax: 01254 826 780

Club Faune 22 rue Duban, 75016 Paris, France; tel: 01 42 88 31 32; fax: 01 45 24 31 29; web: www.club-faune-peche.com

Discovery Initiatives 51 Castle St, Cirencester, Glos GL7 1QD, UK; tel: 01285 643333; fax: 01285 885888; email: enquiry@discoveryinitiatives.com

Explore Worldwide 1 Frederick St, Aldershot, Hants GU11 1LQ, UK; tel: 01252 760000, fax: 01252 760001; web: www.exploreworldwide.com

Geographical Expeditions Garryvenus, Ballycahill, Thurles, County Tipperary, Ireland; tel/fax: 087 81 62947; email: info@geographicalexpeditions.com; web: www.geographicalexpeditions.com

Mistral Voyages 42 cours Pierre Puget, 13006 Marseilles, France; tel: 04 91 54 73 71; fax: 04 91 54 11 26; web: www.ecotourisme.gabon.com

Terra Incognita CP 701 / 36 Quai Arloing, 69 256 Lyon, Cedex 09, France; tel: 04 72 53 24 90; fax: 04 72 53 24 81; web: www.terra-incognita.fr

Tropical Birding 17 Toucan Tropics, Blouberggrise 7441, South Africa; tel: +27 82 400 3400/+27 83 296 0147; fax: +27 21 556 4124; email: tropicalbirding@telkomsa.net; web: www.tropicalbirding.com

Vanga Tours PO Box 38770, Pinelands, 7430 Cape Town, South Africa; tel: +27 21 5317968; fax: +27 21 5311679; email: vangatrs@global.co.za

Vie Sauvage 24 rue Vignon, 75009 Paris, France; tel: 01 44 51 08 00; fax: 01 44 51 08 09. Note that this is a hunting operation.

By land

The most popular road to **Congo** is in the north, via Makokou, Mékambo (where customs is) and Ekata. This would be the right direction for those heading to Odzala National Park for example. Those driving to Ouésso are better off going via Mazingo. The border with **Cameroon** is the River Ntem, and the border village on the Gabon side is Eboro. There's a bridge for vehicles, and for those without their own transport there are plenty of *pagayeurs* taking passengers across the river. To travel by land from Gabon to **Equatorial Guinea**, it is necessary to head west from Oyem or preferably from Bitam via Meyo Kye, where the adjoining road is better. This is the only way to do it, as it is not possible to cross the border at Acurenam.

For any of the above countries, the surest and cheapest approach is to have obtained your visa from your home country in advance. Even if there is no embassy in your home country, however, I have heard stories of non-residents of Gabon having difficulty obtaining visas applied for at these embassies in Libreville. Do not rely on being able to buy a visa at the border, although a day's *laissez-passer* should be straightforward.

By sea

To go to Equatorial Guinea by any means other than by air, you'll need to take a *pirogue* from Cocobeach to Cogo, site of Equatorial Guinean customs and immigration. I know that freight boats leaving Libreville will sometimes take paying passengers. They are usually bound for Bata (Equatorial Guinea), Abidjan (Ivory Coast), São Tomé and, most frequently of all, Douala (Cameroon). Crossings are irregular and you would need to make enquiries at the boats docked at Port Môle and negotiate with the captain. Prepare for a rough ride and take more food and drink than you think you will need.

ENTRY REQUIREMENTS

Needless to say, you must ensure you have a valid passport, and one that is not due to expire for at least six months. An International Certificate of Vaccination against Yellow Fever is also necessary for entry into Gabon. This needs to be the original, not a photocopy.

There has been some recent confusion within the travel industry regarding entry visas for tourists. What is clear is that visas, valid for up to three months, are needed by citizens of the UK, New Zealand, Australia, the United States and Canada. It is also clear that tourists should arrange their visas before they travel. What is less clear-cut is the procedure for obtaining a visa. According to a decree issued by the government in May 2001, both tourist and business visas should be obtained via a travel agent, *not* an embassy. What lies behind this decree is the government's blatant desire to encourage luxury tourists at the expense of backpackers. So-called 'luxury' tourists are those who book a package via a travel agent or tour operator (either in Gabon or elsewhere). These tourists will automatically have their visa arranged for them as part of the trip's services. By contrast, independent backpackers would normally have to obtain their visa from an embassy, and it is they who theoretically lose out under the 2001 decree.

I say theoretically because in reality visas can still be obtained from Gabonese embassies. Applicants need to supply a passport-sized photo, and depending on which embassy you go to, you will probably also need to attach photocopies of your airline ticket and confirmation of your accommodation, such as a hotel booking covering at least the first night(s) of a trip. An absolute minimum of five working days should be allowed for a visa application to be processed, but the time needed to process applications varies between embassies. The cost also varies, but is approximately 55 euros for tourists, more for business travellers. Applicants for a business visa will need a formal invitation letter from their company in order to obtain a visa via the embassy. Alternatively, the company can arrange the visa from Gabon with the necessary photographs and passport photocopies.

If you are intending to leave the country and then return – for example to go to São Tomé – you should apply for a multiple-entry visa, although there is no guarantee that you'll get one. If when you fly back from São Tomé you are connecting to an international flight then a single-entry visa for Gabon is sufficient. Once in Gabon, visa issues are dealt with by the CGDI, or *Centre Gouvernemental d'Immigration* (tel: 76 24 24, 76 24 77), but in the first instance it might be advisable to talk to a travel agent.

Customs
There is no limit to the amount of local or foreign currency that can be brought into the country, although any foreign currency must be declared. You are only allowed to leave with a maximum of 200,000CFA or a sum in foreign currency not greater than the amount you imported. The duty-free allowance for travellers over the age of 17 years is as follows: 200 cigarettes or 50 cigars or 250g tobacco; 2 litres alcohol and 50g perfume.

Gabon's diplomatic missions abroad
Below are the addresses of the Gabonese embassies or high commissions you are most likely to need.

Belgium 112 Av Winston Churchill, 1180 Bruxelles; tel: 02 358 2875; fax: 02 346 4669
Canada 4 Road Range, BP 368, Ottawa, Ontario Kin-8J5; tel: 613 232 5301; 613 232 6916
Cameroon BP 4130, Yaoundé; tel: 20 29 66; fax: 21 01 24
Congo BP 2033, Brazzaville; tel: 83 26 19; fax: 83 30 74
Equatorial Guinea BP 18, Malabo; tel: 08 3180
France 26 bis Av Raphael, 75016 Paris; tel: 01 44 30 22 30; fax: 01 45 20 43 45.
Germany Kronprinzenstr. 52, 5300 Bonn 2; tel: 228 35 92 86; fax: 228 36 58 44

Italy via del Pozzetto 122, 00187 Rome; tel: 06 699 0096/0016; fax: 06 699 0094.
Ivory Coast 01 BP 3765, Abidjan 01; tel: 20 44 51 14; fax: 20 27 70 75
São Tomé e Príncipe CP 394, São Tomé; tel: 12 21 280; fax: 12 23 531
Spain c/Angel de Diego Roldan, no. 14-16, Madrid 280160; tel: 01 413 1153
South Africa PO Box 9222, Pretoria; tel: 02 342 4376/77; fax: 02 342 4375, 322 9429
UK 27 Elvaston Place, London SW7 5NL; tel: 020 7823 9986; fax: 020 7584 0047
USA 2034 20th St, NW Washington DC 20009; tel: 202 797 1000; fax: 202 332 0668
(Consulate in New York, tel: 683 7371.)

WHEN TO VISIT
Gabon can be visited at any time of year. It is hot and humid all year round, but to a lesser degree during the long dry season (May–September). During the rainy season downpours may come at any time of day and can last for several hours.

Travelling
Getting around Gabon at any time of the year can be slow and frustrating, and in the wet season doubly so. Trains and planes – except for light aircraft – should not be affected by wet weather, but the roads pose more of a problem. Only too quickly the tarmac runs out, leaving you struggling on dirt roads.

Flora and fauna
With the coming of spring around mid-September, the forest bursts into flower. By Christmas and the New Year fruit is in abundance. The majority of orchids flower in the savannah and open grasslands between October and January, while some marshy areas are covered in flower during December and January.

If you want to go gorilla trekking, then as a general rule your best bet is to visit during the rains between October and late February. At this time there is more fruit around and the soft ground means gorillas tracks are easier to spot. During the long dry season between mid June and mid September, fruit is scarce and primates and birds spend the majority of their time searching for food in the forest and are less likely to venture into the open savannah. Birdwatchers can sight many migratory birds between November and April coming from Europe or northern Asia or Africa.

The season for whale and dolphin watching is July–October, although the surest time to see them is August–September. To see turtles laying their eggs on the beach at night you should come between mid November and mid January.

Photography
Photographers should bear in mind that the skies are for the most part dull and grey during the dry season, whereas during the rainy season the sky is blue and sparkling after a downpour.

WHAT TO TAKE
The inescapable conundrum of packing is not to overpack and not to leave behind essential items that you won't be able to find on the road. The type of

trip you are intending to do will obviously determine how you distinguish between what is essential and what is a luxury. If you are embarking on an organised trip, you probably needn't share the backpacker's overriding concern about having to walk long distances or struggle in and out of public transport laden with luggage. That said, you will still face a weight restriction if your trip involves a flight in a privately chartered plane at any point, usually of 15kg. Only those travelling in their own vehicle or who have a base where they can store items have the flexibility to bring the kitchen sink, and even then I would advise against it.

Getting the balance right requires careful planning. The classic 'novice traveller' trap is to fill a 75-litre rucksack and a daypack. Not only will you struggle in the heat, feel overburdened and look foolish, but to add insult to injury, you'll probably only use about a third of what you've packed. The trick is not to pack in a rush and not to think you have to take *everything* with you. Clothes can be washed and everyday items replenished or substituted, not to mention that having room for impulse purchases is part of the travel experience. If in doubt leave it out – travelling light is the most liberating. It's a struggle, but I limit myself to a 35-litre rucksack (with lots of pockets) and a daysac. The daysac is one that folds in on itself to make a smaller bag so I can use it at full size on daytrips/treks and at its small size as a handbag substitute. Of course, if you have camera equipment or much in the way of a wardrobe, being this ruthless may not be possible.

Campers will need a large, sturdy rucksack, preferably with an internal frame. Once again, you'll be grateful for a second bag if there are any non-camping sections of the trip when heavy equipment can be temporarily offloaded somewhere that you are returning to. Non-campers on a tight budget may wish to pack a mosquito net and sheet sleeping bag, which can make a less than sparkling room more appealing.

Whatever luggage you decide on in the end, it's a good idea to use a padlock. Bags can of course be slashed or stolen, but a lock is at least some kind of deterrent.

Clothing

Given the high temperatures and humidity throughout the year, cotton is the best fabric to wear. Lightweight, short-sleeved shirts and loose-fitting trousers or flowing skirts make the most comfortable outfits. Outside of the forest people make an effort with their appearance, so it's worth taking at least one nice thing to wear. If you are a woman on your own you will receive extra attention, which at its worst tends to be more annoying than dangerous. In my experience the rule is the same all over the world. The more flesh you bare the more attention you invite, so if you don't want it, don't wear it.

For trekking in the forest, long-sleeved shirts and trousers are a must to avoid scratches and bites. So as not to scare off all the wildlife, browns and khakis should be worn on safari, and white should be avoided. Gaiters will keep you dryish when crossing streams, and are also excellent protection against biting ants and ticks.

Other clothing essentials, irrespective of the season, are a lightweight raincoat or poncho, a floppy hat, swimwear and sunglasses. I would also recommend taking a sweatshirt or fleece as the air conditioning can be fierce in some tourist hotels and restaurants.

Footwear
Boots are essential for forest trekking or any extended walk. Make sure they are lightweight. This is really important as the heat makes heavy footwear unbearable. Breathable canvas is therefore preferable to leather. Wear two thin pairs of socks and ensure your boots are well worn in if you want any reasonable hope of avoiding blisters. The forest floor is uneven and wet, so your boots must also give you sufficient ankle support and preferably be waterproof. Even waterproof boots, however, will not keep you dry when wading through streams or caught in a torrential tropical downpour.

For everyday footwear, take trainers or sandals. Flip-flops can be easily bought.

Camping equipment
Although camping is not allowed in any protected areas, there's nothing to stop you pitching a tent anywhere else. Some of the supplies you might need, such as mosquito nets, can be bought in Libreville, but I would not suggest relying on finding everything you need here. Some of the things you should consider bringing are a Global Positioning System (GPS), Leatherman tool, roll mat, sleeping bag, tin plate, cutlery and mug, firelighters, and of course a lightweight mosquito-proof tent.

Other useful items
As far as documentation is concerned, I would strongly suggest photocopying everything, three or four times, from the numbers of travellers' cheques to your international driving licence and yellow fever certificate (although at immigration you need to be able to show your original). For security purposes it is very important to have a photocopy of the relevant pages of your passport; this can make getting a replacement that much easier should you need to. Leave copies of all this with a couple of people back home, and hide a couple more in the various pouches and pockets around your luggage.

Binoculars are essential for watching birds and monkeys, although if you have a long lens on your camera you could try making do with that instead. Compact 7x21 binoculars weigh very little and fit neatly into a pocket.

Other crucial items are a powerful torch (preferably a head torch), an alarm clock, a basic sewing kit, a towel (I personally don't rate those tiny and supposedly super-absorbent travel towels), a water bottle, a penknife, a medical kit and a handful of energy bars. You may want to include in your reading material a comprehensive wildlife guide (see *Further Reading*). Luxury items you might want to consider are a novel, short-wave radio or personal stereo. Take several strong bin liners; these will keep your kit dry when the skies open.

If you are going to be hiring and driving, cycling or otherwise going it alone, you should add the following to your list of essentials: compass, whistle, electrical insulating tape for all-purpose repairs, biodegradable washing powder and shower gel, and a country or regional map. For more information about maps see *Further Reading*. Given that no map of Gabon is entirely reliable, anyone intending to head anywhere really remote might want to invest in a hand-held GPS navigation system. This battery-powered device can tell you your latitude, longitude and elevation to within 100m anywhere in the world by corresponding with American military satellites. The downside is that in order to do so it needs open, unobstructed access to the sky, which cannot be relied upon if you are in the jungle. In the forest a GPS should be used in conjunction with, not instead of, a guide.

Your bare health essentials should include water-purifying tablets, insect repellent and anti-histamine tablets in case of inset bites and stings. You may also consider a blister-treatment kit in this category. Vegetarians and vegans should seriously consider taking multivitamin supplements. Sunblock, lipsalve and toilet roll are basics that you should carry on you at all times. Women should bear in mind that tampons and sanitary pads are not readily available outside the main towns. See *Chapter 5* for more details of what to include in your medical kit. If you have lots of spare pens and pencils at home you could take some with you and drop them off at a local school.

PHOTOGRAPHY

I suggest you take all the print and slide film you think you will need with you. There are a number of places to buy and process film in Libreville – for example in the Mbolo shopping centre and opposite the BICIG bank in Nombakélé – but the turnover of stocks of film is not always very fast. Check that films are not out of date before you buy.

MONEY

I would suggest you take the bulk of the money you will need as cash, and preferably as CFA francs or euros. I recommend wearing trousers with zip or button pockets – I'm not a great believer in money belts – where you can put small amounts of ready cash in one pocket and the serious money in another pocket that you only open in private. I do not suggest carrying all your money; leave some hidden in your luggage too.

If you feel uncomfortable doing this, and will be spending some time in Libreville, Port Gentil or Franceville, you could bring travellers' cheques as well. In theory, these can now be changed at most big banks, but I have heard stories of people leaving banks disappointed. Your best bet is to bring a widely recognised type in euros, such as American Express or Thomas Cook. At least they have the advantage that they can be refunded if lost, stolen, or taken back home. As always when travelling with travellers' cheques, take a range of cheque denominations, including small denominations. Keep a separate note of refund information and the cheque numbers. Make a note of which cheque numbers you use as you go along, as this will speed up a refund if you need one.

PHOTOGRAPHY
Ariadne Van Zandbergen
Equipment

Although with some thought and an eye for composition you can take reasonable photos with a 'point-and-shoot' camera, you need an SLR camera if you are at all serious about photography. Modern SLRs tend to be very clever, with automatic programmes for almost every possible situation, but remember that these programmes are limited in the sense that the camera cannot think, but only make calculations. Every starting amateur photographer should read a photographic manual for beginners and get to grips with such basics as the relationship between aperture and shutter speed.

Always buy the best lens you can afford. The lens determines the quality of your photo more than the camera body. Fixed fast lenses are ideal, but very costly. A zoom lens makes it easier to change composition without changing lenses the whole time. If you carry only one lens, a 28–70mm (digital 17–55mm) or similar zoom should be ideal. For a second lens, a lightweight 80–200mm or 70–300mm (digital 55–200mm) or similar will be excellent for candid shots and varying your composition. Wildlife photography will be very frustrating if you don't have at least a 300mm lens. For a small loss of quality, tele-converters are a cheap and compact way to increase magnification: a 300 lens with a 1.4x converter becomes 420mm, and with a 2x it becomes 600mm. Note, however, that 1.4x and 2x tele-converters reduce the speed of your lens by 1.4 and 2 stops respectively.

For wildlife photography from a safari vehicle, a solid beanbag, which you can make yourself very cheaply, will be necessary to avoid blurred images, and is more useful than a tripod. A clamp with a tripod head screwed on to it can be attached to the vehicle as well. Modern dedicated flash units are easy to use; aside from the obvious need to flash when you photograph at night, you can improve a lot of photos in difficult 'high contrast' or very dull light with some fill-in flash. It pays to have a proper flash unit as opposed to a built-in camera flash.

Digital/film

Digital photography is now the preference of most amateur and professional photographers, with the resolution of digital cameras improving the whole time. For ordinary prints a 6 megapixel camera is fine. For better results and the possibility to enlarge images and for professional reproduction, higher resolution is available up to 16 megapixels.

Memory space is important. The number of pictures you can fit on a memory card depends on the quality you choose. Calculate in advance how many pictures you can fit on a card and either take enough cards to last for your trip, or take a storage drive on to which you can download the content. A laptop gives the advantage that you can see your pictures properly at the end of each day and edit and delete rejects, but a storage device is lighter and less bulky. These drives come in different capacities up to 80GB.

Bear in mind that digital camera batteries, computers and other storage devices need charging, so make sure you have all the chargers, cables and converters with you. Most hotels have charging points, but do enquire about this in advance. When camping you might have to rely on charging from the car battery; a spare battery is invaluable.

If you are shooting film, 100 to 200 ISO print film and 50 to 100 ISO slide film are ideal. Low ISO film is slow but fine grained and gives the best colour saturation, but will need more light, so support in the form of a tripod or monopod is important. You can also bring a few 'fast' 400 ISO films for low-light situations where a tripod or flash is no option.

Dust and heat

Dust and heat are often a problem. Keep your equipment in a sealed bag, stow films in an airtight container (eg: a small cooler bag) and avoid exposing equipment and film to the sun. Digital cameras are prone to collecting dust particles on the sensor which results in spots on the image. The dirt mostly enters the camera when changing lenses, so be careful when doing this. To some extent photos can be 'cleaned' up afterwards in Photoshop, but this is time-consuming. You can have your camera sensor professionally cleaned, or you can do this yourself with special brushes and swabs made for the purpose, but note that touching the sensor might cause damage and should only be done with the greatest care.

Light

The most striking outdoor photographs are often taken during the hour or two of 'golden light' after dawn and before sunset. Shooting in low light may enforce the use of very low shutter speeds, in which case a tripod will be required to avoid camera shake.

With careful handling, side lighting and back lighting can produce stunning effects, especially in soft light and at sunrise or sunset. Generally, however, it is best to shoot with the sun behind you. When photographing animals or people in the harsh midday sun, images taken in light but even shade are likely to be more effective than those taken in direct sunlight or patchy shade, since the latter conditions create too much contrast.

Protocol

In some countries, it is unacceptable to photograph local people without permission, and many people will refuse to pose or will ask for a donation. In such circumstances, don't try to sneak photographs as you might get yourself into trouble. Even the most willing subject will often pose stiffly when a camera is pointed at them; relax them by making a joke, and take a few shots in quick succession to improve the odds of capturing a natural pose.

Ariadne Van Zandbergen is a professional travel and wildlife photographer specialising in Africa. She runs The Africa Image Library. For photo requests, visit www.africaimagelibrary.co.za or contact her on ariadne@hixnet.co.za.

Personally, I would rather rely on a Visa card as security, for which you *must* have a PIN number. The BICIG bank has cash machines but Visa is the *only* credit card you can use, and without a PIN number your card is just a useless bit of plastic. Credit cards are still only an accepted method of payment in *certain* major hotels, such as the Inter-Continental and The Meridian in Libreville. If you need money wired to you, there are branches of Western Union in Libreville and Franceville (see under the relevant chapters for branch details). They claim that money sent is received immediately, as long as you have identification, and a password and ten-digit number given to you by the sender. It is the sender not the receiver who must pay for this service.

As for advice on how much money to take, any budget will obviously depend on how, where and how long you travel for. The most basic accommodation will set you back as little as 6,000CFA a night. A standard hotel with en-suite facilities, a restaurant of some sort, telephones and sometimes other facilities will set you back about 20,000CFA per room (single or double) per night. You get a bit more for your money in terms of facilities outside Libreville. Top hotels cost just as much as anywhere else in the world.

If you are spending all or most of your time on an organised tour, you will have had to pay in advance for everything except for the occasional meal and tips. Make sure you know exactly what is, and isn't, covered. Food and drink in Gabon are not cheap because virtually everything is imported. A meal in a simple restaurant might set you back less than 4,000CFA, while a two-course meal in a typical tourist restaurant will cost about 15,000CFA, plus an additional 1,500CFA per beer or 15,000CFA per bottle of wine. If you intend to move around, you will need to take into account transport costs. Read the relevant section in *Chapter 4 Getting around* to give you an idea.

Just as elsewhere in Africa, it's on safari that the money really goes. Allow in the region of 100,000CFA for each day you are on safari, and up to 50% more for gorilla trekking.

SUGGESTED ITINERARIES

1 week A day or two in Libreville, then on to Lopé or Langoué Bai, and finally a trip to the beach at Point Denis.

2 weeks From Libreville, head to Lopé or Langoué Bai, returning to Libreville via Lambaréné. Then catch a plane to Iguela or Gamba.

4 weeks Spend a couple of days in Libreville and Point Denis, before heading to Lopé or Langoué Bai. Return to Libreville via Lambaréné and then catch a plane to Iguela or Gamba. Finish up with a week in São Tomé and Príncipe.

Travelling Around

GETTING AROUND
Getting from place to place in Gabon can be difficult, time-consuming, expensive, and sometimes it's all three. It can also be a fantastic way to see the country and meet its people.

By air
There are several airline companies that between them run regular flights from Libreville to the following cities: Bitam, Gamba, Koulamoutou, Makokou, Mayumba, Mouila, Mvengue (Franceville), Ombooué, Oyem, Port Gentil and Tchibanga. The companies frequently change their timetables and should be contacted directly for the most up-to-date information. The main ones are as follows: **Air Service Gabon** (tel: 73 24 08, 73 24 09); **Avirex** (tel: 73 99 20, 73 75 31; fax: 73 66 56); **Air Max** (tel: 20 44 31; fax: 76 28 56); **Gabon Express** (tel: 73 38 40, 73 46 15); and **Transair Gabon** (tel: 24 88 99, 72 63 27). Most of them have offices in the main airport building or in the building to the left, next to the Aeroclub restaurant. This is obviously very handy for comparing times and prices. At present, Air Gabon has a reputation for late and cancelled flights, whilst Avirex has a better track record.

If you have the funds, hiring your own light aircraft will give you even greater flexibility. It's expensive, but the views are amazing – that is unless weather conditions force the pilot to fly above the clouds. Seeing the rainforest from 10–100m above is much more than a means of getting to your destination, it is an attraction in itself. Make enquiries at **Mistral Voyages** or the **Aeroclub**. The hourly rate for a Cessna 402 seating seven passengers is in the region of 2,500 euros, and at a rough estimate it can travel at around 250km/hr if the weather is good. Remember that light aircraft have luggage allowances in the region of 15kg per person. Even if passengers only want a one-way journey they must pay for the aircraft's return trip. Otherwise, if the pilot is required to hang around for a couple of days before the return flight, passengers will be expected to cover his accommodation and food as well.

By rail
Gabon's only railway, the *Transgabonais* (Trans-Gabon Railway), bisects the country east–west, running from Libreville through over 20 stations to its terminus, Franceville. The railroad was the property of the state (run by an

EXPRESS TRAINS FROM OWENDO TO FRANCEVILLE

	Tue, train 11 arr/dep	Fri, train 15 arr/dep	Sun, train 21 arr/dep
Owendo	na/09.00	na/21.00	na/21.00
Ndjolé	11.24/11.26	23.24/23.26	23.24/23.26
Lopé	12.43/12.46	00.43/00.46	00.43/00.46
Booué	13.20/13.25	01.20/01.25	01.20/01.25
Lastoursville	15.01/15.06	03.01/03.06	03.01/03.06
Moanda	16.27/16.32	04.27/04.32	04.27/04.32
Franceville	17.00/na	05.00/na	05.00/na

EXPRESS TRAINS FROM FRANCEVILLE TO OWENDO

	Thu, train 14 arr/dep	Fri, train 16 arr/dep	Sun, train 22 arr/dep
Franceville	na/10.10	na/21.35	na/21.35
Moanda	10.28/10.38	22.03/22.08	22.03/22.08
Lastoursville	11.54/11.59	23.29/23.34	23.29/23.34
Booué	13.35/13.40	01.10/01.30	01.10/01.30
Lopé	14.14/14.17	02.04/02.07	02.04/02.07
Ndjolé	15.34/15.36	03.24/03.26	03.24/03.26
Owendo	18.00/na	05.50/na	05.50/na

SAMPLE TARIFS IN CFA

	VIP	First	Second
Owendo–Lopé	21,500	19,500	16,800
Owendo–Moanda	44,500	40,700	24,700
Owendo–Franceville	48,700	43,000	36,800

NB Train times correct at time of going to press.

office known as OCTRA) until 1999, when it was privatised. The railroad is not without its problems, but it serves a crucial role in the country's economy and in linking the capital to rural areas. In 2001 it transported an estimated three million tonnes of merchandise and 280,000 passengers. On some old maps a railway line is shown heading up through northeastern Gabon. This section of the railway does not exist, and is unlikely ever to do so. Rail bosses prefer the idea of extending the rail network from Franceville to Brazzaville in Congo, a distance of about 100km (62 miles), with a view to transporting wood from the Congo to the coast.

If your itinerary allows, it is well worth taking the *Transgabonais* during the day. Almost as soon as it pulls out of Owendo you're rolling through the forest of the foothills of the Crystal Mountains. The rainforest is so dense in parts that it's not difficult to see why it took 14 years to build the railway. It's even less difficult to understand why it took Count Pierre Savorgnan de Brazza (see page 9) three years to cut a path across the country with his *panga* a century earlier. Just past Ndjolé the tracks lead over the Ogooué River and then follow the course of the river for hours.

According to the timetable the whole journey from Libreville to Franceville takes eight hours on the fast train, but this is very optimistic. Eleven hours is more likely, and that's if there have been no real problems. Delays might be due to any number of factors, for instance sometimes rear carriages come loose and the train has to return to reattach them. The train station is in Owendo south of Libreville. A taxi will cost you 2,000CFA from the city, or 4,000CFA after 21.00. Boarding starts one hour before scheduled departure (get there early if you have a lot of luggage), although it is not unheard of for the train to then sit in the station for several hours.

There are three classes of accommodation: P (Premiere or VIP), 1st and 2nd. The P carriages have very large squashy seats and a stewardess service, and both P and 1st class carriages are air conditioned. In P class is the dubious perk of some entertainment, namely very loud music alternating with second-rate films. As well as ear plugs, you might want to have a jumper or thermal sleeping bag handy – it's not nicknamed the refrigerator for nothing. Children under the age of 4 years travel free of charge. Children between 4 and 12 years pay half fare; children over 12 years pay the full fare. The choice of cooked dishes from the dining car is limited but portions are generous and reasonably priced.

The easiest way to buy a train ticket in Libreville is via a travel agency (the cost is the same). Tickets should be bought at least three days in advance. Times change regularly, so check with a travel agency, in the newspaper *L'Union* or with the Gare d'Owendo (tel: 70 82 43, 70 83 88).

Taxis-brousse and taxis

Apart from the railway, Gabon has no scheduled public transport. It does, however, have upwards of 7,500km (4,670 miles) of road, although only a percentage is tarred and some places, such as Port Gentil, do not feature on the road network at all. During the rainy season, travel on certain roads is difficult, but the absence of surfaced roads does not mean an absence of unscheduled services by *taxis-brousse*, sometimes also called *clandos*. *Taxis-brousse* are the pick-ups and small minibuses that ferry people and their packages between towns, beeping for passengers as they pass through villages. They are easily recognisable as always being in poor condition and very crowded. *Taxis-brousse* are also an integral part of the transport system within Libreville (see under *Getting around* in *Chapter 6*).

Taxis are the lifeblood of the transport system within towns. They differ in colour depending on where you are – red and white for Libreville, blue and white for Port Gentil and so on – but they almost always look as if they are falling apart. '*Une course*' is when you hire an empty taxi and the driver takes you directly to your destination. It's a set fee of 1,000CFA for standard journeys. Each town has a recognised point beyond which the fare increases, for example going to the airport or Owendo in Libreville, or Cap Lopez in Port Gentil, will cost you 2,000CFA. All fares double after 21.00.

Paying for just *une place* (one seat) in a shared taxi is cheaper, slower and usually involves walking the final part of your journey. The system works as follows: hail a taxi and as it slows alongside you, shout out *une place* and the recognised landmark nearest your destination. The driver will hoot if he's going your way. Journeys anywhere in the city centre cost 100CFA, rising to 200CFA for long distances. '*Une demi-course*', or '*une demi*', is where separate passengers in the taxi are dropped directly at their destination in turn. This costs 500CFA per passenger. If you are on a main road and happen to hail an empty taxi, the driver will assume you want a *course* unless you specify otherwise. Try to pay in exact money, as taxi drivers have neither the time nor the inclination to give change.

If you have lots of errands to run you can ask the taxi to wait rather than find a new ride each time. In this instance you should pay 4,000CFA an hour, or 30,000CFA for the whole day (you can bargain for less if you will be hiring the taxi for more than one day). For anything other than a straightforward *course*, the golden rule for happy taxi relations is to give an estimate of time and distance, and then agree the rate before you set off.

Outside of rush hour, taxi drivers are generally very friendly and willing to chat. They are rarely Gabonese, usually coming from Mali, Cameroon, Benin or Nigeria.

Hitching

Getting a lift in the interior with a timber truck is possible, but not necessarily advisable. Truck drivers are renowned for heavy drinking and dangerous driving. A safer and quicker form of hitching is in a private car. Finding such a lift is easiest if you are heading towards Libreville on a Sunday, when weekenders are returning for the working week.

By boat

Pirogues, or dug-out canoes, are the traditional method of transport wherever there is water. Increasingly *pirogues* are now motorised. A man who directs a *pirogue* is called a *piroguier*, or a *pagayeur*, after the *pagaye* or pole used in traditional *pirogues*. There used to be a ferry running between Libreville's Michèle Marina and Port Gentil, but this has stopped for an indefinite period. Ferries still run between Port Gentil and Lambaréné. See the *Getting there and away* sections in the relevant chapters for more details.

Hiring and driving

If you feel ready to brave the fast and furious traffic, it is possible to hire an ordinary car from international companies such as Avis, Hertz or Europcare in Libreville, Franceville and Port Gentil. The insurance usually only covers you within the city (an ordinary car is of limited use outside the city anyway). Prices for the smallest car start at around 50,000CFA per day in Libreville with Hertz, the cheapest company at the time of going to press. This price includes taxes, insurance and unlimited mileage. Port Gentil and Franceville tend to be slightly less expensive. To hire a chauffeur costs an additional 15,000–25,000CFA per day.

Even if you have the road experience and mechanical knowledge to drive a 4WD on rough roads, it is virtually impossible to hire one through a car hire company unless you are looking to sign a long-term contract of two to three years. The travel agency **Equasud** (see under *Useful information* in *Chapter 6*) hires out 4WDs carrying six people, but not without a chauffeur. Rates (including chauffeur and petrol) are 100,000CFA for a half day, 190,000CFA for a full day, 250,000CFA for 24 hours and 400,000CFA for a weekend.

Your International Driving Licence is valid for the first three months, after which point you are supposed to get a Gabonese licence. If caught out at one of the numerous check points with out-of-date papers, an apologetic plea of ignorance – accompanied by a small gift of money – should see you back on the road without incident.

If you are importing your own vehicle, you will need a *Carnet de Passages en Douanes* (CPD). Just one of the invaluable travel aids in *The Traveller's Handbook* (Wexas, 1997) is the comprehensive motorist's checklist for spares and tool kits (including different series of Land Rovers). This is followed by a maintenance list of what to check before departure – an invaluable reminder even for the experienced off-road motorist.

Cycling
Gabon is not a big cycling nation and places to hire or repair bicycles are not much in evidence. Given the state of the roads during the rains, it's not hard to see why – cycling is definitely only an option during the dry season. Bring your own bike, a comprehensive repair kit and an inexhaustible sense of humour.

PUBLIC HOLIDAYS
Everything closes on public holidays – banks, shops and government offices – so it is worth being aware of them. Muslim holidays, which vary from year to year, are also public holidays. Bear in mind that during the lunar month of Ramadan business hours may not always run as normal.

Jan 1	New Year's Day
Mar 12	Renovation Day
Easter	in March or April, depending on the year
May 1	Labour Day
Pentecost weekend	*Fête des Cultures* in Libreville (a singing and dancing extravaganza celebrating the different peoples in Gabon)
Aug 17	Anniversary of Independence
Aug 19	Prophet's Birthday
Nov 1	All Saints' Day
Dec 25	Christmas Day

ACCOMMODATION
There's no shortage of **hotels** in Libreville, a handful of which conform to an international standard of luxury tourist hotels, with the price tags to match. In Libreville the problem lies at the opposite end of the scale, in finding a cheap

hotel. In my experience most hotel rooms, in whatever price category, have en-suite facilities, double bed, and choice of fan or air conditioning. Budget travellers are hard pushed to find a hotel bed for less than 15,000CFA a night. Outside the capital, the urban norm in Franceville, Port Gentil and Lambaréné is for there to be one or two would-be luxury hotels (with swimming pool, nightclub, restaurant and room service) and many more middle range ones (usually with a bar-restaurant). Port Gentil is also unique in the sheer number of its **self-catering apartments**. These are essentially hotels made up of self-contained, furnished flats – one or more bedrooms, bathroom, sitting room, kitchenette – that are charged on a nightly or monthly basis.

Safari accommodation tends to be of a good standard, with attractive solid wooden cabins or tented huts, mosquito nets and running water (not always hot). There may be lighting at certain hours of the day when the generator is operating.

At the cheapest end of the scale are *cases de passage*, which are simple establishments with normally fewer than five rooms at 5,000CFA a night or even less. These are used by truck drivers, sometimes double as brothels, and can be very rowdy. The best have clean sheets, a fan and either a shared shower room or a bucket of water in each room. Toilets – often outside and often long-drops – are always shared. Every town has at least one *case de passage*, often in the market. Just ask. *Cases de passage* and some hotels have a rate for *repos* (rest) for use of the room during the day.

Although not always centrally located, **mission houses** with rooms for visitors are a good bet for just a little bit more than a *case de passage*. Rooms are invariably clean and arranged dormitory-style, and sometimes there are facilities for cooking.

If you find yourself in a **village** in need of a place to sleep, then ask the village chief to help. Chances are he will be very welcoming, inviting you to eat, putting a hut at your disposal or finding you a place to pitch your tent if you have one. If you are able to contribute to the meal with food or wine, or even better whisky, the gesture will be much appreciated.

Having your own **tent** is invaluable for anyone intending to spend prolonged periods in out-of-the-way places, such as the forest. This applies more to researchers than to other visitors. Unauthorised camping is not allowed in protected areas. Anywhere else, just check with whoever seems appropriate, such as the village chief.

EATING AND DRINKING
Eating
It is possible to eat very well in Libreville and Port Gentil if you can afford the international prices. Some of the world's most popular cuisines are readily available, notably Italian, Chinese and, of course, French. There are French-style *boulangeries* selling all manner of croissants and pastries, and the supermarkets are stocked with cheeses, wines and even meat and vegetables imported from France. The choice is supplemented by goods imported from Cameroon, Equatorial Guinea and South Africa. In Libreville, Port Gentil and

other places where there are tourist restaurants and hotels, it is usual to find both European and African dishes on menus, and often tasty *grillades* (barbequed fish or meat) as well. In smaller towns and out-of-the-way places there may be a handful of small African restaurants or *maquis*. These tend to be Senegalese or Cameroonian, and the best serve generous portions of good food for not very much money.

The quickest and cheapest sources of prepared food, however, are *les bédoumeuses*. These are the women selling doughnuts, small brochettes of meat and filled baguettes on the street. Amazingly, fresh baguettes are sold every morning in just about every market in the country, no matter how remote. French baguettes are one of the Gabonese staples, alongside smoked or salted fish, manioc, plantain and rice. Typical sauces are prepared with *arachides* (peanuts), *nyembwe* (the pulp of palm nuts) or *odika* (an oil-producing seed also known as *chocolat*). Bushmeat – antelope, porcupine, monkey, snake and so on – has traditionally been an important part of the Gabonese diet. Very slowly, attitudes are changing, largely because of the bad publicity of ebola (see pages 74–5) and growing awareness about endangered animals.

Strict vegetarians will probably end up relying on omelettes, hard-boiled eggs and avocados (if they are in season) for protein outside of Libreville. In the capital they will be able to vary their diet with pizzas and the occasional pasta dish. Fish-eaters won't have any problems. Even in places where no fresh fish is available there is always that invaluable staple, the tinned sardine.

Drinking

To be on the safe side, it is better not to drink the tap water in Gabon unless you have water-purifying tablets. Most imported fizzy drinks, beers, wines and spirits are easy to find in Libreville and elsewhere. The two local beers, both of them good, are Castel and Régab. The latter, sold in 65cl bottles, is the best value. In rural areas, palm wine is the usual tipple.

SOUVENIR SHOPPING

Gabon is not like some countries where you can't take two paces without tripping over a craftsman and his wares. Here you have to make a bit more effort to find souvenirs and a lot of what you find has been imported from Mali, Cameroon, Benin or even East Africa. You often hear expats lamenting that Gabon is not a nation of craftsmen (or indeed producers of anything at all), and invariably any kind of tourist project involves an attempt to stimulate a local craft industry.

The best place to shop is in Libreville, where there is far and away the greatest choice. As to what there is to buy, it's mostly masks, wooden items, tie-dye clothes, batik tablecloths and stone sculptures. If you are looking for something authentically Gabonese it is worth asking where it was made. The stone carvings, for example, are mostly Mbigou stone, which is quarried around Mbigou in southern Gabon, and a lot of the smaller wooden objects are carved from the different coloured woods found in Gabon forests. The quality of the carving of larger objects, such as chairs and boxes, varies, as do the prices. Bargaining is not always welcome, although it is grudgingly accepted in Libreville's artisans' markets, where shoppers may end up paying just two-thirds of the original quoted price.

As a general rule, most shops open at 08.00 or 09.00 and close for the day by 19.00. The majority shut between 12.30 and 15.30, although some have even longer lunchbreaks.

MEDIA AND COMMUNICATIONS

The government in Gabon takes a keen interest in the country's media and what is not government-controlled is subject to close scrutiny.

Newspapers and magazines

Gabon's newspapers, all published in French, are readily available at kiosks throughout Gabon. The country's only daily newspaper, *L'Union*, is also sold at major traffic junctions in the early morning. *L'Union* is published by the government, the weekly *La Relance* is the paper of the PDG, and the *Gabaon*, which first appeared in 2002, is an independent publication. The opposition papers include the weekly satirical *Le Nganga* and the bi-monthly *Misamu*. *La Croissance* is a bi-monthly paper covering economic issues in Gabon, Cameroon, Congo and DRC. Two interesting French-language Africa-centric magazines are the monthly *Am Afrique Magazine* and the weekly political and economic *Jeune Afrique L'Intelligent*.

If you're going to be in Libreville for any length of time, you might at some point wish to seek out the small pocket guide *Libreville*, published by Sépia, which gives all sorts of useful listings information as well as snippets about the country's history. *Le Pratique du Gabon* is an annually updated pocket publication with listings for Libreville and Port Gentil covering all sorts of practical information, from banks and couriers to schools and hospitals.

Le Cri du Pangolin is concerned with environmental and ecological issues, and is the only periodical of its kind to be exclusively concerned with Gabon. Copies can be read at the Centre Culturel Français Saint-Exupéry (CCF). ECOFAC publishes an excellent environmental magazine, *Canopée*, which deals with the whole of Central Africa. It can also be read on the ECOFAC website (www.ecofac.org).

It is possible to get hold of a good selection of foreign publications in the big hotels and bookshops in Libreville, such as *Time*, *Newsweek*, *The Economist*, the *Herald Tribune* and *Le Monde*, normally for at least twice the price they are sold back home.

Television and radio

Radio-Television Gabonaise (RTVG) is the government-controlled national broadcaster operating the French-language RTVG television station. It also operates the national radio channels, RTG1, or RTG Chaine 1 (broadcasting in French), and RTG2 channel, or RTG Chaine 2, which is a network of provincial stations broadcasting in French and vernacular languages.

RADIO EMERGENCE 91.6FM

Radio Emergence is Gabon's most popular educational radio station, broadcast *by* young people *for* young people. It has an estimated 20,000 listeners tuning in per day, and is the most popular station for those aged 15-25. Not a bad achievement when you consider that the station relies entirely on young volunteers for its successful operation.

The idea for a local school radio station was first conceived in the 1960s, but nothing was done until the late 1990s, when funds were put together by UNESCO, UNICEF, Shell Gabon and the Canadian government. The Ministry of Education donated an abandoned building for its use, right in the centre of Libreville. Some 70 students were trained in researching, interviewing and broadcasting skills. After a year of simulated broadcasting, Radio Emergence went on air for the first time in July 2000. Its broadcast radius is about 25km outside Libreville.

The primary purpose of the station is to serve as a place where important issues affecting the young can be tackled openly. Alongside educational programmes on Gabon's environment and African fashions, there are regular question-and-answer sessions on health issues, everything from nutrition, sex, AIDs and teenage pregnancy. In the mornings there's generally music (a mixture of African and American), but if you tune in after 14.00, you'll catch the programmes. For an up-to-date schedule of what's on, see the website www.f-i-a.org/emergence.

In March 2002 I was interviewed by 17-year-old Yves-Judicaël Mboumba-Mboumba about my visit to Gabon. Afterwards I asked him why he thought Radio Emergence was important. 'Gabon is more modern than the rest of West Africa,' he said, 'but tradition is still important. Programmes like Inter-Culture teach young people the customs of their tribe: how to walk, eat, dress, show respect.'

Although subject to change, the following are some useful radio frequencies at the time of going to press. Africa No. 1 first broadcast on February 7 1981 at 06.00 and quickly became the most listened-to station on the continent, and it's also popular in France.

RTG1/RTG Chaine 1	86.5FM
Africa No.1 (Gabon)	94.5FM
Africa No.1 (France)	107.5FM
Radio France Internationale (RFI)	104FM
Voice of America	105.5FM (07.30-22.30)
Radio Emergence	91.6FM

Post

There is a post office in every town, usually open Monday–Friday 08.00–12.00 and 15.00–18.00. In theory, airmail post to the UK takes one to two weeks.

Sending post to Gabon can take forever. Even within Gabon it is not very reliable, which is why *taxi-brousse* drivers are always given letters to deliver.

Telecommunications

International direct dialling is available to Gabon. The country code from anywhere in the world is +241. There are plenty of *cabine telephoniques* from where it is possible to make phone calls and send faxes.

There are now a number of **internet cafés** in Libreville, Franceville, Port Gentil and in theory soon elsewhere, although I wouldn't count on it. The usual rate is about 1,000CFA an hour. Connections used to be consistently very unreliable, and often very slow, especially at peak times, ie: anytime after 21.00. Things have improved in recent times, largely because of the efforts of Gabon Telecom. Even so, if you are going to be in Gabon for any length of time it may be worthwhile setting up an account with the local server Assala, which is quite quick.

TOURISM AND THE GABONESE
The tourist industry

The government has supposedly made a firm commitment to furthering tourism in Gabon, although sights are set on attracting the upper end of the market as opposed to backpackers. Unfortunately, some of the faces working in tourism are not as smiling and welcoming as they might be at present. Libreville airport is a case in point. More generally, however, the people you meet on the course of your travels tend to be friendly, curious and honest with travellers. This is especially true outside the capital, away from the hectic and impersonal big-city syndrome. (Note: My particular experience has been positive, but African visitors from neighbouring countries have frequently complained to me that the Gabonese demonstrate a superior and dismissive attitude towards them.)

Tipping

Tipping is not yet usual in Gabon, except in Libreville, where a 10% tip has become the norm in tourist restaurants and hotels. Tipping is not necessary in petrol stations. Tips for good service on excursions and safaris are of course always welcome, if not expected. The amount of a tip should be left to the discretion of the tipper, but for your background knowledge, note that most guides receive a salary in the region of 6,000CFA a day.

CRIME AND SECURITY

Carry your passport with you at all times. Random controls are a feature of life in Gabon and everybody and anybody are checked. I have heard some unpleasant stories of nights spent in gaols for those without papers. These may not be true, or may not be usual, but it's not worth the risk.

Muggings and hold-ups are still comparatively rare, but unfortunately are on the increase in Libreville, which is why certain posh restaurants lock the door after letting in their customers. Outside Libreville, travellers should guard against petty crime. As anywhere in the world there are certain areas that are more prone to security problems than others. Also, be sure to use reputable guides who know the forest or rivers well as *faux guides* posing as experts put their clients' and their own lives in danger.

Women travellers

Travelling alone as a woman in Gabon does not pose any particular security problems, although, as anywhere in the world, there are always *drageurs* on the prowl. Expect attention from those who are simply curious about who you are, where you come from, where you are going and, above all, why you are alone. There is also no shortage of people keen to practise their English.

EMBASSIES AND DIPLOMATIC MISSIONS

Major embassies and high commissions in Libreville are listed below. Note that there is no British government representation in Gabon.

British Honorary Consul David Harwood, MBE, c/o Brossette Z.I. Oloumi, BP 486 Libreville; tel: 76 22 00; fax: 76 57 89; email: harwood@internetgabon.com
Cameroonian Embassy BP 14001, near the Omar Bongo University; tel: 73 28 00
Canadian Embassy PO Box 4037, Libreville; tel: 74 34 64/5; fax: 74 34 66
Congo Embassy BP 269, quartier Batterie IV, behind Citibank; tel: 73 29 06 or 73 01 09
French Embassy BP 2125, bd Bord de la Mer, Libreville; tel: 76 10 64, 76 20 31 or 76 48 78; fax: 74 55 33
Italian Embassy BP 2251, Immeuble Personaz et Gaerdin, next to CK2 shop; tel: 74 28 92/93; fax: 74 80 35
Spanish Embassy BP 1157, Immeuble Diamant; tel: 72 12 64, 77 30 68; fax: 74 88 73
Swiss Embassy BP 2254, Hotel Okoumé Palace; tel: 73 26 19
Embassy of São Tomé and Príncipe BP 489, bd de la mer; tel: 72 09 94
Embassy of the United States of America BP 4000, bd Bord de la Mer, Libreville; tel: 76 20 03, 74 34 92 or 76 20 04; fax: 74 55 07

LOCAL NGOS

Aventures Sans Frontières (ASF) BP 7248 Libreville; tel: 76 84 12, 26 06 66; email: asf@inet.ga; web: www.environnement-gabon.org. This local NGO was founded in 1991 by childhood friends Guy-Philippe Sounguet and Serge Akagah after they had completed a 1,200km (745 mile) tour of Gabon on foot. ASF confined itself to introducing children to the nature surrounding them, until a kayak trip from Libreville to Port Gentil highlighted the plight of turtles. Now ASF has a team of 14 men conducting surveys in a number of sites around Gabon, including Point Pongara, Mayumba, Iguela and Gamba.
Brainforest BP 2103 Libreville; tel: 24 78 48; fax: 76 28 16; email: brainforest.gabon@assala.com; web: www.brainforest.org. This environmental organisation is committed to protecting the biodiversity of the Ipassa Mingouli forest in the region of Ogooué-Ivindo. Its aim is to encourage new ways, other than logging,

to use the forest, including pharmaceutical research and ecotourism. It is also concerned to introduce social and economic development in the areas around the forest.

Handicaps Sans Frontières (HSF) BP 4474 Libreville; tel: 24 78 48; fax: 76 28 14; email: hsf.gabon@assala.com; web: www.f-i-a.org/hsf. This organisation was set up in 1994 by a group of handicapped friends in Libreville. Their mission is to raise awareness about the plight of the handicapped in Gabon, moving towards an integrated society where the handicapped are not marginalised. Contact the Director, Marc Ona Essangui, for more information.

Health

with Dr Felicity Nicholson and Philip Briggs

PREPARATIONS

Preparations to ensure a healthy trip to Gabon and STP require checks on your immunisation status: it is wise to be up to date on tetanus (ten-yearly), polio (ten-yearly) and diphtheria (ten-yearly). Meningococcus, rabies and hepatitis A are also recommended and immunisations against yellow fever are mandatory as a condition of entry for those over one year of age.

Hepatitis A vaccine (Havrix Monodose or Avaxim) is comprised of two injections given about a year apart. The course costs about £100, but protects for ten years. It is now felt that the vaccine can be used even close to the time of departure and has replaced the old-fashioned gamma globulin. The newer typhoid vaccines (eg: Typhim Vi) last for three years and are about 85% effective. They should be encouraged unless the traveller is leaving within a few days for a trip of a week or less when the vaccine would not be effective in time. Meningitis vaccine (containing strains ACW and Y) is also recommended, especially for trips of more than four weeks (see *Meningitis*). Immunisation against cholera is no longer recommended for either Gabon or STP. Vaccinations for rabies are advised for travellers visiting more remote areas (see Rabies). Hepatitis B vaccination should be considered for longer trips (two months or more) or for those working with children or in situations where contact with blood is likely. Three injections are needed for the best protection and can be given over a four-week period if time is short. Longer schedules give more sustained protection and are therefore preferred if time allows. A BCG vaccination against tuberculosis (TB) is also advised for trips of two months or more.

Ideally you should visit your own doctor or a specialist travel clinic (see page 64) to discuss your requirements about eight weeks before you plan to travel.

Protection from the sun

Give some thought to packing suncream. The incidence of skin cancer is rocketing as Caucasians are travelling more and spending more time exposing themselves to the sun. Keep out of the sun during the middle of the day and, if you must be exposed to the sun, build up gradually from 20 minutes per day. Be especially careful of sun reflected off water and wear a T-shirt and lots of waterproof SPF15 suncream when swimming; snorkelling often leads to scorched backs of the thighs so wear bermuda shorts. Sun exposure ages the skin and makes people prematurely wrinkly; cover up with long, loose clothes

LONG-HAUL FLIGHTS, CLOTS AND DVT
Dr Jane Wilson-Howarth

Long-haul air travel increases the risk of deep vein thrombosis. Although recent research has suggested that many of us develop clots when immobilised, most resolve without us ever having been aware of them. In certain susceptible individuals, though, large clots form and these can break away and lodge in the lungs. This is dangerous but happens in a tiny minority of passengers.

Studies have shown that flights of over five-and-a-half-hours are significant, and that people who take lots of shorter flights over a short space of time form clots. People at highest risk are:

- Those who have had a clot before – unless they are now taking warfarin
- People over 80 years of age
- Anyone who has recently undergone a major operation or surgery for varicose veins
- Someone who has had a hip or knee replacement in the last three months
- Cancer sufferers
- Those who have ever had a stroke
- People with heart disease
- Those with a close blood relative who has had a clot

Those with a slightly increased risk:

- People over 40
- Women who are pregnant or have had a baby in the last couple of weeks
- People taking female hormones or other oestrogen therapy
- Heavy smokers
- Those who have very severe varicose veins
- The very obese
- People who are very tall (over 6ft/1.8m) or short (under 5ft/1.5m)

and wear a hat when you can. The glare and the dust can be hard on the eyes, too, so bring UV-protecting sunglasses and, perhaps, a soothing eyebath.

Malaria prevention

There is no vaccine against malaria, but there are other ways to avoid it; since most of Africa is very high risk for malaria, travellers must plan their malaria protection properly. Seek current advice on the best antimalarials to take. If mefloquine (Lariam) is suggested, start this two-and-a-half weeks (three doses) before departure to check that it suits you; stop it immediately if it seems to cause depression or anxiety, visual or hearing disturbances, severe headaches, fits or changes in heart rhythm. Side effects such as

A deep vein thrombosis (DVT) is a blood clot that forms in the deep leg veins. This is very different from irritating but harmless superficial phlebitis. DVT causes swelling and redness of one leg, usually with heat and pain in one calf and sometimes the thigh. A DVT is only dangerous if a clot breaks away and travels to the lungs (pulmonary embolus). Symptoms of a pulmonary embolus (PE) include chest pain that is worse on breathing in deeply, shortness of breath, and sometimes coughing up small amounts of blood. The symptoms commonly start three to ten days after a long flight. Anyone who thinks that they might have a DVT needs to see a doctor immediately who will arrange a scan. Warfarin tablets (to thin the blood) are then taken for at least six months.

Prevention of DVT
Several conditions make the problem more likely. Immobility is the key, and factors like reduced oxygen in cabin air and dehydration may also contribute. To reduce the risk of thrombosis on a long journey:

• Exercise before and after the flight
• Keep mobile before and during the flight; move around every couple of hours
• Drink plenty of water or juices during the flight
• Avoid taking sleeping pills and excessive tea, coffee and alcohol
• Perform exercises that mimic walking and tense the calf muscles
• Consider wearing flight socks or support stockings (see www.legshealth.com)
• Take a meal of oily fish (mackerel, trout, salmon, sardines, etc) in the 24 hours before departure to reduce blood clotability and thus DVT risk

If you think you are at increased risk of a clot, ask your doctor if it is safe to travel.

nightmares or dizziness are not medical reasons for stopping unless they are sufficiently debilitating or annoying. Anyone who is pregnant, who has suffered fits in the past, has been treated for depression or psychiatric problems, has diabetes controlled by oral therapy or who is epileptic (or who has suffered fits in the past) or has a close blood relative who is epileptic, should avoid mefloquine.

Malarone (proguanil and atovaquone) is a new drug that is almost as effective as mefloquine. It has the advantage of having few side effects and need only be continued for one week after returning. However, it is expensive and because of this tends to be reserved for shorter trips although a licence has been granted for up to three months use. Paediatric Malarone is now available for children under 40kg. The number of paediatric tablets required is calculated by weight. Malarone may not be suitable for everybody so advice should be taken from a doctor.

The antibiotic doxycycline (100mg daily) is a viable alternative when either mefloquine or Malarone are not considered suitable for whatever reason. Like Malarone it can be started one day before arrival. Unlike mefloquine, it may also be used in travellers with epilepsy, although certain anti-epileptic medication may make it less effective. Users must be warned about the possibility of allergic skin reactions developing in sunlight which can occur in about 3% of people. The drug should be stopped if this happens. Women using the oral contraceptive should use an additional method of protection for the first four weeks when using doxycycline. It is also unsuitable in pregnancy or for children under 12 years.

Chloroquine and proguanil are not considered to be very effective for Gabon or STP. However, they may still be recommended if no other regime is suitable.

All prophylactic agents should be taken with or after the evening meal, washed down with plenty of fluid and with the exception of Malarone (see above) continued for four weeks after leaving.

Travellers to remote parts would probably be wise to carry a course of treatment to cure malaria. Experts differ on the costs and benefits of self-treatment, but agree that it leads to over-treatment and to many people taking drugs they do not need; yet treatment may save your life. Discuss your trip with a specialist to determine your particular needs and risks, and be sure you understand when and how to take the cure. If you are somewhere remote in a malarial region you probably have to assume that any high fever (over 38°C) for more than a few hours is due to malaria (regardless of any other symptoms) and should seek treatment. Diagnosing malaria is not easy, which is why consulting a doctor is sensible: there are other dangerous causes of fever in Africa, which require different treatments. However, malaria-testing kits are now available in the UK from some travel clinics and pharmacies for diagnosing falciparum malaria – the most serious form of the disease. So consider taking a testing kit with you if your trip includes visiting remote, inaccessible regions. (See box *Malaria in Gabon and STP* on pages 70–1 for more advice.)

Presently quinine and doxycycline, or quinine and Fansidar, are the favoured regimes, but check for up-to-date advice on the current recommended treatment. And remember malaria may occur anything from seven days into the trip to up to one year after leaving Africa.

The risk of malaria above 1,800m above sea level is low. It is unwise to travel in malarial parts of Africa whilst pregnant or with children: the risk of malaria in many parts is considerable and these travellers are likely to succumb rapidly to the disease.

In addition to antimalarial medicines, it is important to avoid mosquito bites between dusk and dawn. Pack a DEET-based insect repellent, such as Repel (roll-ons or stick are the least messy preparations for travelling). You also need either a permethrin-impregnated bednet or a permethrin spray so that you can 'treat' bednets in hotels. Permethrin treatment makes even very tatty nets protective and prevents mosquitoes from biting through the impregnated net when you roll against it; it also deters other biters. Putting on long clothes at dusk means you can reduce the amount of repellent you need to put on your skin, but be aware that malaria mosquitoes hunt at ankle level and will bite through socks, so apply repellent under socks too. Travel clinics usually sell a good range of nets, treatment kits and repellents.

Travel clinics and health information
A full list of current travel clinic websites worldwide is available from the International Society of Travel Medicine on www.istm.org. For other journey preparation information, consult www.tripprep.com. Information about various medications may be found on www.emedicine.com. For information on malaria prevention, see www.preventingmalaria.info.

UK
Berkeley Travel Clinic 32 Berkeley St, London W1J 8EL (near Green Park tube station); tel: 020 7629 6233
Cambridge Travel Clinic 48a Mill Rd, Cambridge CB1 2AS; tel: 01223 367362; email: enquiries@travelcliniccambridge.co.uk; www.travelcliniccambridge.co.uk. Open Tue–Fri 12.00–19.00, Sat 10.00–16.00.
Edinburgh Travel Clinic Regional Infectious Diseases Unit, Ward 41 OPD, Western General Hospital, Crewe Rd South, Edinburgh EH4 2UX; tel: 0131 537 2822; www.link.med.ed.ac.uk/ridu. Travel helpline (0906 589 0380) open weekdays 09.00–12.00. Provides inoculations and antimalarial prophylaxis, and advises on travel-related health risks.
Fleet Street Travel Clinic 29 Fleet St, London EC4Y 1AA; tel: 020 7353 5678; www.fleetstreetclinic.com. Vaccinations, travel products and latest advice.
Hospital for Tropical Diseases Travel Clinic Mortimer Market Bldg, Capper St (off Tottenham Ct Rd), London WC1E 6AU; tel: 020 7388 9600; www.thehtd.org. Offers consultations and advice, and is able to provide all necessary drugs and vaccines for travellers. Runs a healthline (tel: 0906 133 7733) for country-specific information and health hazards. Also stocks nets, water purification equipment and personal protection measures.
Interhealth Worldwide Partnership House, 157 Waterloo Rd, London SE1 8US; tel: 020 7902 9000; www.interhealth.org.uk. Competitively priced, one-stop travel health service. All profits go to their affiliated company, InterHealth, which provides health care for overseas workers on Christian projects.
Liverpool School of Medicine Pembroke Pl, Liverpool L3 5QA; tel: 051 708 9393; fax: 0151 705 3370; www.liv.ac.uk/lstm
MASTA (Medical Advisory Service for Travellers Abroad) Moorfield Rd, Yeadon LS19 7BN; tel: 0870 606 2782; www.masta-travel-health.com. Provides travel health advice, anti-malarials and vaccinations. There are over 25 MASTA pre-travel clinics in Britain; call or check online for the nearest. Clinics also sell mosquito nets, medical kits, insect protection and travel hygiene products.

NHS travel website www.fitfortravel.scot.nhs.uk. Provides country-by-country advice on immunisation and malaria, plus details of recent developments, and a list of relevant health organisations.

Nomad Travel Store/Clinic 3–4 Wellington Terrace, Turnpike Lane, London N8 0PX; tel: 020 8889 7014; travel-health line (office hours only) tel: 0906 863 3414; email: sales@nomadtravel.co.uk; www.nomadtravel.co.uk. Also at 40 Bernard St, London WC1N 1LJ; tel: 020 7833 4114; 52 Grosvenor Gardens, London SW1W 0AG; tel: 020 7823 5823; and 43 Queens Rd, Bristol BS8 1QH; tel: 0117 922 6567. For health advice, equipment such as mosquito nets and other anti-bug devices, and an excellent range of adventure travel gear.

Trailfinders Travel Clinic 194 Kensington High St, London W8 7RG; tel: 020 7938 3999; www.trailfinders.com/clinic.htm

Travelpharm The Travelpharm website, www.travelpharm.com, offers up-to-date guidance on travel-related health and has a range of medications available through their online mini-pharmacy.

Irish Republic

Tropical Medical Bureau Grafton Street Medical Centre, Grafton Bldgs, 34 Grafton St, Dublin 2; tel: 1 671 9200; www.tmb.ie. A useful website specific to tropical destinations. Also check website for other bureaux locations throughout Ireland.

USA

Centers for Disease Control 1600 Clifton Rd, Atlanta, GA 30333; tel: 800 311 3435; travellers' health hotline 888 232 3299; www.cdc.gov/travel. The central source of travel information in the USA. The invaluable Health Information for International Travel, published annually, is available from the Division of Quarantine at this address.

Connaught Laboratories PO Box 187, Swiftwater, PA 18370; tel: 800 822 2463. They will send a free list of specialist tropical-medicine physicians in your state.

IAMAT (International Association for Medical Assistance to Travelers) 1623 Military Rd, 279, Niagara Falls, NY14304-1745; tel: 716 754 4883; email: info@iamat.org; www.iamat.org. A non-profit organisation that provides lists of English-speaking doctors abroad.

International Medicine Center 920 Frostwood Drive, Suite 670, Houston, TX 77024; tel: 713 550 2000; www.traveldoc.com

Canada

IAMAT Suite 1, 1287 St Clair Av W, Toronto, Ontario M6E 1B8; tel: 416 652 0137; www.iamat.org

TMVC Suite 314, 1030 W Georgia St, Vancouver BC V6E 2Y3; tel: 1 888 288 8682; www.tmvc.com. Private clinic with several outlets in Canada.

Australia, New Zealand, Singapore

IAMAT PO Box 5049, Christchurch 5, New Zealand; www.iamat.org

TMVC Tel: 1300 65 88 44; www.tmvc.com.au. Clinics in Australia, New Zealand and Singapore, including:

MEDICAL FACILITIES IN GABON AND STP

Private clinics, hospitals and pharmacies can be found in most large towns. In Gabon in all likelihood you will need to speak French with the doctors, and in STP you will probably need some Portuguese, although you may manage in French or English. If you are not confident of your language level, you might want to enlist the help of someone to act as your translator. Note that consultation fees and laboratory tests are almost comparable to those in most Western countries. Commonly required medicines such as broad-spectrum antibiotics are widely available throughout the region, as are malaria cures and prophylactics. Quinine and doxycycline, or quinine and Fansidar, are best bought in advance – in fact it's advisable to carry all malaria-related tablets on you, and only rely on their availability locally if you need to restock your supplies.

If you are on any medication prior to departure, or you have specific needs relating to a known medical condition (for instance if you are allergic to bee stings or you are prone to attacks of asthma), then you are strongly advised to bring any related drugs and devices with you.

Auckland Canterbury Arcade, 170 Queen St, Auckland; tel: 9 373 3531
Brisbane 6th floor, 247 Adelaide St, Brisbane, QLD 4000; tel: 7 3221 9066
Melbourne 393 Little Bourke St, 2nd floor, Melbourne, VIC 3000; tel: 3 9602 5788
Sydney Dymocks Bldg, 7th floor, 428 George St, Sydney, NSW 2000; tel: 2 9221 7133

South Africa and Namibia
SAA-Netcare Travel Clinics P Bag X34, Benmore 2010; www.travelclinic.co.za. Clinics throughout South Africa.
TMVC 113 D F Malan Drive, Roosevelt Park, Johannesburg; tel: 011 888 7488; www.tmvc.com.au. Consult website for details of other clinics in South Africa and Namibia.

Switzerland
IAMAT 57 Chemin des Voirets, 1212 Grand Lancy, Geneva; www.iamat.org

Personal first-aid kit
The more I travel, the less I take. My minimal kit contains:

- A good drying antiseptic, eg: iodine or potassium permanganate (don't take antiseptic cream)
- A few small dressings (Band-Aids)
- Suncream
- Insect repellent; malaria tablets; impregnated bednet
- Aspirin or paracetamol
- Ciprofloxacin antibiotic, 500mg x 2 (or norfloxacin) for severe diarrhoea
- Tinidazole (500mg x 8) for giardia or amoebic dysentery (see below for regime)

TREATING TRAVELLERS' DIARRHOEA

It is dehydration which makes you feel awful during a bout of diarrhoea and the most important part of treatment is drinking lots of clear fluids. Sachets of oral rehydration salts give the perfect biochemical mix to replace all that is pouring out of your bottom but other recipes taste nicer. Any dilute mixture of sugar and salt in water will do you good: try Coke or orange squash with a three-finger pinch of salt added to each glass (if you are salt-depleted you won't taste the salt). Otherwise make a solution of a four-finger scoop of sugar with a three-finger pinch of salt in a glass of water. Or add eight level teaspoons of sugar (18g) and one level teaspoon of salt (3g) to one litre (five cups) of safe water. A squeeze of lemon or orange juice improves the taste and adds potassium, which is also lost in diarrhoea. Drink two large glasses after every bowel action, and more if you are thirsty. These solutions are still absorbed well if you are vomiting, but you will need to take sips at a time. If you are not eating you need to drink three litres a day plus whatever is pouring into the toilet. If you feel like eating, take a bland, high carbohydrate diet. Heavy greasy foods will probably give you cramps.

If the diarrhoea is bad, or you are passing blood or slime, or you have a fever, you will probably need antibiotics in addition to fluid replacement. A single dose of ciprofloxacin (500mg) repeated after 12 hours may be appropriate. If the diarrhoea is greasy and bulky and is accompanied by sulphurous (eggy) burps, the likely cause is giardia. This is best treated with tinidazole (four x 500mg in one dose, repeated seven days later if symptoms persist).

- Antifungal cream (eg: Canesten)
- Antibiotic eye drops, for sore, 'gritty', stuck-together eyes (conjunctivitis)
- A pair of fine pointed tweezers (to remove hairy caterpillar hairs, thorns, splinters, coral, etc)
- Condoms or femidoms
- Maybe a malaria treatment kit and thermometer

MAJOR HAZARDS

People new to exotic travel often worry about tropical diseases, but it is accidents that are most likely to carry you off. Road accidents are very common in many parts of Gabon and STP, so be aware and do what you can to reduce risks: try to travel during daylight hours and refuse to be driven by a drunk. Listen to local advice about areas where violent crime is rife, too.

COMMON MEDICAL PROBLEMS
Travellers' diarrhoea

Travelling in Gabon and STP carries a risk of getting a dose of travellers' diarrhoea; perhaps as many as half of all visitors will suffer and the newer you are to travel, the more likely you will be to suffer. By taking precautions against travellers' diarrhoea you will also avoid typhoid, cholera, hepatitis, dysentery, worms, etc. Travellers' diarrhoea and the other faecal-oral diseases come from getting other peoples' faeces in your mouth. This most often happens from cooks not washing their hands after a trip to the toilet, but even if the restaurant cook does not understand basic hygiene you will be safe if your food has been properly cooked and arrives piping hot. The maxim to remind you what you can safely eat is:

PEEL IT, BOIL IT, COOK IT OR FORGET IT.

This means that fruit you have washed and peeled yourself, and hot foods, should be safe but raw foods, cold cooked foods, salads, fruit salads which have been prepared by others, ice-cream and ice are all risky. And foods kept lukewarm in hotel buffets are often dangerous. If you are struck, see box above for treatment.

Water sterilisation
It is much rarer to get sick from drinking contaminated water but it happens, so try to drink from safe sources.

Water should have been brought to the boil (even at altitude it only needs to be brought to the boil), or passed through a good bacteriological filter or purified with iodine; chlorine tablets (eg: Puritabs) are also adequate although theoretically less effective and they taste nastier. As a rule, mineral water is safer than contaminated tap water.

Malaria
Whether or not you are taking malaria tablets, it is important to protect yourself from mosquito bites (see box, *Malaria in Gabon and STP*, on pages 70–1 and *Malaria prevention*, page 62), so keep your repellent stick or roll-on to hand. Be aware that no prophylactic is 100% protective but those on prophylactics who are unlucky enough to catch malaria are less likely to get rapidly into serious trouble. It is easy and inexpensive to arrange a malaria blood test.

Dengue fever
This mosquito-borne disease may mimic malaria but there is no prophylactic medication available to deal with it. The mosquitoes that carry this virus bite during the daytime, so it is worth applying repellent if you see any mosquitoes around. Symptoms include strong headaches, rashes, excruciating joint and muscle pains, and high fever. Dengue fever lasts only for a week or so and is not usually fatal. Complete rest and paracetamol are the usual treatment; plenty of fluids also help. Some patients are given an intravenous drip to prevent dehydration. It is especially important to protect yourself if you have had dengue fever before, since a second infection with a different strain can result in the potentially fatal dengue haemorrhagic fever.

Insect bites
It is crucial to avoid mosquito bites between dusk and dawn; as the sun is going down, don long clothes and apply repellent on any exposed flesh. This

MALARIA IN GABON AND STP
with Philip Briggs

Along with road accidents, malaria poses the single biggest serious threat to the health of travellers in most parts of tropical Africa, Gabon and STP included. The *Anopheles* mosquito that transmits the parasite is most abundant near marshes and still water, where it breeds, and the parasite is most prolific at low altitudes. In mid-altitude locations, malaria is largely but not entirely seasonal, with the highest risk of transmission occurring during the rainy season. Those heading for moist and low-lying areas, such as along the coast and the waterways between Port Gentil and Lambaréné in Gabon, and of course anyone spending long periods deep in the forest in Gabon or STP, are at high risk throughout the year, but the danger is greatest during the rainy season. Even if this does not apply to you, all travellers to Central Africa should assume that they will be exposed to malaria and should take precautions throughout their trip (see page 62 for advice on prophylactic drugs and avoiding mosquito bites).

Even those who take their malaria tablets meticulously and do everything possible to avoid mosquito bites may contract a strain of malaria that is resistant to prophylactic drugs. Untreated malaria is likely to be fatal, but even strains resistant to prophylaxis respond well to prompt treatment. Because of this, your immediate priority upon displaying possible malaria symptoms – which might include any combination of a headache, flu-like aches and pains, a rapid rise in temperature, a general sense of disorientation, and possibly even nausea and diarrhoea – is to establish whether you have malaria.

The blood test for malaria takes ten minutes to produce a result. A positive result means that you have malaria. A negative result suggests that you don't have malaria, but bear in mind that the parasite doesn't always show up on a test, particularly when the level of infection is mild or is 'cloaked' by partially effective prophylactics. For this reason, even if you test negative, it would be wise to stay within reach of a laboratory until the symptoms clear up, and to test again after a day or two if they don't. It's worth noting that if you have a fever and the malaria test is negative, you may have typhoid, which should also receive immediate treatment. Where typhoid-testing is unavailable, a routine blood test can give a strong indication of this disease.

will protect you from malaria, elephantiasis and a range of nasty insect-borne viruses. Otherwise retire to an air-conditioned room or burn mosquito coils or sleep under a fan. Coils and fans reduce rather than eliminate bites. During the day it is wise to wear long, loose (preferably 100% cotton) clothes if you are pushing through scrubby country; this will keep ticks off and also tsetse flies and day-biting Aedes mosquitoes which may spread dengue and yellow fever. Tsetse flies hurt when they bite and are attracted to the colour blue;

It is preferable not to attempt self-diagnosis or to start treatment for malaria before you have tested, but there are few places outside the main towns where you will be able to have a test carried out. With malaria, it is normal enough to go from feeling healthy to having a high fever in the space of a few hours (and it is possible to die from falciparum malaria within 24 hours of the first symptoms). In such circumstances, assume that you have malaria and act accordingly – whatever risks are attached to taking an unnecessary cure are outweighed by the dangers of untreated malaria.

It is imperative to treat malaria promptly. The sooner you take a cure, the less likely you are to become critically ill, and the more ill you become the greater the chance you'll have difficulty holding down the tablets. There is some division about the best treatment for malaria, but the quinine/doxycycline regime is safe and very effective. Alternatively quinine and Fansidar can be used if doxycycline is unavailable. And if there is no quinine either then Fansidar alone can be used. The latter is widely available in Gabon and STP. One cure that you should avoid is Halfan, which is dangerous, particularly if you are using Lariam as a prophylactic.

In severe cases of malaria, the victim will be unable to hold down medication, at which point they are likely to die unless they are hospitalised immediately and put on a drip. If you or a travelling companion start vomiting after taking your malaria medication, get to a hospital or clinic quickly, ideally a private one. Whatever concerns you might have about African hospitals, they are used to dealing with malaria, and the alternative to hospitalisation is far worse.

Malaria typically takes around two weeks to incubate (minimum time seven days), but it can take much longer, so you should always complete the prophylaxis as recommended after returning home. If you display possible malaria symptoms up to a year later, then get to a doctor immediately and ensure that they are aware you have been exposed to malaria.

Every so often I run into travellers who prefer to acquire resistance to malaria rather than take preventative tablets, or who witter on about homoeopathic cures for this killer disease. That's their prerogative, but they have no place expounding their ill-informed views to others. Travellers to Africa cannot acquire any effective resistance to malaria, and those who don't make use of prophylactic drugs risk their life in a manner that is both foolish and unnecessary.

locals will advise on where they are a problem and where they transmit sleeping sickness.

Minute pestilential biting blackflies spread river blindness in some parts of Africa between 190°N and 170°S; the disease is caught close to fast-flowing rivers since flies breed there and the larvae live in rapids. The flies bite during the day but long trousers tucked into socks will help keep them off. Citronella-based natural repellents do not work against them.

Mosquitoes and many other insects are attracted to light. If you are camping, never put a lamp near the opening of your tent, or you will have a swarm of biters waiting to join you when you retire. In hotel rooms, be aware that the longer your light is on, the greater the number of insects will be sharing your accommodation.

Tumbu flies or putsi are a problem where the climate is hot and humid. The adult fly lays her eggs on the soil or on drying laundry and when the eggs come in contact with human flesh (when you put on clothes or lie on a bed) they hatch and bury themselves under the skin. Here they form a crop of 'boils' which each hatches a grub after about eight days, when the inflammation will settle down. In putsi areas either dry your clothes and sheets within a screened house, or dry them in direct sunshine until they are crisp, or iron them.

Jiggers or sandfleas are another flesh-feaster. They latch on if you walk barefoot in contaminated places, and set up home under the skin of the foot, usually at the side of a toenail where they cause a painful, boil-like swelling. They need picking out by a local expert; if the distended flea bursts during eviction the wound should be dowsed in spirit, alcohol or kerosene, otherwise more jiggers will infest you.

Bilharzia or schistosomiasis
with thanks to Dr Vaughan Southgate of the Natural History Museum, London
Bilharzia or schistosomiasis is a disease that commonly afflicts the rural poor of the tropics who repeatedly acquire more and more of these nasty little worm-lodgers. Infected travellers and expatriates generally suffer fewer problems because symptoms will encourage them to seek prompt treatment and they are also exposed to fewer parasites. However, it is still an unpleasant problem that is worth avoiding.

The parasites digest their way through your skin when you wade, bathe or

QUICK TICK REMOVAL
African ticks are not the prolific disease transmitters they are in the Americas, but they may spread Lyme disease, tick-bite fever and a few rarities. Tick-bite fever is a non-serious, flu-like illness, but still worth avoiding. If you get the tick off whole and promptly the chances of disease transmission are reduced to a minimum. Manoeuvre your finger and thumb so that you can pinch the tick's mouthparts, as close to your skin as possible, and slowly and steadily pull away at right angles to your skin. This often hurts. Jerking or twisting will increase the chances of damaging the tick, which in turn increases the chances of disease transmission, as well as leaving the mouthparts behind. Once the tick is off, dowse the little wound with alcohol (local spirit, whisky or similar are excellent) or iodine. An area of spreading redness around the bite site, or a rash or fever coming on a few days or more after the bite, should stimulate a trip to a doctor.

even shower in infested fresh water. Unfortunately, many African lakes, rivers and irrigation canals carry a risk of bilharzia.

The most risky shores will be close to places where infected people use water, wash clothes, etc. Winds disperse the cercariae, though, so they can be blown some distance, perhaps up to 200m from where they entered the water. Scuba-diving off a boat into deep offshore water, then, should be a low-risk activity, but showering in lake water or paddling along a reedy lake shore near a village is risky.

Although absence of early symptoms does not necessarily mean there is no infection, infected people usually notice symptoms two or more weeks after parasite-penetration. Travellers and expatriates will probably experience a fever and often a wheezy cough; local residents do not usually have symptoms. There is now a very good blood test which, if done six weeks or more after likely exposure, will determine whether you need treatment. Since bilharzia can be a nasty illness, avoidance is better than waiting to be cured and it is wise to avoid bathing in high risk areas.

Avoiding bilharzia

- If you are bathing, swimming, paddling or wading in fresh water which you think may carry a bilharzia risk, try to get out of the water within ten minutes.
- Dry off thoroughly with a towel; rub vigorously.
- Avoid bathing or paddling on shores within 200m of villages or places where people use the water a great deal, especially reedy shores or where there is lots of water weed.
- If your bathing water comes from a risky source try to ensure that the water is taken from the lake in the early morning and stored snail-free, otherwise it should be filtered or Dettol or Cresol added.
- Bathing early in the morning is safer than bathing in the last half of the day.
- Covering yourself with DEET insect repellent before swimming will protect you.
- If you think that you have been exposed to bilharzia parasites, arrange a screening blood test (your GP can do this) MORE than six weeks after your last possible contact with suspect water.

Skin infections

Any mosquito bite or small nick in the skin gives an opportunity for bacteria to foil the body's usually excellent defences; it will surprise many travellers how quickly skin infections start in warm humid climates and it is essential to clean and cover even the slightest wound. Creams are not as effective as a good drying antiseptic such as dilute iodine, potassium permanganate (a few crystals in half a cup of water), or crystal (or gentian) violet. One of these should be available in main towns. If the wound starts to throb, or becomes red and the redness starts to spread, or the wound oozes, and especially if you develop a fever, antibiotics will probably be needed: flucloxacillin (250mg four times a day) or Augmentin (250–500mg three times a day). For those allergic to penicillin, erythromycin (500mg twice a day) for five days should help. See a doctor if the symptoms do not start to improve in 48 hours.

EBOLA VIRUS

Bushmeat – that includes gorilla, chimpanzee, monkey, snake, porcupine, crocodile, forest antelope and lizard – is a traditional source of protein in Central Africa. Alternative sources of protein, such as domestic animals, are scarce and too expensive for forest dwellers. That's not to say that forest dwellers are the only market. In fact, with urbanisation the demand for bushmeat has, if anything, increased. Bushmeat is eaten in the cities not because there are no alternatives, but from habit, cultural attachment, or simply because consumers like the taste. Commercial hunting to supply city markets has become an important means of making money for forest dwellers, and hunting in the forest is easier than ever. Guns are widely available and logging roads have opened up parts of the forest that once were unreachable. The American-based Bushmeat Crisis Task Force (BCTF) estimates that one million tonnes of wildlife are killed and eaten each year in Central Africa. Needless to say, this represents a very worrying decrease in animal populations.

Gorilla and chimpanzee populations have also been struck by a terrifying disease. The health consequence of humans handling or eating dead infected apes has been equally dire (some might say retributional). Ebola is a deadly virus that causes its victims to bleed to death. It was first identified in 1976 in western Sudan and the Congo, and since then over 1,000 people have been killed by it. The first outbreak of Ebola in Gabon was in 1994, near an area in the forest where many apes were said to have died for no clear reason. In 1996 there were two outbreaks several months apart. In the first, 13 people fell ill after butchering a dead chimpanzee that they had found. In December 2001 there was another outbreak in Gabon in which 34 people were killed. Mékambo was the town at the heart of this epidemic, and the World Health Organisation (WHO) issued a warning to visitors strongly recommending against travel to northeast Gabon. In early 2003 there was another outbreak in the northwest of the neighbouring Republic of the Congo.

All the evidence points to the source of the Ebola virus as being the rainforests of Africa and Asia, but much more research is required to

Fungal infections also get a hold easily in hot moist climates so wear 100% cotton socks and underwear and shower frequently. An itchy rash in the groin or flaking between the toes is likely to be a fungal infection. This needs treatment with an antifungal cream such as Canesten (clotrimazole); if this is not available try Whitfield's ointment (compound benzoic acid ointment) or crystal violet (although this will turn you purple!).

Eye problems

Bacterial conjunctivitis (pink eye) is a common infection in Africa; people who wear contact lenses are most open to this irritating problem. The eyes feel sore and gritty and they will often be stuck together in the mornings. They will identify its exact origin. There have been a number of different hypotheses, and rodents, bats and even plants have all been suspected. What scientists do know is that Ebola is transmitted by direct contact with infected blood, secretions, organs or semen, whether the carrier is a dead chimpanzee or a living person. The first symptoms are sudden fever and weakness, accompanied by aching muscles, headache and sore throat. The next stage of the illness is vomiting, diarrhoea, rashes, reduced kidney and liver functions, and finally internal and external bleeding. The usual scenario is that within two weeks the patient has died from massive blood loss.

There is currently no treatment or vaccine for Ebola. Prevention and containment, not cure, are the current goals. For this reason dead patients should be immediately buried or cremated, suspected cases should be isolated for 21 days to prevent contamination, and people should be made aware of the link with bushmeat. Unfortunately efforts to combat Ebola can be hampered by politics – the government is reluctant to talk about it for fear of bad publicity, while there have also been rumours of scientists exaggerating their findings in an underhand bid for international research grants. It is also proving difficult to make people turn their backs on traditional food sources. In some remote areas, the local communities may even be unaware of the link because they have no access to radios. At the recent outbreak in December 2001 the WHO quarantined the small village of Ntolo, near Mekambo, in an attempt to halt the spread of the virus. The village chief Isidore Nkoto is reported to have complained: 'The medical teams are forcing us to live on a diet without bushmeat and in the dry season it is not easy to catch fish in the rivers. We are not vegetarians.'

Ebola is a virulent and terrifying disease that originates deep in the jungle, and the reaction it provokes is usually an overly alarmist one. At the latest outbreak the Peace Corps quickly withdraw all its volunteers from Gabon and tourists changed their holiday plans. The responsible tourist can, and should, still travel in Central Africa, taking care to abstain from bushmeat, keep away from any specific epidemic areas cited by WHO, and be aware of the first symptoms.

need treatment with antibiotic drops or ointment. Lesser eye irritation should settle with bathing in salt water and keeping the eyes shaded. If an insect flies into your eye, extract it with great care, ensuring you do not crush or damage it otherwise you may get a nastily inflamed eye from toxins secreted by the creature.

Prickly heat

A fine pimply rash on the trunk is likely to be heat rash; cool showers, dabbing dry, and talc will help. Treat the problem by slowing down to a relaxed schedule, wearing only loose, baggy, 100% cotton clothes and sleeping naked under a fan; if it's bad you may need to check into an air-conditioned hotel room for a while.

OTHER MEDICAL ISSUES
Meningitis
This is a particularly nasty disease as it can kill within hours of the first symptoms appearing. The telltale symptoms are a combination of a blinding headache (light sensitivity), a blotchy rash and a high fever. Immunisation protects against the most serious bacterial form of meningitis and the tetravalent vaccine ACWY is recommended for Central Africa. Other forms of meningitis exist (usually viral) but there are no vaccines for these. Local papers normally report localised outbreaks. A severe headache and fever should make you run to a doctor immediately. There are also other causes of headache and fever; one of which is typhoid, which can occur in travellers to Central Africa. Seek medical help if you are ill for more than a few days.

Safe sex
Travel is a time when we may enjoy sexual adventures, especially when alcohol reduces inhibitions. Remember that the risks of sexually transmitted infection are high, whether you sleep with fellow travellers or locals. About 40% of HIV infections in British heterosexuals are acquired abroad. Use condoms or femidoms; spermicide pessaries help reduce the risk of transmission. If you notice any genital ulcers or discharge, get treatment promptly since these increase the risk of acquiring HIV.

Rabies
Rabies is carried by all mammals (beware the village dogs and small monkeys that are used to being fed in the parks) and is passed on to man through a bite,

MARINE DANGERS
Before assuming a beach is safe for swimming, always ask local advice. It is always better to err on the side of caution if no sensible advice is forthcoming, since there is always a possibility of being swept away by strong currents or undertows that cannot be detected until you are actually in the water.

Snorkellers and divers should wear something on their feet to avoid treading on coral reefs, and should never touch the reefs with their bare hands – coral itself can give nasty cuts, and there is a danger of touching a venomous creature camouflaged against the reef. On beaches, never walk barefoot on exposed coral. Even on sandy beaches, people who walk barefoot risk getting coral or urchin spines in their soles or venomous fish spines in their feet. If you do tread on a venomous fish, soak the foot in hot (but not scalding) water until some time after the pain subsides; this may be for 20–30 minutes in all. Take the foot out of the water to top up; otherwise you may scald it. If the pain returns, re-immerse the foot. Once the venom has been heat-inactivated, get a doctor to check and remove any bits of fish spine in the wound.

scratch or a lick of an open wound. You must always assume any animal is rabid (unless personally known to you) and seek medical help as soon as possible. In the interim, scrub the wound with soap and bottled/boiled water, then pour on a strong iodine or alcohol solution. This helps stop the rabies virus entering the body and will guard against wound infections, including tetanus.

If you intend to have contact with animals and/or are likely to be more than 24 hours away from medical help, then pre-exposure vaccination is advised. Ideally three doses should be taken over four weeks. Contrary to popular belief these vaccinations are relatively painless!

If you are exposed as described, treatment should be given as soon as possible, but it is never too late to seek help as the incubation period for rabies can be very long. Those who have not been immunised will need a full course of injections together with rabies immunoglobulin (RIG), but this product is expensive (around US$800) and may be hard to come by. Another reason why pre-exposure vaccination should be encouraged in travellers who are planning to visit more remote areas!

Tell the doctor if you have had pre-exposure vaccine, as this will change the treatment you receive. And remember that, if you do contract rabies, mortality is 100% and death from rabies is probably one of the worst ways to go!

Snakes

Snakes rarely attack unless provoked, and bites in travellers are unusual. You are less likely to get bitten if you wear stout shoes and long trousers when in the bush. Most snakes are harmless and even venomous species will dispense venom in only about half of their bites. If bitten, then, you are unlikely to have received venom; keeping this fact in mind may help you to stay calm. Many so-called first-aid techniques do more harm than good: cutting into the wound is harmful; tourniquets are dangerous; suction and electrical inactivation devices do not work. The only treatment is antivenom. In case of a bite that you fear may have been from a venomous snake:

- Try to keep calm – it is likely that no venom has been dispensed.
- Prevent movement of the bitten limb by applying a splint.
- Keep the bitten limb BELOW heart height to slow the spread of any venom.
- If you have a crepe bandage, bind up as much of the bitten limb as you can, but release the bandage every half hour.
- Evacuate to a hospital which has antivenom.

And remember:

NEVER give aspirin; you may offer paracetamol, which is safe.
NEVER cut or suck the wound.
DO NOT apply ice packs.
DO NOT apply potassium permanganate.

If the offending snake can be captured without risk of someone else being bitten, take this to show the doctor – but beware since even a decapitated head is able to bite.

des
ailes...

...de nouveaux
horizons

Conception : **HDA** Communication - hdacommunication@wanadoo.fr - crédit photos : agence BIOS

AIR GABON
LA MEILLEURE SOLUTION

Part Two

Gabon

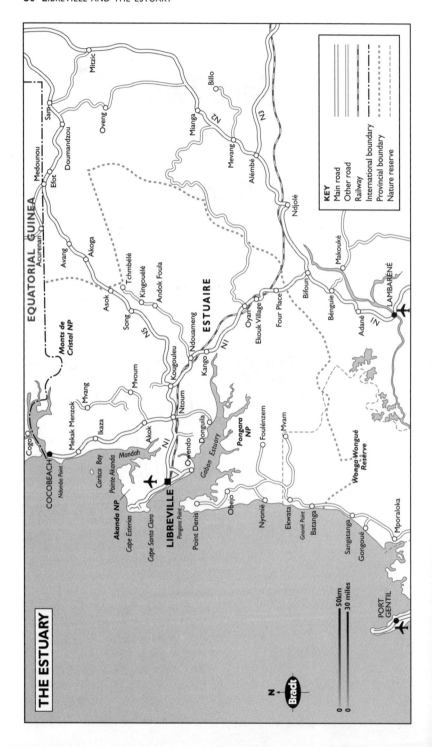

Libreville and the Estuary

LIBREVILLE

Gabon's capital lies in the far northwest of the country, spread along the Atlantic Ocean for some 15km (9 miles). Libreville is French for 'free town'. The French lieutenant Bouët-Willaumez chose the name – inspired by the example of Freetown in Sierra Leone – when slaves freed from the captured slave ship *L'Elizia* were settled here in 1849. This date is generally regarded as when the city was founded, although people, mostly the Mpongwé, had been living here long before then. In fact, in preceding years the French had been making great efforts to increase their power on this part of the coast. In 1839 the local Gabonese chief Rapontchombo put his mark to a treaty placing his territory under the French flag, the first of many such treaties signed with local chieftains.

By 1860 Libreville is thought to have consisted of the village of the freed slaves, a trading post and a handful of missionaries. The city grew a bit after World War II, but the real sparks to its growth were independence in 1960 and the petrol boom in the 1970s, which made the city an irresistible magnet for immigrants from neighbouring countries. The city's population increased in great leaps: 31,000 in 1960, 77,000 in 1970, 185,000 in 1980 and 337,700 in 1990. Today Libreville has an official population of 450,000, which accounts for about 40% of the country's inhabitants.

So, what's where? The coastal road runs from the airport – located 11km (7 miles) to the north of the city centre – through the city and on to the port of Owendo, 20km (12.5 miles) to the south on the Gabon estuary. On the way, roads lead away from the waterfront to the different *quartiers*. Batterie IV is the city's grandest area full of embassies and large houses and Quartier Louis is primarily an entertainment district. The grand boulevard Triomphal Omar Bongo was built on what was once the marshland of the Sainte Marie valley. The next big road junction leads up to Mont-Bouët, the busiest part of the city. Stretching from the Presidential Palace as far as avenue Felix Eboue is the commercial centre of the city, known as Nombakélé, and butting up to it is the old colonial Quartier Glass, where many trading companies once had their headquarters. Continuing brings you to the industrial area Oloumi, then the lively residential area Lalala, and finally the train station and port of Owendo. All distances in Gabon are measured from the Bessieux roundabout, *'le point*

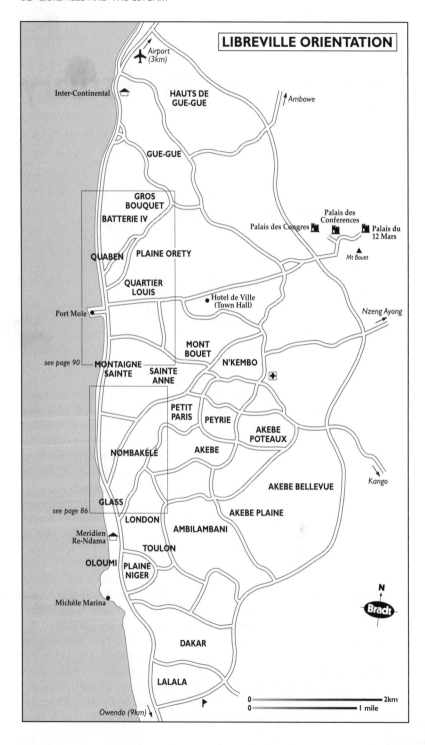

LIBREVILLE ORIENTATION

Airport
(3km)

Inter-Continental

HAUTS DE
GUE-GUE

Ambowe

GUE-GUE

GROS
BOUQUET

Palais des
Conferences

BATTERIE IV

Palais des Congres

Palais du
12 Mars

QUABEN

PLAINE ORETY

Mt Bouet

QUARTIER
LOUIS

Hotel de Ville
(Town Hall)

Port Mole

Nzeng Ayong

MONT
BOUET

see page 90

MONTAIGNE
SAINTE

N'KEMBO

SAINTE
ANNE

PETIT
PARIS

PEYRIE

AKEBE
POTEAUX

NOMBAKÉLÉ

AKEBE

Kango

AKEBE BELLEVUE

GLASS

see page 86

LONDON

AKEBE PLAINE

AMBILAMBANI

Meridien
Re-Ndama

TOULON

OLOUMI

PLAINE
NIGER

N

Michèle Marina

Bradt

DAKAR

LALALA

0   2km
0   I mile

Owendo (9km)

kilométrique zéro du Gabon'. When people refer to *quartiers* PK5, PK8 and PK12 they mean the area 5km, 8km or 12km from point zero.

President Bongo had big ideas for his capital back in the days when the coffers were overflowing with petrol money. For most of the 1970s the city resembled a massive building site. A new presidential palace was built, the first skyscrapers, big roads, new ministries, luxury hotels, plus the futuristic buildings of boulevard Triomphal. Recession in the mid 1980s slowed construction, but there's no denying that on one level Libreville lives up to the image of the flourishing international capital that Bongo envisaged. The buildings and hotels are still impressive, and you can dine on food from anywhere in the world if you can stomach the international prices – *les Librevillois*, immigrants and expats all agree the city is '*très, très cher*'. But of course, there is another, less visible side of the city behind the modern buildings, '*les matitis*' or shanty towns.

Getting there and away

Libreville is the hub of Gabon's transport system, such as it is. It's the home of the country's only international airport and has reasonable links by air, rail and road to the rest of the country. For a detailed breakdown of getting to and from other parts of the country, see under the relevant place in this guide, but there is a brief overview below.

By air

For details of international connections see the *Getting there* section of *Chapter 3 Planning Your Trip*. For details of national flights see under *By air* in *Chapter 4 Travelling Around*.

By boat

There used to be a boat leaving for Port Gentil from Michèle Marina in Glass (4 hours/15,000CFA one way), but the service has stopped for an unknown period. There are boats to Point Denis from Michèle Marina and Port Môle, from where you can also get to Ekwata. Boats also leave Port Môle bound for more far-flung destinations. For more information see under *By sea* in *Chapter 3*.

By rail

Gabon's only railway runs between Libreville and Franceville. It has made the southwestern region, and everything on route in-between, much more accessible from the capital. If the proposed track to the northeast is ever built that region will similarly be brought that much closer. See the *By rail* section in *Chapter 4* for more details on the railroad.

By taxis-brousse

Most of the unscheduled minibus services operating between Libreville and other towns leave from PK5 (*point kilometre* 5) or PK8 (*point kilometre* 8) further out of the city centre. Head to PK5 to pick up transport to Ntoum (2,500CFA) and Kango (2,500CFA), and to PK8 for more far-flung destinations, such as Cocobeach (4,000CFA), Lambaréné (5,000CFA), Mitzic (10,000CFA) and Mouila (12,000CFA). The *gare routière* just north of the Mont-Bouët marketplace is more commonly used for travel within Libreville, for getting to PK5, PK12 or the airport.

Getting around Libreville

Without your own car, the only way to get around town is to use a shared taxi, a private taxi or a *taxi-brousse*. *Taxis-brousse* are the minibuses that stick to certain routes and connect the city centre to the furthest reaches of town. Almost any journey will set you back just 100CFA.

There are masses of red-and-white taxis. You can either hire the whole taxi and be taken direct to your destination, or just *une place* (one seat). See under *Taxis* in *Chapter 4* for more details. It can be a bit hit-and-miss using collective taxis at first, as until you know your way around it is difficult to know where you want to get off. Although they exist, street names are not used much in Libreville and instead people orientate themselves in relation to key road junctions (such as *carrefour etranger* near Mbolo) and prominent buildings (CK2, *la poste*, *hôpital Jeanne Ebori*). In the rush hour (12.00–13.30 and 18.00–19.30) it's much harder to get a ride and the waterfront is choked up with cars. There are crowds of people at the main road junctions desperately signalling their required direction of travel in the hope that a taxi will pick them up.

The core city centre – where you'll find banks, travel agencies, clothes shops, souvenir shops and the Score supermarket – can be easily tackled on foot. Once again, directions to each place are given not in relation to streets but in relation to one another – opposite, around the corner from, behind, and so on.

It is possible to hire a car for use within the city. **Europcar** (tel: 74 58 45/46; fax: 77 25 78) and **Avis** (tel: 73 20 11; fax: 73 05 35) are both in the Oloumi *quartier* of town, and Avis also has an office at the Meridien Hotel (tel: 76 53 28). **Hertz** (tel: 73 20 11; fax: 73 05 35) has an office in the Hotel Intercontinental. All three have counters at the airport to deliver pre-arranged bookings, but cars cannot be booked here. The only manned car-hire company at the airport is **EGCA** (tel/fax: 73 97 08), which seems to prefer supplying cars to companies rather than individuals. See under *Hiring and driving* in *Chapter 4 Travelling Around* for general information.

Where to stay
Upper range
Résidence Hôtelière Le Maïsha La Sablière quartier; tel: 73 03 33; fax: 73 03 69. This is accommodation at its most sumptuous. It is located beyond the airport in amongst the city's grand houses and embassies. Every room has a different themed décor, such as French, Oriental or African. Stay in a standard room for 71,000CFA or the royal suite for 451,000CFA. Rates are negotiable for long stays. See under *Where to eat* for details of the restaurant.

Previous page Gabon coastline near Gamba (JT)
Above Lac Onangué (DH)
Right Whale breaching (LW)
Below right Goliath heron, Offooué River (JT)
Bottom right Duiker in the Offooué River (TI)
Below Goliath heron (TI)

Hôtel Méridien Re-Ndama Glass; tel: 76 61 61; fax: 74 29 24. Built in 1987, the hotel has recently been given a facelift. The hotel has well-maintained facilities that you would expect from a four-star hotel, including a sparklingly clean pool and a large restaurant. Rooms start at 86,000CFA for a standard room. Residents are eligible for a 50% discount on room rates at weekends.

Monts de Cristal Place de l'Indépendance; tel: 72 02 83/84/85/86; fax: 73 16 29. For 46,000CFA per room guests can enjoy cable TV, room service and a puddle of a swimming pool. Step out of the hotel right into the city centre. The reception and restaurant are nicely decorated, but the rooms could do with new carpets, curtains and bedspreads.

Le Novotel Rapontchombo Near the French Embassy; tel: 76 47 42; fax: 76 13 45. The hotel is gloomy, old-fashioned and much in need of modernisation. There is a boring restaurant and a car-hire counter in the lobby. A single/double is 53,500CFA/60,000CFA, or 80,000CFA for a suite.

Hotel Intercontinental Okoumé Palace Waterfront; tel: 73 26 19, 73 20 23, 73 21 25; fax: 73 16 29. The Intercontinental is one of the larger landmarks on Libreville's waterfront. Its grandeur is definitely of the faded variety, although it does have all the facilities (pool, gym, tennis courts, restaurant, souvenir boutiques). Lunchtimes at weekends there is a boring-looking buffet. Room prices start from 65,000CFA for a standard and 85,000CFA for a deluxe, but negotiations are sometimes possible.

Hotel Atlantique Opposite the airport; tel: 73 24 48/50; fax: 73 24 36/60. The Atlantique is blessed with a large, breezy restaurant directly on the beach, a swimming pool, conference facilities for 600, and even a thalasso water therapy centre. That said, to my mind it is overpriced at 85,000CFA for a sea-view room and 65,000CFA for a road-view. For stays of several days discounts are possible. A day room costs 42,500CFA. There's a buffet lunch every day from midday for 15,000CFA.

L'Alisé Michèle Marina; tel/fax: 72 92 22, 76 57 98. A welcoming hotel-restaurant on the waterfront, with small garden, pool and children's play area. Renovated rooms cost 45,000CFA and non-renovated rooms 35,000CFA. The restaurant serves good French food and wine (breakfasts cost 5,000CFA and the midday menu 7,000CFA).

Moderate
Hotel Equateur Not far from Mont-Bouët; tel: 72 55 46; fax: 76 12 53. A clean, welcoming hotel with 15 large rooms at 28,000CFA each kitted out with large double bed, air conditioning, bath and telephones. A sixteenth room at 30,000CFA has little extras, such as a carpet, a fridge and pictures on the wall. There is a bar and restaurant.

Le Patio Rue Pierre Barro; tel: 73 47 16; fax: 73 22 68. The Spanish owner of this lovely little hotel makes sure the hotel is well maintained and inviting. The rooms surround a small patio garden of potted plants. They are simply furnished, but all have air conditioning and telephone. The restaurant is romantic, with subtle lighting and arches draped with flowing curtains. The menu has some Spanish specialities, such as paella. Rooms cost 24,000CFA/28,000CFA a single/double. A television in the room costs an extra 3,000CFA.

Hotel Louis Rue Pierre Barro; tel: 73 25 69; fax: 73 04 00. Rooms at 19,000CFA, 21,000CFA and 26,000CFA. All rooms are air conditioned. The restaurant is popular

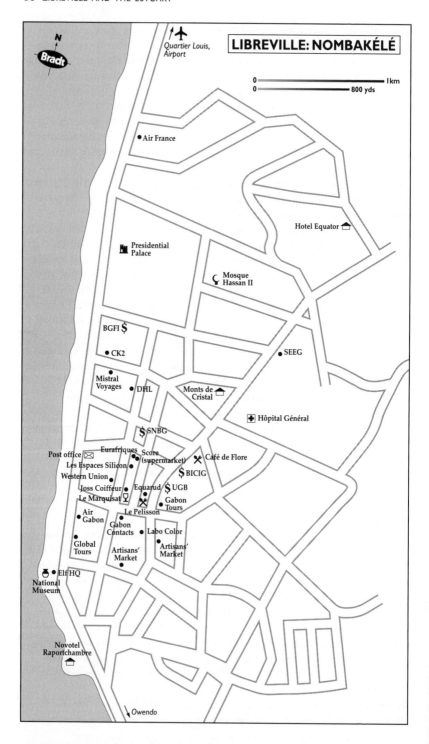

N

Bradt

Quartier Louis,
Airport

LIBREVILLE: NOMBAKÉLÉ

0 ————————————— 1km
0 ————————————— 800 yds

● Air France

Hotel Equator 🏠

Presidential
Palace

ᶜ Mosque
Hassan II

BGFI $

● CK2

SEEG ●

Mistral
Voyages ● DHL

Monts de
Cristal 🏠

✚ Hôpital Général

$ SNBG

Eurafriques
Post office ✉   Score
Les Espaces Silicon ● (supermarket)   ✗ Café de Flore
Western Union ● $ BICIG
Joss Coiffeur ●   Equarud ○ $ UGB
Le Marquisat 🏺   ✗   ● Gabon
            Le Pelisson   Tours
● Air   Gabon
Gabon   Contacts ● Labo Color
Global   ● Artisans'
Tours   Artisans'   Market
           Market
🏺 ● Elf HQ   ●
National
Museum

Novotel
Raportchambre
🏠

↙ Owendo

for business lunches during the week, when a three-course meal will set you back 10,000CFA.

Hotel Eclipse Paces from Hotel Louis; tel: 39 81 80. A new hotel with an inviting bar (but no restaurant) and bright, clean rooms simply decorated in black and white. The six rooms range in price from 20,000CFA to 28,000CFA, all with air conditioning and en-suite facilities.

Hotel Tropicana Near the airport; tel: 73 15 31/32; fax: 73 65 74; email: tropicana@inet.ga. The Tropicana is my personal favourite. What the hotel lacks in luxury it makes up for in charm. Soothing jazz plays in the bar-restaurant, which opens directly onto the beach. The food is very good, and Monday–Saturday there is an excellent value 3-course midday menu for 6,500CFA. The rooms are no-frills, with en-suite facilities and noisy air conditioning (16,000–36,000CFA). This is where many expats working outside Libreville stay when they come to the city, so reservations are recommended. Sundays the restaurant is always very crowded with families who come for the buffet lunch.

Hotel Somotel Mont-Bouët Rue Félix Eboué, near the Léon Mba roundabout; tel: 76 58 46/47/48; fax: 72 20 08. This hotel is in a very busy part of town, near the Mont-Bouët market. The 24-hour reception makes it a very useful place for those arriving in Libreville in the dead of night. It's a 15-minute walk to the centre of town (left out of the hotel and straight down). Clean en-suite rooms are 13,000CFA with a fan and 18,000CFA with air conditioning. Not suitable for those with an aversion to lumpy mattresses or flooded bathroom floors. There is a laundry service and a restaurant-bar with TV (open 07.00–22.30). The menu serves reasonably priced, if not very exciting, fast foods and traditional African dishes.

Hotel Bilbouqet Quartier Louis; tel: 73 53 13. This small hotel has rooms for 18,000–28,000CFA. There is a reasonable terraced restaurant (pizzas, grills, some Asian dishes) and a small bar with booths.

Budget

Maison Liebermann Bd Bessieux (*avant l'ancien gare routière, en face des Soeurs Bleues et du Petit Seminaire Saint Jean*); tel: 76 19 55; fax: 72 43 68; email: libermanngab@internetgabon.com. It's worth having the directions down pat in French as this is not a place that taxi drivers tend to know. Once exclusively a *Maison d'Accueil* (welcome house) for new Roman Catholic missionaries arriving in West Africa, the Maison Liebermann is now the saving grace for budget travellers in Libreville. There are five rooms with three beds, a fan and use of communal toilets and showers (6,000CFA for the first person and an additional 2,000CFA each for occupants two and three). There are also three air-conditioned singles with sink and shower in the room (10,000CFA). The first night there is an extra 2,000CFA per person for the sheets. It's clean, spartan, cheap and friendly. There is no restaurant, and not much in the immediate vicinity either. Be extra vigilant if you are wandering around the *gare routière* at night, as muggings are not uncommon.

Where to eat

There are so many restaurants in Libreville that it's not possible to list them all, or indeed to keep track of them all. This is a city that's growing and changing all the time, and inevitably places disappear and are replaced. Quartier Louis is the city's most happening district in the evenings, so you could just wander around until somewhere takes your fancy. It's not very well lit, but it's a safe area. Below I mention a few reliable places in different price categories. Bear in mind that some restaurants close on Sundays.

Upper range

Le Maïsha La Sablière quartier; tel: 73 03 33; fax: 73 03 69. This is Libreville's most expensive restaurant and it is found in the city's most expensive hotel. On Sundays there is a three course buffet for 20,000CFA, when non-residents also come to make a day of it and enjoy the pool and the beach. This is very good value compared to the restaurant's à la carte menu, which might features starters of *foie gras*, smoked salmon or langoustines for 14,000CFA.

La Tomate Quartier Louis; tel: 73 64 77. Many gourmands consider La Tomate to serve the best food in Libreville. The menu is heavily French, and there is always a good choice of specials (the soufflés are superb). The chef, David, is in fact English, although his habit of speaking English with a French accent often fools people. For a 3-course meal not including drinks expect to spend around 25,000CFA per person.

La Paillotte Waterfront; tel: 73 26 60. I haven't actually eaten here but have heard very good reports. The menu is largely international, with some African specialities. There is often live music at the end of the week. Prices comparable to La Tomate.

Le Jardin Gourmand Waterfront; tel: 73 02 73. Pricey, gastronomic French *haute cuisine* in a stiff and formal décor. There is an extensive wine list with bottles ranging from 13,000CFA to 1 million CFA.

Moderate

Dolce Vita On the left-hand side of Port Môle; tel: 72 42 38. This lovely Italian restaurant serves fresh pizzas, pastas and risottos for about 6,000CFA a dish. Meat and seafood dishes are slightly more expensive. If you sit at one of the window tables, it feels a bit like being in the cabin of a large boat – the décor is all wood, and there is a view over the water towards the city centre.

L'Odika Montée Louis; tel/fax: 73 69 20. This refreshingly breezy open-sided restaurant serves a mixture of European and African dishes, such as salt fish and creamed aubergine. Not only is the food good, but so is the décor (interesting wooden statues, soft lighting, greenery). There are even a few of the old favourites for dessert – chocolate mousse, ice cream, profiteroles. Prices from about 6,000CFA for a main course.

Costa Sylvia Montée Louis, opposite L'Odika; tel: 25 63 08. A friendly restaurant named after the Romanian owner and chef, Costa (Sylvia is his daughter). In the evenings he and his French wife do the rounds of the tables chatting to diners. Costa cooks a lot with fresh pasta and seafood, particularly gambas and crab. Good food for about 7,000CFA a main dish. Closed Sunday.

L'Aubergine Near La Maringa; tel: 73 03 59. Excellent-value pizzas in a relaxed atmosphere.

Papa Union II At the bottom of Montée Louis; tel: 73 86 80. Tasty steaks and fish at excellent value (main courses ranging from 3,000–8,000CFA). There are two other Papa Union restaurants in town but this is the most popular.

Le Barracuda Turn right at the sign for the company called La Sablière, just before the train station in Owendo; tel: 70 13 00. Breezy restaurant on a sandy beach. There is a midday menu at 6,500CFA and special dishes such as paella and couscous on Sundays. Popular with businessmen at lunchtime during the week.

Garden Caffé Quartier Louis; tel: 73 89 89. This restaurant feels like a cross between a modern French brasserie and a sports bar. There's a zinc bar (complete with boiled eggs), an open kitchen, billiards and a large television screen. The garden at the back has tables and 9-hole mini-golf.

C'est pas facile Descente Louis; tel: 73 31 89. Choice of pastas, pizzas, fish and meat from 7,000CFA. Plus on Friday nights there is *bouillabaisse* and on Saturday nights paella. At the road junction in front of the restaurant there is a slightly bizarre statue of André Raponda-Walker, the man hailed as Gabon's foremost historian and writer.

Café del Mar Montée Louis; tel: 73 41 25. The usual mixture of European and African choices, with a smattering of fancy gastronomic recipes. Main dishes starting at around 7,000CFA. There are sometimes themed evenings with special buffets. The *confit de canard* is excellent.

Aeroclub Restaurant In the row of buildings to the left of the main terminal building; tel: 73 57 77. This pilot's hang-out is also open to the public. A good place to watch planes take off and land. The menu is large and the food good. Main dishes cost around 5,500CFA.

Chez Marie-qui-fait-chaud Across from the Meridien Re-Ndama in Glass; tel: 32 13 59. Marie is very warm and friendly, which can make a welcome change. She cooks excellent langoustines and local dishes from her home country Cameroon. Sometimes she sings for her clients.

Le Paradiso Montée Louis. Considered by some to serve the best pizzas in town.

Chez Weng Montée Louis. Chinese fare with a popular all-you-can-eat buffet on Friday nights.

L'Indochine Montée Louis. The food here is much better than at Chez Weng, but more expensive. It also does a popular buffet on Friday nights.

Le Debarcadère Quartier Charbonnages. A slightly out-of-the-way seafood restaurant overlooking the mangroves. You can hire a *pirogue* here to explore the mangroves of Mondah Bay.

Cheap eats and snacks

Boga'to At Port Môle. Buy some goodies to take away from this great little bakery, or go to the café-bar next door and order the same pastries with your breakfast coffee.

Le Palmier Doré Rue de la Mairie. This is a nice boulangerie and coffee shop in the city centre selling freshly baked pastries, quiches, croques, sandwiches and ice creams. There's even a choice of teas and coffees. Ludicrously it's closed over lunch, from 13.00–15.30.

La Tasse d'Or In Mbolo shopping centre, the CCF end; tel: 71 81 81. Tiny but sophisticated coffee shop serving quality teas and coffees. Alternatively, there is an outdoor café at each end of Mbolo. Opening hours as per Mbolo, therefore closed at lunchtimes.

Le Pelisson Nombakélé. This popular *salon de thé* is something of a Libreville institution, having been around since 1936. In May 2002 it was entirely

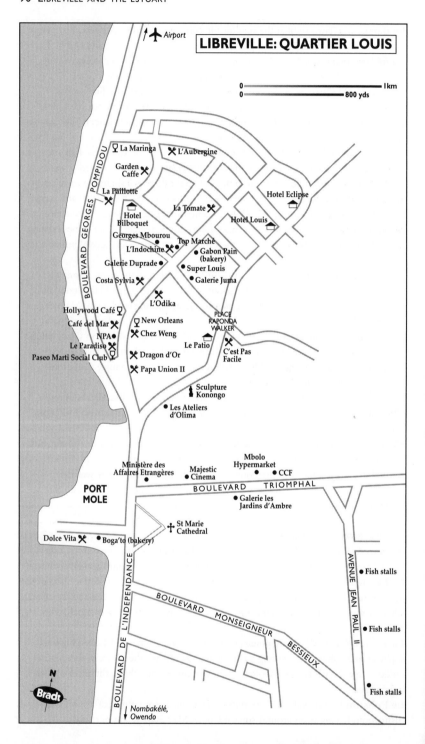

LIBREVILLE: QUARTIER LOUIS

Airport

0 ————————— 1km
0 ————————— 800 yds

BOULEVARD GEORGES POMPIDOU

La Maringa
L'Aubergine
Garden Caffe
La Paillotte
Hotel Eclipse
La Tomate
Hotel Bilboquet
Hotel Louis
Georges Mbourou
Top Marché
L'Indochine
Gabon Pain (bakery)
Galerie Duprade
Super Louis
Costa Sylvia
Galerie Juma
L'Odika
Hollywood Café
PLACE RAPONDA WALKER
Café del Mar
New Orleans
NPA
Chez Weng
Le Paradiso
Le Patio
C'est Pas Facile
Paseo Marti Social Club
Dragon d'Or
Papa Union II
Sculpture Konongo
Les Ateliers d'Olima

Ministère des Affaires Etrangères
Mbolo Hypermarket
Majestic Cinema
CCF

PORT MOLE
BOULEVARD TRIOMPHAL
Galerie les Jardins d'Ambre

St Marie Cathedral
Dolce Vita
Boga'to (bakery)

BOULEVARD DE L'INDEPENDANCE

AVENUE JEAN PAUL II
Fish stalls

BOULEVARD MONSEIGNEUR BESSIEUX
Fish stalls

N
Bradt

Nombakélé, Owendo

Fish stalls

redecorated. There is a mouthwatering adjoining boulangerie-patisserie. Open 06.30–20.00.

Le Marquisat Just across from Le Pelisson. This little wine bar is nicely decorated in creams and greens, with wrought-iron furniture completing the garden feel. Unfortunately the menu is limited and very expensive – salads start at 5,700CFA and puddings at 4,000CFA.

Les Jardins d'Ambre Galerie les Jardins d'Ambre, opposite Mbolo. A quiet place to have a snack or a cocktail. Sit in the cosy bar inside or under the inviting gazebo-type shelter outside. There is a good selection of savoury snacks and crepes, as well as sickly ice-cream sundaes. Open Monday–Saturday 08.00–22.00.

Le Café de Flore Av du Colonel Parent, near the BICIG bank. This is a good place to pause and unwind in the city centre. There's a nice breeze on the covered terrace, although you'll also get a lungful of the fumes from the street. The chalkboard menu offers fish and meat dishes for about 5,000CFA.

Le Centrale Down the alley to the right of Le Café de Flore. This small Lebanese café serves *schwarma*, salads and fish at very reasonable prices. Try the excellent fruit juice.

Le Dakota On the main road heading from the airport into town, just after the Tropicana Hotel. The décor is uninspiring but the pizzas are good and inexpensive. If you're staying nearby you could always eat the pizza at your hotel.

Avenue Jean-Paul II Linking Bd Omar Bongo with Bd Bessieux. From 19.00 this street is transformed into a string of small open-air restaurants. Each establishment sells the same thing – fried fish, fried rice, fried bananas and chips – so the only real choice is where to sit. It's a simple, tasty, filling and good value supper at around 2,000CFA for a large plateful. Your drinks order will be taken and paid for separately. The first 'fryings' of the evening can have a whiff of petrol about them, so I recommend not ordering as soon as they have set up.

Bars and nightspots

Quartier Louis is Libreville's most concentrated entertainment area, with venues staying open from early evening until 04.00, or until the punters can no longer stand. As you turn off the seafront into Quartier Louis, immediately on the left is the **Paseo Marti Social Club**, the place to go for those in search of a bit of salsa. It also serves what it claims is Cuban food. Jazz nights are Wednesdays and Thursdays. Next door is the **NPA** (*nul par ailleurs*, not found elsewhere), a bar-club complete with flashing lights and glittering balls. The music is mostly rock, techno and rap, and there are theme nights every second Thursday with cheap drinks. Other nights, a beer will set you back 2,500–3,500CFA. Diagonally opposite is **Le New Orleans**, which is more of a pub than a club. There are seven pool tables and a juke box with English and French music (three tunes for 500CFA). The majority of clients in both NPA and Le New Orleans are expat pilots and French legionaries. For clubs with a broader mix of tunes and clientele, try the **Hollywood Café** or **La Maringa**.

Le **Couloir de la Mort** (corridor of death) in Lalala may sound threatening, but in actual fact people are very friendly at this small strip of cheap terrace bars with very loud music and small restaurants serving fried fish. It gets crowded towards the end of the night, and the dancing only stops around 06.00, when drunken bodies litter the street (hence the name). Saturday night it's at its most crowded.

The **Casino La Croisette** (open 11.00–04.00) has roulette, blackjack, poker and masses of machines. It's pretty seedy inside, but the outside terrace is a nice place for an early evening drink.

Where to shop

Bear in mind when contemplating a shopping trip that Libreville virtually comes to a standstill over lunchtime and nothing is open (see under *Souvenir shopping* in *Chapter 4 Travelling Around*).

Libreville is well catered for by supermarkets, where you'll find a lot of imported goods and fruit and vegetables of a better quality than what is being sold on the streets. Prices are steep – imported yoghurts, cheeses and crisps are usually more than twice the price of back home. In the city centre there's the Score supermarket, in Glass there's Superglass, and in Quartier Louis there's Superlouis and Top Marché.

Quartier Louis also has two shopping centres – **Galerie Juma** and **Galerie Duprade** – which between them have a pharmacy, a branch of Western Union, a telephone/internet café and various shops. There is an ambitious South African project to redevelop **Port Môle** into a shopping and entertainment complex in the style of Cape Town's Victoria and Albert Waterfront. In all likelihood this project won't be completed for several years. Until then, **Mbolo** on boulevard Triomphal, is *the* shopping centre of the capital. Not only is there a supermarket, there's also a newsagent/bookshop, pharmacy, photography shop, travel agency, a couple of souvenir boutiques and a decent coffee shop, all under one roof. Mbolo's **Grand Pharmacie des Forestiers** is very well stocked with insect repellents, vitamins, baby foods and every recognised brand of face cream. Everything is imported, and as a result is astronomically expensive. A landmark by virtue of its size, **CK2** (on the waterfront in the city centre) sells everything, from tools to furniture.

Every *quartier* in the city has its own market. These markets sell everything you might need (shoes, spices, household goods) and more besides (bushmeat, ivory, rotten vegetables). Feel free to haggle. The largest of these local markets is **Mont-Bouët**, which takes its name from the hill commemorating Commandant Bouët-Willaumez, who named the city back in 1849. You can find just about anything here, and there are plenty of snack stands to choose from, but leave your valuables elsewhere. There was a massive fire here some years ago and sadly the market has failed to recover some of its former vibrancy.

There are two covered artisan's markets in the city centre, selling tie-dye clothes, CDs, masks, stone statues, as well as wooden bowls, boxes and chairs. Behind the Charles de Gaulle military camp not far from the airport is a shop with the best choice of finely carved African chairs and other wooden items. Next door is Art-Batik, where Alade (tel: 35 80 54) will make to order fabulous tablecloths, napkins and bedspreads that clients choose from a photo catalogue. Further along the same road is a sculptor's workshop. The best sculptor I know of, however, is Maitre Konongo, whose workshop is on Descente Louis in

Quartier Louis. Practically next door is the lovely shop Les Ateliers d'Olima, which sells, amongst other things, beautiful wooden lamps. Take the second left off the hill Montée Louis in Quartier Louis and you'll find Georges Mbourou's contemporary art gallery, next door to a cane-furniture workshop.

Useful information
Tourist information
The closest thing Gabon has to a tourist office is the Centre Gabonais de Promotion Touristique, otherwise known as **Gabontour** (see under *Tourist information* in *Chapter 3* for contact details). This is supposedly the information arm of the Ministry of Tourism, but unfortunately they're a bit short on information. They may be able to give you a map (don't count on it) or supply you with the odd leaflet, but that's about it. Nor do they run any trips to the country's interior. For this sort of service see the travel agencies listed below.

Mistral Voyages (BP 2106, up the exterior stairs of the Diamant building, opposite CK2; tel: 76 04 21; fax: 74 77 80; email: mistral.lbv@internetgabon.com) is an established and reputable firm, which also has branches in Marseille and São Tomé town. They offer trips to anywhere where there is a tourist infrastructure, including Lopé, Petit Loango, Sette Cama, Nyonie, Ekwata and Lékédi Park. They also organise day trips (Mondah Forest and Akanda National Park), rail and air tickets, and the chartering of light aircraft. As the most experienced travel agency in the country, they are recommended as the first port of call to anyone with a difficult or unusual travel proposition.

Equasud (tel: 76 86 86/99; fax: 76 86 77; email: aquasud.tourisme.gabon.com) is a relatively new company with a friendly and enthusiastic team. In addition to organising car hire, rail and air tickets, they propose a series of short trips to Lopé, Lambaréné, Franceville, Point Denis, Ekwata, Sette Cama and Kango. They also organise afternoon/day trips to the Mondah Forest, the Arboretum of Sibang and to Corisco Bay. For the day trips a minimum of six people is usually required.

Eurafrique Voyages (BP 4026; in the city centre; tel: 76 27 87; fax: 76 18 97; email: euravoyages@inet.ga) is an established and reliable agency offering trips to La Lopé, Parc de Lékédi and Point Denis. They will also happily organise trips to Cap Esterias or Mondah Forest. Needless to say, they also cover the usual air and train tickets.

Gabon Contacts (Immeuble des Arcades, BP 17012; tel: 74 68 90; fax: 74 68 89; email: gabon.contact@inet.ga) clearly has Agence de Voyages on its sign, but don't be misled. In actual fact the only travel service they currently do is booking flights. Train tickets are expected to be on offer in the near future. Their real business is organising conferences.

Global Tours (Immeuble Concorde next to Air Gabon on waterfront; tel: 76 19 01, 75 69 73, 74 64 02; fax: 76 00 84; email: globule@solsi.ga, globalservice@assala.com) offers trips to Nyonie, Gamba, Sette Cama and Petit Loango. They also organise visas for business travellers.

SDV Voyages (Mbolo centre, BP 77; tel: 74 31 28/29; fax: 77 21 80) is primarily a shipping company, and doesn't offer tourist packages as such. They do take airline and train bookings, however, and claim they can get clients preferential airline rates.

Safety

For the most part, Libreville is a calm, friendly place. As in any city there are places where extra care should be taken, and which should preferably be avoided altogether after dark, such as along the beach, around the *gare routière*, Mont-Bouët market and Petit Paris. Avoid being a target by not wearing jewellery, even a watch, and carrying the bare minimum in the way of money and bags in very crowded places.

Cinemas

There is one operational cinema in Libreville, **Le Majestic**, next door to Mbolo. It has two screens showing American blockbusters, which may or may not have been dubbed into French. Check *L'Union* for what's on. Films are also shown at the CCF. They favour recent French films and arty 'foreign' films, which are screened in their original language with French subtitles.

Money

It's not difficult to find banks in Libreville. For starters, there are at least three branches of the BMBG (Concorde building on bd de l'Indépendance, Okoumé Palace, Mont-Bouët) and two of the UGB (av Colonel Parant, Mbolo shopping centre), plus the big Citibank next to St André church. Bank opening times vary slightly, but as a general rule, opening hours are Monday–Friday 07.45–11.30, 14.45–16.45. Be warned that they always close on the dot. For this reason, I have fallen into the habit of always changing money at the **BGFI Bank/Bureau de Change**, which has the longest opening hours I know of and doesn't close for lunch (07.30–19.00 Monday–Saturday).

If I had to choose, however, my favourite bank would be the **BICIG**, for the simple reason that this is currently the only bank where you can withdraw money from a cash machine with a Visa card. There are branches of BICIG just before the airport, on avenue Colonel Parant in the city centre and at Mont-Bouët. There are also cash-point machines at Mbolo and in the airport, although a leaking roof has meant the airport machine has long been out of service. Queues at machines can be long and tense – particularly on Fridays – as the machines quite frequently fall out of service. The machine in BICIG Prestige (under the walkway to the left of the branch in the city centre) tends to be less crowded. If none of the machines is working, you can try withdrawing cash by having your card swiped through a credit-card machine – ask someone at the bank to direct you to the right counter.

The main branch of **Western Union** is in the city centre, but there are also branches elsewhere, such as in Quartier Louis.

Books, maps, newspapers

There are permanent kiosks selling national papers at the following places (as well as elsewhere) in Libreville: opposite the Hotel Dialogue, inside the airport, inside the supermarket Score, next to the shop CK2. Most of the big hotels in the capital have small newspaper kiosks selling (almost) up-to-date issues of foreign papers and magazines for about twice the price they would cost back home. The widest selections can be found in the bookshops opposite the Meridien Hotel, in the Galeries les Jardins d'Ambre opposite Mbolo, and inside the Mbolo shopping centre itself. These bookshops also sell coffee-table books about Gabon, children's books and French novels.

In theory these bookshops should sell the 1:1,000,000 map of Gabon, complete with a 1:50,000 inset of Libreville, published by the Institut Geographique National (IGN). The map was last revised and reprinted in 1994, but since stocks have run dry, you now have to go directly to the national mapping office, or Institut National de la Cartographie (INC). It is located on the road leading away from Citibank into Batterie IV, just past the school Gros Bouquet I on the left (open Monday–Friday 08.00–12.00, 15.00–18.00). They'll make you a colour photocopy that is more expensive and of poorer quality than the original (plead poverty and you might be able to haggle the price). They also sell large maps of Libreville and other major cities and regions, some of which can also be found at the book kiosk in the Hotel Atlantique.

Post and communications

The main post office is in the city centre. The opening hours are 08.00–12.00 and 15.00–18.00 Monday–Friday. To make phone calls or send faxes head to one of many *cabines telephoniques* in the city centre.

Wandering around Libreville you'll stumble upon a growing number of cybercafés, all charging 1,000CFA an hour and all with long opening hours. Some sell fizzy drinks and stale biscuits, but they are more cyber than café. There are two in the shopping concourse opposite Mbolo, which are both open every day 08.00–22.00. There is also a cyberroom upstairs at the Centre Culturel Français (see under *What to see and do* on page 97 for more information).

If you are in the city centre, go to **Les Espaces Silicom** (tel: 26 14 66, open Monday–Friday 08.00–21.00), just around the corner from the main post office. It tends to be quieter here than in some of the larger ones that are often inundated with school kids. They also have a couple of private offices that can be hired for 3,000CFA an hour or 29,000CFA a day (weekly rates negotiable).

Sports

The Hotel Meridien Re-Ndama and the Hotel Intercontinental Okoumé Palace have gyms/tennis courts that can be used by non-residents. The facilities at the Intercontinental are superior, and the cost is 5,000CFA a visit. The capital's best fitness club is **Club Saoti** (tel: 73 03 95), which is located in the Hauts de Gué Gué quartier. There is a gym, swimming pool, and tennis and squash courts. There are also dance classes run by Laurence Gatto (tel: 06 60 90).

There is a golf course (18 holes, 38 hectares) outside Libreville. Head in the direction of Owendo, turn left at the IAI roundabout, then the first right. For more information call 76 03 78.

For alternative activities and watersports, refer to Point Denis and Ekwata in *The estuary* section below.

TRADITIONAL BELIEFS AND PRACTICES

According to traditional beliefs in Gabon, the natural and the supernatural are inextricably linked, and there are special and powerful forces at play in a person's everyday life. There are a number of different male and female religious societies in Gabon that share this premise. These initiation societies have traditionally played a crucial social role, determining social order, settling disputes and dispensing knowledge. The most widespread male secret society is **Bwiti**. Through the philosophy of *Bwiti* a man acquires the knowledge, discipline and strength necessary for life. He is taught to respect the powers of nature and the spirits, and to value the forest. He is also taught how to communicate with his ancestors.

It is through the **cult of ancestors** that the cosmic cycle of life and death operates, which is the basis of religion. The skulls of important people, and sometimes also teeth and bone fragments, are kept in baskets and bags by the Kota, and bark receptacles by the Fang. These receptacles are usually then surmounted by small statues meant to symbolise the ancestors. They are kept under a shelter away from the village. When an event demands it – for example birth, marriage, illness, an initiation, the beginning and end of a period of mourning – the bones are brought out and the ancestors are consulted.

In each village there is a *Bwiti* temple called a *mbandja*, or *corps de garde* by the French. This is an open-sided hut where the ground is consecrated. Special ceremonies take place here, in which initiates seek to enter into contact with the spirits in the other world in order to further their spiritual enlightenment, their understanding of themselves and their understanding of the world. The initiates facilitate their contact with the other world by eating the sacred wood, the root of the *iboga* shrub. *Iboga* induces hallucinations when consumed in sufficient quantities (and death when consumed in excessive quantities).

At all ceremonies there is traditional music and dancing. The sacred music includes drums, the *ngombi* (a harp with eight strings) and a musical bow that is plucked with the mouth and tapped with a stick. Only the male dancers wear **masks**, their identity usually a secret. A mask is another tool

What to see and do

For most people, Libreville is just a stepping stone to the interior and the coast. If you do wind up staying here a couple of days, however, there's enough to keep you busy. And if busy is the last thing you want to be, then you could spend the day at a hotel with a pool or beach for the price of your lunch (see under *Where to stay* in this chapter). Alternatively, head out of town for the day (see page 99 and under *The Estuary* for ideas).

As far as tourist attractions in the city go, the most obvious place to start is the **Musée National des Arts et Traditions** (National Museum), which is hidden at the rear of the towering Elf building on the waterfront. The for establishing contact between the spiritual and earthly worlds. It is a physical manifestation of a mythical concept, namely the spirits of the ancestors or the spirits of the forest. It can be in the form of a human or animal – man, woman, snake, crocodile, gorilla or elephant – and each mask has a different expression to indicate whether it is good or bad. The style and materials of the mask depend on why and where they were made. For example, in the Coastal Ogooué masks are traditionally carved out of wood in the shape of a helmet, and are often painted white and adorned with mirrors, feathers and horns. African masks have been a source of inspiration to artists worldwide for years. The sale of a *Mbede* mask for one billion four hundred million CFA in 2001 is a clear indicator of the value the art world currently places on Gabonese masks.

The *nganga* is a traditional practitioner who has spent years studying the art of healing and the links between this world and the other. It is the *nganga* who administers the *iboga*, as well as all other forest remedies. He does not have absolute power. He is a man with the weaknesses of a man. The *nganga*'s gift lies in his ability to feel a person's illness, and his intimate knowledge of the forest enables him to prepare a remedy. A *nganga* will tell you that that human and the forest are one, and that everything in the forest has an important role to play, from termites and bees, to pythons and panthers. **Jean-Claude Cheyssial**, a French film-maker, has produced a series of fascinating documentary films since the early 1990s focusing on subjects such as the importance of the forest in Gabonese society and the role of the *nganga*.

Traditional beliefs and practices suffered enormously at the hands of the missionaries, who taught people to be ashamed of their culture and to destroy the instruments of their beliefs, such as the masks. The frequency of rituals has decreased enormously, and naturally there are fears for what is being lost and questions as to whether there is a future for authentic masks (meaning masks created for religious as opposed to artistic purposes). That said, the young *Gabonais* exhibit a growing recognition and pride about their traditions, even if they do not all choose to participate. This home-grown interest is paralleled outside Gabon, and there is a steady trickle of foreigners who come to Gabon to be initiated into *Bwiti*.

museum is small but full of little gems, notably the photographs, musical instruments and the amazing masks. It is open 09.00–12.00 and 15.00–18.00 Monday–Friday. The entrance fee is 1,000CFA, or 2,000CFA for a guided tour.

Libreville has a number of buildings of architectural interest. The boulevard Triomphal El Hadj Omar Bongo, for example, has several impressive structures, not least the glass-and-tile **Ministère des Eaux et Forêts** decorated with palm trees and birds. The building with the wavy roof is the **Centre Culturel Français Saint-Exupéry** or CCF (tel: 76 11 20), which hosts regular exhibitions, talks and film screenings, and also has a library and internet facilities. The library and cyberroom are open Tuesday–Saturday 09.30–12.00 and 15.00–18.30 (closed Thursday morning).

On a hill looking down on the *carrefour etrangère* and Port Môle is **Saint-Marie cathedral**, seat of the archbishop. The current cathedral was built in 1958 on the site of the old Aumale fort, and is now much in need of a lick of paint. The old church, consecrated approximately a century earlier, was fortunately preserved behind it. The capital's most beautiful church is **Saint Michel's church in Nkembo** (on the left at the STFO roundabout), whose intricately carved wooden pillars depict Christian and African legends. Above the entrance Saint Michael fells the dragon in a blaze of colour. The church can seat up to 1,000 people.

Arboretum de Sibang
In 1931, 16 hectares of the trees to be found in Gabon's forests were planted just beyond PK8 for the purpose of scientific research. A visit to the arboretum is an interesting introduction to the different species of the forest. Hervé Ovono (tel: 23 46 68; email: ovono50@assala.com, vogbwiti69@yahoo.fr), who used to manage the arboretum, will take small groups on tours for around 10,000CFA an hour.

Cultural villages
There are currently two cultural villages in Libreville, which aim to give visitors a greater understanding of Gabonese culture and religion. Ceremonies for anyone wishing to be initiated into *Bwiti* can be arranged at both.

Mbeng-Ntame is run by Christophe (tel: 27 09 90; email: kooldayele@assala.com; web: www.assala.com/etincelle) and his wife Marie-Claire (tel: 24 06 10). They are committed believers in the spiritual and physical benefits of *Bwiti*, and are keen to bring the intense music and dancing that accompanies it to a wider audience. They organise 90-minute shows followed by a traditional Gabonese meal served on manioc leaves for groups of around 30 people (20,000CFA per person). Smaller groups are welcome to visit for less formal evenings, and they hope soon to be able to welcome guests for overnight stays. The village is very much a family affair. The dance troupe is made up of their children and Marie-Claire's sisters. Marie-Claire makes all the dance costumes, as well as the jewellery and clothes on sale. The village is located at PK12. To get there, take a bus from Sainte Marie or the *gare routière*. At PK12, take a left turn off the surfaced road and walk for 300m along the old Lambaréné road as far as the black wooden gate. A *course* in a taxi will cost 2,000CFA.

Resident at **Festivillage** are a *nganga* (see box on *Traditional beliefs and practices*, pages 96–7) and several young Gabonese being instructed in traditional skills, including dance, music, cooking, basketry and jewellery. Visitors are welcome to consult the *nganga* (10,000CFA plus three drinks) or to watch a consultation. Contact Hugues Poitevin for further information (tel: 25 09 17; fax: 73 35 80; email: asso_ebando@assala.com; web: www.f-i-a.org/ebando). The village is beyond the airport, on the road parallel to the Capes Santa Clara and Esterias road, but on the side of the waterfront (next to

the Bananas hotel and the lovely beach of **La Sablière)**. It's very popular with
mosquitoes after sundown so be sure to use plenty of repellent.

THE ESTUARY

Within the Estuary (Estuaire) region are a number of places where it's only too
easy to forget the proximity of the big smoke. Just minutes out of Libreville on
the airport road the forest begins. Both along this coast and on the other side
of the estuary, there are dreamy beaches where it's possible to walk for miles
along the shore at low tide. On the southern side of the estuary is **Pongara
National Park**, which incorporates the tourist resort of **Point Denis**.
Neither side of the estuary is short on birdlife – kingfishers, little egrets, reef
herons, sanderlings and other fast-moving waders abound.

Cape Santa Clara

About a 15-minute drive from Libreville's airport is the left turn-off to Cape
Santa Clara. The turn-off is difficult to miss for two reasons: there is a large
sign and invariably a crowd of small vendors selling palm wine. From here the
road is very poor. It's just passable in an ordinary car in the dry season, but in
the rainy season a 4WD is essential. Because of the state of the road this stretch
of coast has been little developed, even though the beach is lovely and
swimming is possible at low tide. At the time of writing, there were no
functioning hotels, although this is set to change soon. Le Poulet Fermier
hotel-restaurant is indefinitely closed, and its owner is in the throes of
building a second hotel of bungalows on the site next door. Call Mr Okouaghe
on 76 40 16 or 76 60 21 for more details. Beyond Le Poulet Fermier is **La
Nerina** (tel: 24 87 67, 26 90 93), a crumbling, converted colonial building. At
present, the staff can prepare you something to eat, but until there is running
water they are not catering for overnight guests. The plan is eventually to have
four en-suite rooms in the main building and a handful of bungalows.

Mondah Forest

Just a 20-minute drive from Libreville is the beautiful Forêt de la Mondah, a
fantastic escape from the big city. Continue past the turn-off to Cape Santa
Clara until you see the colourful board on the left. The board outlines five
walks, ranging from 0.8km to 4.6km. The longest circuit takes about 1.5 hours,
not including any stops. There are a couple of places with rustic benches for
those who have picnics. The Ministère des Eaux et Forêts have done a tree list
identifying the trees you pass according to their number, although it's quite
difficult to get hold of. The most frequent number is 123, for the Okoumé.

It's not obligatory to have a guide, but if you want to learn more about the
trees and their different uses then contact the Ecole Nationale des Eaux et
Forêts at Cape Esterias (tel: 48 02 11), explaining that you wish to have a
guided visit of the Parcelle des Conservateurs. Some travel agencies will
arrange a half-day trip to the forest for you, including a guide and transport
and a *pirogue* trip in the mangroves of Mondah Bay, but they normally require
a minimum of six people. Either arrangement will require at least a couple of

days' notice. Alternatively, hire a *pirogue* at Le Débarcadère restaurant (see under *Where to eat* on page 89).

Cape Esterias

Continuing past the turn-off to Cape Santa Clara will bring you to Cape Esterias. This was the place people came to from Libreville to get away from it all ten years ago. Now the same clientele go to Point Denis, and the restaurants are to all intents and purposes closed during the week when there are rarely any diners. At weekends things pick up a bit, when families come for a day on the beach, and on New Year's Eve it's still a happening venue. It's a long, sandy beach fringed by the obligatory palm trees and strewn with tree trunks that have run aground. Accessible from Cape Esterias is beautiful **Corisco Bay**, with its picture-postcard islets of sand and coconut palms, including Corisco Island. This island of about 15km² (6 square miles) is actually part of Equatorial Guinea. It can be reached in 1.5 hours from Cape Esterias by boat.

The following are the restaurants and hotels in the order in which they lie on the Cape Esterias beach.

Le Nautic BP 2049; tel: 37 61 00. At weekends Le Nautic serves a popular lunchtime buffet for 12,000CFA (without drinks) with a large choice of seafood and barbecued dishes.

L'Auberge du Cap BP 9465; tel: 48 04 47. This is an inviting restaurant on a covered terrace right on the beach. The food is very good. An à la carte meal for one costs around 14,000CFA. Behind the restaurant there are *rondavels* sleeping up to 4 people (15,000–26,000CFA). Camping is also allowed (there are outdoor showers). The restaurant is closed Mondays and in the evenings when there are no clients.

Le Relais du Phare BP 3529; tel: 48 04 48. Situated right on the peninsula, next to the rather squat lighthouse, the Relais is the grandest that Cape Esterias has to offer. The colonial-style bar-restaurant opens on to a manicured lawn, beyond which there is the best ocean view yet. Rooms are 25,000CFA for a double, and there is one studio sleeping up to 8 people for 50,000CFA. The hotel can organise walks in the forest and fishing trips to the offshore islands of Corisco Bay, although prices aren't cheap.

La Balise Beyond Le Relais du Phare; tel: 48 04 28. This relaxed joint is slightly cheaper than the others, but unfortunately there is only an obscured view of the water. The house speciality is shellfish, in particular *palourdes*, a triangular shellfish that the chef usually cooks in garlic butter. At weekends a craftsman sets up his wares for sale alongside the tables – lampshades and masks made from raffia, wood and peanut shells.

Akanda National Park

The area bordering the Mondah and Corisco Bays is protected as the **Akanda National Park** since 2002 (although this might prove difficult given the density of villages here). The park is said to harbour the largest populations of migratory birds in Gabon, as well as being a vital feeding zone for turtles. There is currently no tourist infrastructure here (the only tourist camp is not operational) but Mistral Voyages can arrange birdwatching day trips from Libreville.

Point Denis

The silky sand beach on the southern side of the estuary is part of **Pongara National Park**. The village of Point Denis has become Gabon's most established seaside resort and is very popular at the weekends. Many French expats have built holiday homes notable for their double aspect, overlooking the estuary on one side and mangrove swamps on the other. But not to worry if you don't have a holiday home, as there is a good choice of places to stay although remember that most of them are only open at the weekend.

The largest is the **Ndjogu Assala Lodge**, a former minister's house and now a hotel with 28 air-conditioned rooms, *paillottes* on the beach and a large restaurant. Fishing, quad biking, jet skiing and excursions into the forest can all be arranged. Rooms cost 45,000CFA a night. Next door is the **Restaurant Moustache**, and then **Chez Ayo**, the least expensive hotel-restaurant, with a good Sunday buffet and rooms with fan. The next stop is **Cocoloco** hotel-restaurant, which has air-conditioned rooms and Creole dishes on its menu. Finally there is **La Maringa**, also known as **Sonnet's**, after the owner Robert Sonnet (tel: 32 17 45). La Maringa restaurant serves a buffet on Sundays for 10,000CFA. There are four small and clean bungalows with double bed and en-suite shower room at 35,000CFA a night.

If you fancy forest-walking or fishing by day, and campfires or turtle-watching by night, then contact a young and enthusiastic 'eco-guide' Hervé Ovono, who will organise for someone to take you if he is busy. The cost is 10,000CFA a day for the guide and 5,000CFA for a tent. See under the Arboretum de Sibang in the *What to see and do* section on page 98 for Hervé's contact details. The more notice you give him the better.

Keep walking beyond the Maringa to reach **Pongara Point**, where the estuary meets the ocean. This beach, which is famous for the large number of turtles that lay their eggs here, gives its name to the national park. **Pongara National Park**, which extends for 1,200km² (463 square miles), was granted protective status because of its diverse scenery – vast mangrove flats, forest, savannah, and of course the beach itself. The local environmental organisation Aventures sans Frontières (see page 59) conducts annual surveys here throughout the turtle season (November–February).

It's a 25-minute journey from Libreville to Point Denis. A *navette* leaves **Port Môle** on Saturday and Sunday mornings at 09.00 and 10.00, returning both evenings at 16.00 and 17.00. The cost is 8,000CFA for the return trip. It is advisable to book with Muriel in advance, indicating where you want to be dropped off (tel: 24 25 01, 31 40 40, 24 34 34, 73 12 75). There is also a *navette* departing from **Michèle Marina** (tel: 31 80 80) at the following times: 09.00 Tuesday–Friday, 09.30 Saturday, and 09.30 and 11.00 Sunday. The *navette* leaves Point Denis at 17.00 Tuesday–Friday, 17.30 Saturday, and 16.00 and 17.00 Sunday. A round-trip costs 10,000CFA. All the establishments at Point Denis are close together along the same stretch of beach, so if you're not sure where you want to go, just get off the boat anywhere and make up your mind on foot.

Ekwata

South of Point Denis, facing the ocean, is Ekwata. The setting of this lodge is spectacular – white sand and ocean in front, dense forest behind. For this reason, access from Libreville is usually made by boat to Point Denis and then by 4WD. There are plenty of activities to choose from, including wind-sailing, water-skiing, fishing and guided walks in the forest. The water in front of the lodge can be a bit rough for swimming at times.

A weekend (Saturday morning to Sunday late afternoon) at Ekwata costs 80,000CFA, with supplementary nights at 40,000CFA. A day trip is 25,000CFA. These rates include meals and, where appropriate, accommodation in air-conditioned bungalows. Some of the activities are included, some of them cost extra. The Ekwata *navette* leaves Port Môle at 09.00 and returns at about 17.00. Bookings are necessary, even for day trips, and are most easily made through travel agents in Libreville. There are special rates for children.

Wonga-Wongué Reserve and Nyonié

Wonga-Wongué has been a Presidential Reserve since 1972. It covers a massive 500,000 hectares (1,235,500 acres) of beautiful beaches, dense forest, open savannah, hills and valleys. There are plenty of animals, including elephants, buffaloes, chimpanzees, bongos, sitatungas, even panthers, and an extensive network of roads. Unfortunately Wonga-Wongué is only open to presidential parties, although it is possible that all or part of it might be made into a national park at some point. Until such a time, the paying public must content itself with skirting the edges of the reserve from Nyonié camp, in the hope of catching glimpses of the wildlife. Fortunately, Nyonié is a welcoming and relaxing camp on the beach run by Monsieur Beti. The barbecues are very good and can also be very entertaining, as Monsieur Beti regularly takes in baby gorillas orphaned by poachers.

A weekend will set you back 90,000CFA, with each supplementary night costing 35,000CFA. Unless you have your own means of transport, day trips from Libreville are not possible. Weekends start at 09.00 on Saturday – when the boat leaves Libreville's Michèle Marina – and last until about 17.00 on Sunday. The price includes all food, accommodation in air-conditioned rooms, plus a game drive and fishing for those interested. Visitors may see turtles coming to lay their eggs November–February. Bookings are essential, either through a travel agent or via Monsieur Beti direct (tel: 02 36 36). Those arriving in their own light aircraft or boat pay 10,000CFA less, and children pay half price.

Kango

Kango is a small town on the bank of the Komo River. It is located 100km southeast of Libreville along an excellent road that runs through numerous villages. There's nothing particular about the town – fewer than 1,500 inhabitants – except for the **Hotel Assok** (tel: 40 00 03). The tranquil riverside location and stunning view make a refreshing contrast to the city. On a *pirogue* trip along the Komo you might catch a glimpse of crocodiles, monkeys or birds. The cost is 22,000CFA per person per night, or 45,000CFA per person (based on two people sharing) for Saturday through to Sunday, with dinner, breakfast and Sunday lunch buffet included. Book direct at the hotel or through Equasud travel agency in Libreville.

Cocobeach

A good three hours' drive north of Libreville is the small coastal town of Cocobeach, on the frontier with Equatorial Guinea. There's very little to see or do here, but it's a nice enough place to spend a couple of days. It's so small there are no taxis, just a market, the beach and a couple of picturesque fishing villages nearby. The catch of the day arrives directly at the beach behind the market. Approach the fishermen if you want to hire a *pirogue* for a spin, or to find out when the next *pirogue* will be heading up the Mouni River to the old Spanish colonial town of Cogo in Equatorial Guinea (about 4,000CFA). The best beach for swimming is a 20-minute walk along the road left of the market – keep an eye out for fossilised fish on rocks at low tide.

Getting there and away

There are *taxis-brousse* doing the return journey between Libreville and Cocobeach every day. They leave Libreville from PK8. The journey takes over three hours – sometimes a lot longer if the control checks don't go smoothly – and costs about 4,000CFA each way. The road is surfaced until Ntoum, after which it is mostly very good dirt road, and drivers tend to travel way faster than is safe. I personally wouldn't want to be on this road after dark.

Where to stay and eat

The largest hotel in town is the **Motel Esperance**, which is next to the market on the waterfront. There are seven rooms with air conditioning at 12,300CFA and two rooms with fan at 10,300CFA. All rooms have en-suite facilities and small balconies that open out into a garden. The hotel has seen better days, but is none the less good value. There is a bar, and a nightclub that only opens on special occasions. Breakfast – and possibly other meals – can be served if enough advance warning is given. Opposite one another on the main street are **Motel Iboga** and **Au Beau Sejour**, which both have an assortment of different rooms with fan in the region of 5,000–8,000CFA. The Iboga Motel also has the town's most popular dance club. The only other place to stay is **Chez Mado**, located out of the town centre on the road towards Libreville. The hotel restaurant serves the most expensive and fancy food in town.

The food options are not extensive. The most popular restaurant in town is the Togolese restaurant, which serves meat brochettes and grilled fish. The Cameroonian lady at Au Beau Sejour will cook a good fried fish supper if you order it in the morning.

Crystal Mountains National Park

The forests of the Crystal Mountains (les Monts de Cristal) are amongst the oldest in Gabon. Strictly speaking the mountain range is mostly in the region of **Woleu-Ntem**, but because access is easier and more usual from Libreville,

I have included it in this chapter. This ancient forest at an altitude of over 900m (2,950ft) served as a botanical refuge for plants, birds, insects and snakes during the last Ice Age. Specific research still needs to be done on its biological diversity and the high concentration of its endemic plants. Orchids and begonias are particularly prolific; also expect to see many mosses and lichens on the trees. Research is also needed into the unique flora that grows on the bizarre inselbergs found around the village of Medouneu.

The SEEG (Société d'Energie et d'Eau du Gabon or electricity and water board) have built two hydro-electric dams in the area, at Kinguélé and Tchimbélé. The second site is the more interesting of the two, with its impressive lake, its orchid garden of more than 200 different species, and the *sentier botanique* (botanical path) in the surrounding forest. The best time to see flowers in bloom is between September and January. At any time of year, take plenty of insect repellent and be sure to wear long sleeves, long trousers and socks. Seeing animals in the forest here is rare, as this is historically an area of concentrated poaching, which is hardly surprising given its proximity to the markets of Libreville.

How to visit

Until a basic tourist infrastructure is in place, there is no prescribed way of visiting the Crystal Mountains. That is not to say it is impossible. A round-trip in a 4WD from Libreville to Tchimbélé, for example, is possible in a long day (3.5 hours each way). Tchimbélé is now remote controlled and there is vacant SEEG accommodation that at some point will be renovated for use by tourists and researchers. Until then, committed nature enthusiasts *might* be able to arrange basic overnight accommodation with SEEG. The best thing to do is to ask Mistral Voyages how the plans to welcome tourists for short stays at Tchimbélé have progressed.

If you end up driving independently, the route is very pretty, with great views of mountains and roadside waterfalls. The worst part of the road is between Ndouameng and Kinguélé, where you could stop at the village and ask the village chief to give you a walking guide for a few hours. The road is private beyond this point and you will need to check with the SEEG electricity plant here if you wish to continue. This is the only access road to Tchimbélé. It was once possible to reach Tchimbélé via Assok on the national road, but a landslip has blocked that section of the road. The national road itself is in a very poor state of repair. At its closest point to Equatorial Guinea lies Medouneu, although it is not officially possible to cross the border here. Between Medouneu and Sam is the village of Efot, which lies sandwiched between two inselbergs called Voma and Fene.

The Middle Ogooué

The Ogooué splits into two channels at Lambaréné, before rejoining in a large alluvial plain with a series of picturesque lakes fringed by papyrus marshes, reedbeds and dense forests. This is one of the largest deltas in Africa, extending from Lambaréné to Port Gentil, and it is hoped it will be granted protective status as a Biosphere Reserve. Lake excursions can be made from either Lambaréné or Port Gentil, but the Lambaréné lakes are more accessible and less pre-planning is required. Aside from the lakes this region is known for two reasons: the hospital founded by Albert Schweitzer and the peculiar fierceness of its mosquitoes.

LAMBARÉNÉ

This is a river-island city. The three parts of the city – the Rive Gauche (Left Bank), Ile Lambaréné (the Central Island), and the Rive Droite (Right Bank) – are divided by water and united by bridges and *pirogues*. Each section feels different from the others. *Quartier* Isaac on the Left Bank has the highest concentration of small eateries and bars, but also the most rubbish and hustlers. As soon as you cross over Isaac Bridge on to Lambaréné island the city feels cleaner and greener. Continuing over Adouma Bridge brings you to the Right Bank and the site of Albert Schweitzer's hospital, which put Lambaréné on the European map. *Quartier* Isaac aside, there is a relaxed, friendly atmosphere here, the sort of place you feel like strolling around purposelessly. It is well worth a stay of a couple of days or more.

Getting there and away

Road access to Lambaréné is now so good that flights to other parts of the country have been suspended. The approach to Lambaréné both from Libreville and from the south is a lovely one, with forests on either side of the road and small roadside villages selling chillies, bushmeat, pineapples and tarrow. There are *taxis-brousse* several times a day between Lambaréné and Libreville (5,000CFA/3 hours) and at least once a day with Mouila (7,000CFA/4 hours on a dirt road). Change at Mouila for Ndendé, Tchibanga and Mayumba. *Taxis-brousse* leave from in front of the Shell station in *quartier* Isaac, one side of the road for Libreville, the other for Mouila. Transport to

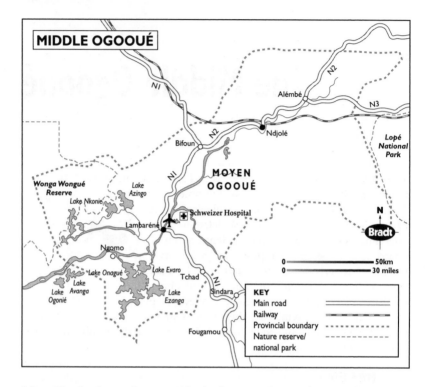

Libreville also leaves from outside the hypermarket on the waterfront of Ile Lambaréné.

It is possible to travel by boat between Lambaréné and Port Gentil. Boats leave Port Gentil on Friday and Monday mornings at 06.30 and arrive in Lambaréné around 13.00. Departures from Lambaréné are on Sundays and Thursdays at 06.00, arriving in Port Gentil at about 11.00. There are agents selling tickets the day before departure in the Marché du Port, near the Isaac Bridge in Lambaréné, or at Port Môle in Port Gentil. Tickets cost 10,000CFA/12,000CFA one way in the low/high season. No food or drink is available on board, but there are always sandwich sellers at the port before a departure.

Getting around

Lambaréné island is small enough and green enough to make getting about on foot a real pleasure. To move between the different parts of the city, there are plenty of blue-and-white taxis picking up and dropping off customers for a basic fare of 100CFA. The compact size of the town makes taking a *course* redundant. *Pirogues* ferry passengers between the market on Lambaréné island and the market on the Left Bank for 100CFA.

Where to stay and eat

The best hotel in town is the **Ogooué Palace Hotel** (tel: 58 18 64; mobile: 22 11 06, 24 42 32; fax: 58 18 65; email: ogooue.palace@assala.com), a colonial-style hotel directly overlooking the Ogooué. Rooms range from 25,000CFA with no view, to 35,000CFA with river view and TV. There is a pool, tennis court, a bar and a good restaurant. Main dishes in the restaurant are priced at 6,000CFA and up. Non-residents may use the pool for a charge of 2,000CFA, or 2,500CFA at weekends.

Not far from the Ogooué Palace Hotel, separated from the river by the road, is the **Mission Soeurs de l'Immaculée Conception** (tel: 58 10 73), a magnificent complex of cloistered, red-brick buildings surrounding a courtyard garden alive with birdsong. This is a wonderfully relaxing place to stay. There are six rooms with fan and between two and five single beds each, as well as a dormitory of 18 beds. A bed costs 6,000CFA per night. The mission is often full so it is advisable to book in advance. There are kitchen facilities for guests to cook for themselves, or it's a short walk to the Ogooué Palace Hotel or over the bridge to the eateries in *quartier* Isaac. At one time, the fathers next door to the sisters also welcomed visitors, but this is no longer the case.

The rooms at the **Hotel Schweitzer** (tel: 58 10 33) all have small balconies overlooking the river from up high. A twin room with fan costs 15,000CFA and a larger room with double bed and air conditioning costs 18,000CFA. All rooms have en-suite facilities. The reception area and bar-restaurant (main dishes for about 5,000CFA) are rather sparse and shabby. Alternative eating possibilities can be found along the waterfront, at the **Cafeteria Diallo**, the bakery and the small food stands.

The **Auberge le Millenium** (tel: 04 04 85) is a clean, friendly and good-value establishment with just three rooms, all of them air conditioned. The first two rooms (10,000CFA) share a toilet and shower, while the third room (12,000CFA) has en-suite facilities, including a bath, and a view over the treetops. There is an airy bar with comfy armchairs and a restaurant serving pizzas starting at 2,500CFA.

Of the hotels on the other side of town, in *quartier* Isaac, **Le Bananas** (tel: 58 12 28) is the best bet, although I found the staff to be anything but welcoming. Rooms with air conditioning and en-suite facilities cost 15,500CFA. There is a restaurant-bar, and I have heard the food is quite good, although I didn't stick around to find out.

The **Motel Bop-Bébé** (tel: 58 19 63) has five small, stuffy rooms with air conditioning and en-suite facilities for 15,000CFA. At the **Motel Pakita** (tel: 58 19 17), a basic room costs 6,000CFA, a room with fan 8,000CFA, and an air-conditioned room with en-suite facilities 14,000CFA. Otherwise there is the rather gloomy **Auberge du Marché** where rooms with fan and en-suite facilities cost 8,500CFA.

Where to shop

For a town of its size, Lambaréné has more than its fair share of markets. The most animated – particularly before a boat is due to leave – is the **Marché du Port**, where just about everything is sold. Directly across the river on the other side of town is the **Marché d'Isaac**, the place where fishermen come ashore

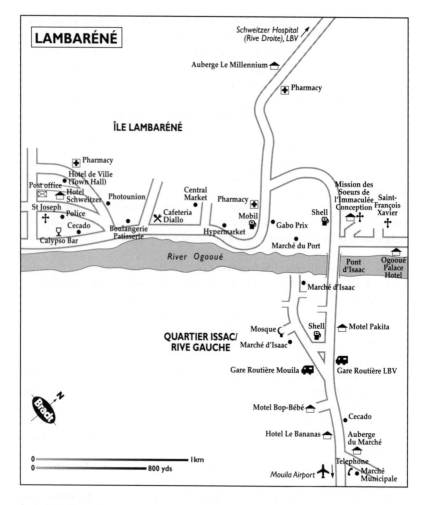

and therefore the best place to buy fresh fish. The nearby covered **Marché Municipale** was built by the city officials to replace the Marché d'Isaac, but it was an unpopular move and consequently has never really taken off.

What to see and do
The Schweitzer Hospital
The hospital founded in 1924 by Albert Schweitzer is still operating today. The atmosphere is as lively and relaxed as a small village, with women selling fruit near the entrance, patients' kids playing in the dust and a small shop stocking basic provisions. As well as being a place of healing it has also become a place of pilgrimage. Admirers of '*le grand docteur*' come to see the museum that since 1987 has occupied his former lodgings. His room is simplicity and order itself: his white doctor's apron, his pharmaceutical cabinet, his narrow bed, his parrot's cage. Visitors can also visit his study, his wife's room and the

conference room that before his death served as a dormitory for nurses. There is a small shop selling books, T-shirts and items made at the leprosy village. Behind the house is a cemetery with the doctor's grave.

The Gabonese government contributes approximately a quarter of the hospital budget, while the Schweitzer Foundation and private donations cover the rest. Most of the doctors and nurses are volunteers from abroad, working for between three months and two years. (Gabonese medics work for the state hospitals, which pay better for fewer hours.) There is an extensive programme of renovation underway at present. The aim is to retain the historical importance of the site – the visual exteriors of the buildings will be kept the same as they were in Schweitzer's time – whilst updating buildings for modern use. Once completed, the works will boast a new refectory, visitors' rooms and two more small museums, amongst other things. To make a donation to the Schweitzer Foundation to assist with the renovation work, visit the website www.schweitzer.org.

The museum is open Monday–Friday 09.00–12.30, 14.30–17.30, and Saturday–Sunday 09.00-18.00. It is possible to get to the hospital in a shared taxi for 100CFA, or by *pirogue*. There is always a stream of taxis dropping people off at the hospital so it's very easy to get a ride back to town.

A road leading off to the right as you approach the hospital leads to the leprosy village. At its peak there were about 600 inhabitants. Today there are about 250 village residents, of which only 40 are sufferers – nowadays leprosy can be treated – and the rest their families. A handful of the sufferers have been here since Schweitzer founded the village, including the village chief.

The Lakes

An excursion into the lakes by motorised *pirogue* is a wonderful way of passing the time. **Lake Zilé** is the closest lake to the city. It's small, but very pretty, and its handy location makes it the most popular introduction to the region for those pressed for time. The northern lakes (Deguelié, Azingo, Gomé) tend to be less visited than the southern ones (Evaro, Ezanga, Onangué, Oguemoué), perhaps because access is trickier, with sandbanks, rapids and whirlpools in places. It's possible to visit **Lake Azingo** in a day's round-trip, but to properly explore the northern lakes visitors will need camping gear and to be prepared to spend the night at a fishing village.

At present, most visitors take day or half-day trips to the southern lakes, focusing their attention on **Lake Oguemoué** if they are ornithologists, as this lake is particularly prized as an excellent spot to observe birds. Those with an interest in architecture invariably allow time to stop at the village of **Ngomo** on the Ambila river, site of a Protestant mission that was abandoned at independence. Peace Corps volunteers have now restored some of the dilapidated buildings to their original elegance. The trend of daytripping may change if the luxury tourist camp under construction on the banks of **Lake Evaro** opens as planned.

The appearance of the lakes differs depending on the time of year. February is a good month. For one thing, the light is so piercing, making the greens

ALBERT SCHWEITZER

On the basis of an article published in the Paris Missionary Society's monthly journal Albert Schweitzer decided to become a doctor and dedicate himself to working in Gabon. The year was 1904, and Schweitzer was 29 years old. He was very religious, and the article extolling the need for proper health care near the Andendé Mission had struck a chord with his belief that true Christianity meant helping one's fellow man. It was nearly a decade later before he had completed his medical training and raised the necessary funds to cover passage for himself and his wife, Hélène Bresslau, from Alsace in Germany, to Lambaréné in Gabon.

The doctor's – and Gabon's – first clinic was located in a converted henhouse at the Andendé Mission, but it wasn't long before war broke out and Schweitzer was arrested for being a German on French soil. Schweitzer did not return to Gabon until April 1924. The new Schweitzer Hospital was built on the site of Trader Horn's (see page 8) old Hatton and Cookson factory, on the Right Bank of the River Ogooué at Lambaréné. The factory had been moved some 40 years previously and the land left to grow wild. Funnily enough, at the same time that Schweitzer was clearing the old factory site, Trader Horn was having his tales recorded in South Africa, and the book *Trader Horn* was published in 1927, the same year that the new hospital opened. The Trader Horn connection tickled Schweitzer, who was a big fan of this 'enterprising but

greener and the blues bluer. During the dry season (July–September) the colours are duller and the water level is lower, which means that birds do not come to the banks to fish in the same numbers. At all times, keep an eye out for hippos in areas of low water, and an ear cocked for the telltale splash of manatees. Birds to look out for include herons, spoonbills, skimmers, egrets, pelicans, cormorants and pratincoles, including the grey pratincole.

Trips can be booked through the Ogooué Palace Hotel. The hotel offers set excursions in a *pirogue* for up to six passengers: a four-hour 'grand tour' of the southern lakes (75,000CFA); a three-hour tour concentrating on lakes Evaro and Onangué (60,000CFA); a mini one-and-a-half-hour tour of Lake Zilé (35,000CFA); and a trip taking in the Schweitzer Hospital and the bridge famous for the enormous number of *chauves-souris* (bats) nesting underneath it (25,000CFA).

It is usually a bit cheaper to deal directly with a *piroguier* at the Marché du Port. This is probably advisable anyway if you are hoping to make a deal for several days or have specific plans not covered by the hotel tours. Do ensure that you trust in the *piroguier*'s competence to undertake your chosen route(s). The cost will vary according to the distance, the time and the number of passengers, and both parties should be absolutely clear on the itinerary before setting off. This is the time to establish the desired pace, and to make it clear if you would like the motor to be cut for quiet periods so you can observe the self-willed agent', and he dedicated a whole chapter to him in *From My African Notebook* (1938).

Unlike the Europeans who had descended on Africa before him, Schweitzer was motivated by a desire to help 'the black peoples'. His motto was 'Reverence for life' and he was determined they should have access to medical treatment. That is not to say he considered the local people as equals. As a young man he had excelled at philosophy, theology and music, and after a day's work at the hospital he would write on these disciplines to spare him from loneliness. From these works we have a clear picture of how he viewed the African man and his world. The African was not in fact lazy or stupid, he was simply no different from a child who must be directed with a firm and kind authority. Schweitzer was incredulous and pitying in the face of 'primitive' African taboos and fetishes, announcing 'it is our duty to endeavour to liberate them from these superstitions'.

Schweitzer was awarded the Nobel Peace Prize in 1952 and used the money from the award to found the adjoining leprosy village, at a time when sufferers were driven from their villages. He died in Lambaréné in 1965. His legacy lives on in the hospital and in his prolific writings. There are now state hospitals in Gabon, but the Schweitzer Hospital is still one of the country's best and most popular. It's not free, but patients are only asked to pay what they can afford, and that *after* they have been treated, an important continuation of Schweitzer's founding ethos.

birds. For small journeys requiring little petrol, such as the Schweitzer Hospital or even Lake Zilé, you could open negotiations by asking the *piroguier* how much he usually makes in an hour of ferrying passengers, and then add 1,000–2,000CFA to make an hourly rate.

With the possible exception of very localised trips, all excursions will need to be arranged, and partially paid for, at least a day in advance so that petrol can be bought. Passengers should come prepared with suncream, sunglasses, insect repellent, a windbreaker and appropriate provisions.

NDJOLÉ

After Lambaréné, the only settlement of any size in the Middle Ogooué is Ndjolé, built on the bank of the River Ogooué. In itself this is not a reason to visit. In fact, it's the sort of place where you might find yourself killing a bit of time on your way somewhere else. Being the largest town for a good stretch in either direction, however, it does have the advantage of certain amenities, including a petrol station, telephone exchange, pharmacy, police station, church, mosque and supermarkets, as well as places to eat and sleep. Ndjolé is also on the railway line; the station is a little way out of town in the direction of La Lopé. Traditionally Ndjolé was the place where logging companies emptied their cargo into the Ogooué for transportation to the coast. This system is still practised today, although the good state of the road now means you will also see numerous logging trucks. Given all this, it's hardly surprising that it's a popular stopping point.

The main road junction is where it all happens. This is the location of the market, the petrol station, food stalls, and the pick-up and drop-off point for *taxis-brousse* to Libreville or Lambaréné (would-be passengers should ask about likely times and be prepared to wait). There's usually music and a lot of people milling around. Just paces from here is the **Hotel Papaye** (tel: 59 33 15), which has rooms with fan starting at 10,500CFA and air-conditioned rooms from 15,500CFA. If you head past the market and over the bridge, you'll see the church on a hill. This is the town's most attractive building, a simple design with pleasing lattice brickwork. If, on the other hand, you turn right immediately past the petrol station you'll reach the **Auberge Saint Jean**. Reasonable rooms and the best food in town are found here, and it's on a nice birdwatching spot overlooking the small island of Samory Touré. You can ask here about hiring a *pirogue* if you fancy an outing on the river.

www.tourismconcern.org.uk

LIFE'S A BEACH...

There is a flipside to tourism

We have nearly all travelled and seen the negative effects of tourism. For many people who live in tourist destinations around the globe their culture and homes are being destroyed through a lack of consideration of their interests and rights.

Tourism Concern campaigns to raise awareness of the many abuses that take place and encourage change to eradicate these negative effects on the indigenous population. Through our educational work, campaigning and challenging the tourism industry we aim improve the quality of life in the host locations.

You can help by becoming a Tourism Concern supporter, member or donor and help us change tourism for the better.

For more info, visit our website or call or E-mail us below.

E-mail: info@tourismconcern.org.uk
Call: 020 7753 3330

TourismConcern
Transforming the negatives into positives

The Ngounié

The Ngounié region takes its name from the River Ngounié – an important tributary of the Ogooué – which feeds its forests and lakes. It is sometimes also known as Mitsogho country, after the people who have traditionally lived here. To the south lies the Congo, along the region's eastern flank rise the du Chaillu mountains, and along its western flank the Ikoundou mountains. Sandwiched between these forested mountains lies the grassy Ngounié valley, location of the town of Ndendé. The Ngounié must be one of the least visited regions of Gabon. If it welcomes any visitors they are invariably passing through on their way to or from Mayumba, or making a brief southerly foray from Lambaréné to Fougamou and Sindara. Those who linger a while, however, and venture deeper into the Mitsogho country, are rewarded with the beauty of a little-changed part of the country.

FROM LAMBARÉNÉ TO NDENDÉ

The Route Nationale 1 cuts through Ngounié, leading travellers directly from Lambaréné to the Congo border or, as is usually the case, to Ndendé, from where there are roads leading west to the coast and east to the mountains of the interior. The road between Lambaréné and Mouila is not yet entirely surfaced, but already it has been greatly improved.

The missions

About 17km (10.5 miles) south of Lambaréné, before arriving in Fougamou, there is a left turn leading to the pretty village of **Sindara**. Sindara is worth a visit mainly because of its beautiful, abandoned mission. The mission is reached via a grand avenue lined with mango trees. The main building has arched colonnades on two levels and is built in brick and wood. Opposite is a small and crumbling whitewashed church, painted with touches of blue, making it look Greek in style. Continue past the mission to see the surging rapids of the River Ngouniéits. If you do not have your own 4WD, you should wait on the main road by the Sindara turn-off for a *taxi-brousse* to pick you up. Ask for a guide in the village.

Continuing along the main road brings you to another green and pretty place, surrounded by forested hills. The small town of **Fougamou** is a linear

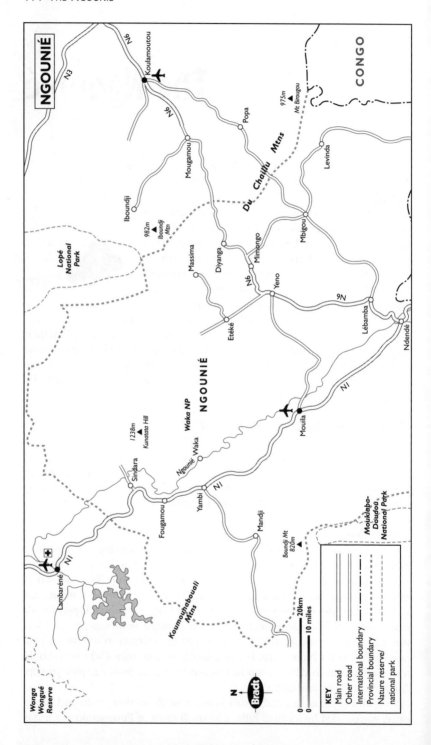

town, stretching for a couple of kilometres along the bank of the Ngounié. The mission, market, pharmacy, shops, as well as places to stay and eat, are all on the main street. If you find yourself here overnight, a good place to stay is the Ngounié Hotel, a large place with a fantastic view of the river. Visitors are also welcome at the Saint-Famille Mission, although they prefer some advance warning. Near Fougamou are some falls, which some say are the husband to the wife-rapids at Sindara. The falls are known either as the Samba falls, or as the *chutes de l'Imperatrice* (the name given them by the explorer du Chaillu in the 19th century). *Taxis-brousse* pass through Fougamou several times a day in both directions. It's just a question of hailing one and squeezing in.

Mouila

South of Fougamou, the road has fantastic views of mountains on both sides – to the west are the Koumounabouali mountains and the ones far away to the east are the du Chaillu mountains. The next town of note, Mouila, is capital of the region and has a population of about 20,000. The town is divided in two by the River Ngounié. The Lambaréné and Ndendé roads enter Mouila at different points of the Rive Gauche (Left Bank), while the Koulamoutou road enters town in the Rive Droite (Right Bank). All administrative and government buildings are on the Right Bank, while most of the shops, hotels and restaurants are on the Left Bank. Just 5km (3 miles) out of town is Mouila's principle attraction, the Lac Bleu, a lake famed for the blueness of its water. It is a popular bathing, fishing and picnicking spot at weekends.

Getting there and away

There are flights to Mouila several times a week, as well as *taxis-brousse* from Lambaréné (4 hours/7,000CFA) and Tchibanga (3.5 hours/6,000CFA).

Getting around

For the most part, the choice is to walk or take a taxi. There are also *pirogues* that ferry people between the two banks, leaving from near the Prefecture on the Right Bank and the landing stage near the top of the main commercial street on the Left Bank. This landing stage is also the place to negotiate for a *piroguier* to take you to the Lac Bleu, about two hours away.

Where to stay and eat

The **Hotel du Lac Bleu** (tel: 06 29 59) is right on the river and has a tennis court and swimming pool, as well as a restaurant and bar. Ordinary rooms/suites are at 20,500CFA/65,500CFA. All the rooms have air conditioning, TV and en-suite facilities. The hotel offers all-inclusive weekend deals, depending on the number of people booking.

Further down the same street is **La Matisse** (tel: 86 18 06), which is clean, friendly and good value. Large rooms with en-suite facilities and fan/air conditioning are 7,000CFA/13,000CFA. Breakfast is served for 1,000CFA and other meals for around 2,500CFA. Next door is the **Motel Ikouma Village** (tel: 06 83 84), which offers rooms with fan/air conditioning for

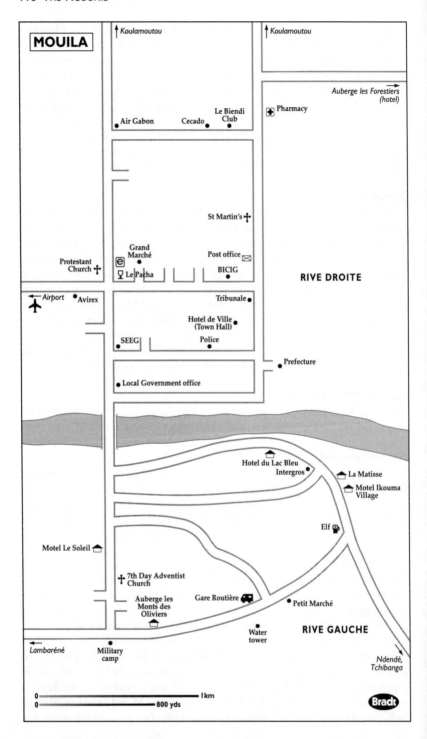

6,000CFA/10,000CFA, all with shared bathroom facilities. There is a restaurant-bar.

The **Auberge les Monts des Oliviers** has slightly pricier rooms with fan/air conditioning for 6,500CFA/12,500CFA, once again all with shared bathroom facilities. The hotel has a restaurant, and is located in a quiet area of town. **Motel Le Soleil** (tel: 06 25 18) has rooms with en-suite facilities for 8,000CFA/15,000CFA with fan/air conditioning. There is a restaurant-bar serving African dishes for 2,500CFA.

A little bit off the beaten track, but well worth the effort, is a new establishment, the **Auberge les Forestiers** (tel: 86 16 39), which currently has six en-suite rooms at 15,000CFA. The large rooms are light and nicely painted, and come with air conditioning, TV and potted plants outside the door. The area is quiet and the staff are friendly. There is a good restaurant serving both African and European dishes for about 2,500CFA. **Le Pacha** is a popular bar on the Right Bank.

Ndendé

Ndendé lies in an area of gentle hills, overshadowed from the northeast by the du Chaillu mountains. It is the last town before the border with Congo to the south and the regional border with Nyanga to the west, and is linked by road to Koulamoutou. Ndendé functions as a crossroads for travellers who change *taxis-brousse* here, refill their own vehicles with petrol, and stock up on provisions in the small market. If you find yourself needing a place to stay, ask for the Relais de Saint-Hubert, which is central and has a restaurant.

THE MASSIF DU CHAILLU

The area east of Route Nationale 1 is dominated by the du Chaillu mountain range, which can be seen as a continuation of the Crystal Mountains to the south of the River Ogooué. The mountains are dissected northeast to southwest by two roads from Koulamoutou, which eventually merge for the final stretch to Ndendé. Some claim these roads are among the country's prettiest because of the breathtaking scenery of mountains and valleys. A 4WD is essential in this area, particularly in the rainy season. The northern section of the du Chaillu range, between Fougamou and Lopé National Park, has been decreed the **Waka National Park**, while the southern end has become the **Birougou National Park**. The southern park takes its name from Mount Birougou, a peak of 975m (3,200ft).

The whole of this area has plenty of tourism potential, although at present there are no facilities, and Waka in particular is difficult to access. It is primarily great walking country – there are footpaths throughout the du Chaillu mountains – but as yet there are no tourist routes or guides. Today the vast majority of villages have moved to the roadsides, but signs of old cultivation indicate where there were once settlements. Not all the villages in the forest have been deserted. There are still villages in the forest that can only be accessed on foot, including traditional pygmy villages. This area is most heavily populated by the Mitsogho people, who claim to be the most

'Gabonese' of all the tribes living in Gabon and the original practitioners of *Bwiti* (see pages 96–7). **Mimongo**, for example, is a typical Mitsogho village and centre for *Bwiti*. If the evidence is to be believed then this area is the cradle of Gabonese culture. Travellers can stay in the *case de passage* here for about 3,000CFA.

North of Yéno is a gold-panning area. There is an old mining town at Etéké, and the gold panners have apparently moved on towards Massima. Visitors are not expected to drop by uninvited. Near the village of **Lébamba** are a couple of massive underground cave networks, most famously the Bongolo caves. The Catholic mission in the village can direct you towards a guide and offer you a bed for the night. Just under half-way along the Ndendé to Koulamoutou road you will pass **Mbigou**, home of the Mbigou soapstone favoured by Gabonese sculptors.

The du Chaillu mountains are also covered in *Chapter 14 The Ogooué-Lolo*.

Bradt Travel Guides is a partner to the 'know before you go' campaign, masterminded by the UK Foreign and Commonwealth Office to promote the importance of finding out about a destination before you travel. By combining the up-to-date advice of the FCO with the in-depth knowledge of Bradt authors, you'll ensure that your trip will be as trouble-free as possible.

www.fco.gov.uk/knowbeforeyougo

Coastal Ogooué

The Ogooué Maritime, or Coastal Ogooué, is a region that combines economic resources and diverse beauties in its 23,000km². The region's capital is Port Gentil. From the late 15th century, Europeans, notably the Portuguese, descended on the coastal peoples to trade in ivory and timber. Later, in the 17th century, their commercial interest turned to slaves, while by the 19th century the missionaries were arriving to battle for souls. In the 20th century the attraction was oil, and that of the 21st century looks set to be tourism, thanks to the spectacular scenery and plentiful wildlife. The camps here have long been a place of pilgrimage for tarpon fishermen, and are now broadening their net to welcome birdwatchers and wildlife enthusiasts.

The Coastal Ogooué region has many different ecosystems harbouring enormous biodiversity. It is a region that includes forests, lagoons, lakes, floodplains, savannahs and over 200km (124 miles) of coastline. This is one of the richest and most beautiful areas in Central Africa, and preliminary research has shown it to have one of the highest densities of elephants and apes. Yet such riches have not been a guarantee against exploitation. The government has in the past given logging and oil companies the right to operate in the region, and their presence has both improved access routes for poachers and increased the demand for illegally hunted meat. Now the Gabonese government, in conjunction with conservation agencies (in this case WWF in particular), has given the region the two national parks of Loango and Moukalaba-Doudou. They are keen to find a workable solution to the twin issues of conservation and economics by encouraging tourism. Loango National Park is probably the only place on the African continent where western lowland gorillas, forest elephants, buffalo and hippopotami can all, with luck, be seen on the same beach. Even leopard have been spotted on the beach. There is also the chance to see manatees and crocodiles, and at the right times of year, nesting leatherback sea turtles, humpback whales and dolphins.

PORT GENTIL

Port Gentil is located on the northeastern edge of an island some 30km by 6km (19 miles by 4 miles), an island surrounded by ocean and swamps. At the end of the 15th century it was named Lopez Island by a Portuguese sailor,

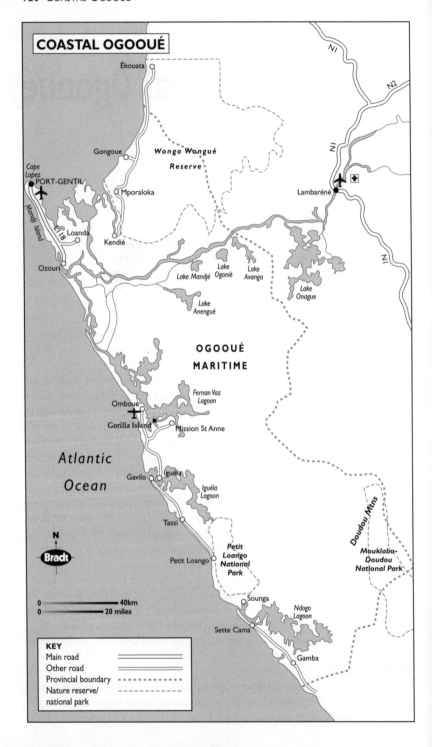

COASTAL OGOOUÉ

Ékouata

Gongoue

Cape Lopez
PORT-GENTIL

Mporaloka

Wonga Wongué Reserve

Lambaréné

Mandji Island

Loanda

Kendié

Ozouri

Lake Mandjé

Lake Ogonié

Lake Avanga

Lake Onague

Lake Anengué

OGOOUÉ MARITIME

Fernan Vaz Lagoon

Omboué
Gorilla Island
Mission St Anne

Atlantic Ocean

Gavilo
Iguéla

Iguéla Lagoon

Tassi

N
Bradt

Petit Loango
Petit Loango National Park

Doudou Mtns

Mouklaba-Doudou National Park

0 ——— 40km
0 ——— 20 miles

Sounga

Ndogo Lagoon

Sette Cama

Gamba

KEY
Main road
Other road
Provincial boundary ·············
Nature reserve/ — — — —
national park

Lopez Gonzalvez. The name didn't stick, although the island's furthest point is still known as Cape Lopez. Instead, the island became known as Mandji Island, a name chosen by the Myené people because of the concentration of mandji trees growing here.

The city itself takes its name after a certain Frenchman, Emile Gentil, an administrator for Afrique Equatoriale Francaise (AEF) who was sent to perform a mission here between 1890 and 1892. Port Gentil at this time was little more than a handful of villages and a mission, and was to remain so until at least the end of World War I. Today Port Gentil is the economic capital of Gabon, a city that got rich quick, and in the process acquired a disproportionate number of hotels, restaurants and expats (mostly French and Lebanese). The city's meteoric financial growth is based on wood and *l'or noir* (black gold). The residents of Port Gentil claim there are three separate groups of people here: the Gabonese, the expats and those working for Elf. The question on everybody's mind is, what will happen to the city when the petrol runs out?

Getting there and away

Port Gentil is not accessible by road. The most common way of getting there is by plane. There are several flights a day from Libreville, and connections at least once a week with Omboué, Gamba, Mayumba and Tchibanga. A while ago there was also a ferry running between Libreville and Port Gentil but this service has been cancelled indefinitely. There are, however, twice-weekly boat runs between Port Gentil and Lambaréné. For more details, see the *Getting there and away* section for Lambaréné in *Chapter 7*.

Getting around

There is no shortage of taxis in Port Gentil. The usual rates apply for shared taxis or *une course* (see under *Taxis* in *Chapter 4 Getting Around*). If you stumble across a taxi that doesn't feel as if it's about to fall apart and you want to hang on to it, the going rate is 3,000CFA per hour or 25,000CFA per day. There are car-hire agencies renting vehicles at the usual rates (see *Chapter 4 Getting Around*) but the condition is town use only, which is rather pointless since the city centre is small and safe enough to walk around on foot.

Where to stay
Upper range
The centrally located **Meridien Mandji** (tel: 55 21 03; fax: 55 28 06) is Port Gentil's only corporate, international hotel, with all the facilities you would expect of a three- or four-star establishment, including restaurants, a swimming pool, a meeting room for 200 people, and rooms with balconies and sea view. Non-residents are welcome to use the pool for the princely sum of 3,500CFA, or the cost of lunch. Rooms are 75,500CFA/90,500CFA for a standard/executive. Continental/American breakfast is an extra 5,500CFA/7,000CFA.

After the Meridien, there's the **Hotel du Parc** (tel: 55 25 28, 56 11 30; fax: 56 02 95), which has six categories of room, from a basic room at 20,000CFA

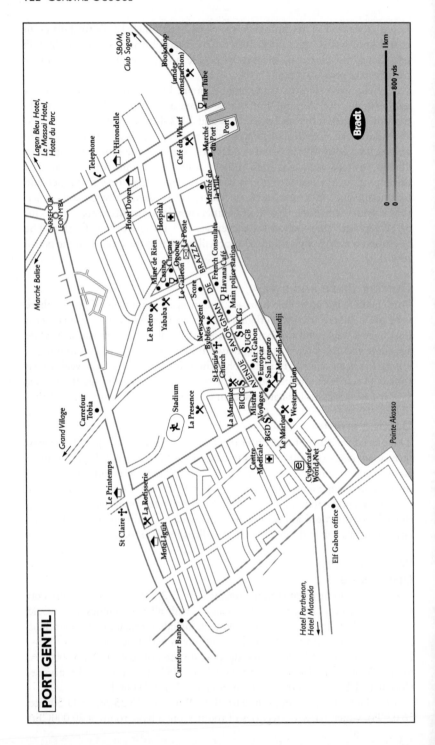

PORT GENTIL

a night to an apartment at 71,000CFA. Part of the hotel complex is a zoo (see under *What to see and do* on pages 126–7). It does not have its own restaurant but right next door is **Le Ranch** (tel: 55 08 27), which has not only a popular restaurant, but a gym and tennis courts as well. Rates are 42,000CFA/53,000CFA for a room/apartment. The restaurant is open 06.00–00.00 every day, serving a midday menu at 7,500CFA, couscous on Fridays and paella the first Sunday of every month.

Self-catering apartments

One more indicator of the high concentration of business expats in Port Gentil is the number of hotels with self-catering apartments. All have air conditioning, TV and telephone as standard and deals can be negotiated for stays of more than a month at all of them. **Residence Mbandja** (tel: 56 02 53/59; fax: 56 53 23) has large one- and two-bedroom apartments at 30,500CFA/51,000CFA a night. There is a breakfast, bar and laundry service, and 24-hour reception. The apartments at the **Lagon Bleu** (tel: 56 06 61; fax: 55 26 69) are comfy and homely and 30,000CFA a night. The most attractive apartments – bright and modern – are those at the **Residence Parthénon** (tel: 55 04 51, 56 08 10; fax: 55 53 66). Rates start from 41,300CFA a night. A bar-restaurant is under construction. The Parthénon is a ten-minute walk from the Elf building heading out of town. It is easy to catch a taxi into town from here.

Moderate to budget

The **Hotel L'Hirondelle** (tel: 55 17 82; fax: 55 17 82) has clean and inviting rooms at 24,000CFA/29,000CFA a single/double. All rooms have air conditioning, cable TV and fridge, while the doubles also have a small kitchen area. The hotel flower beds are well tended and a snack bar is currently being built. Opposite Hotel L'Hirondelle is the **Hotel Doyen**, a quiet place with 19 rooms starting at 17,000CFA. The largest rooms (23,000CFA) have cable TV, an armchair, and bath, and some even have a fridge. A restaurant is under construction next door.

The **Hotel Matanda** (tel: 39 52 62) is the latest project of the energetic French expat, Jean-Pierre Sage, and in my opinion the best-value and most welcoming hotel in this category. Most of the rooms have been refurbished and by the time this guide comes out a restaurant and a new floor of apartments will have been completed. Most evenings the hotel bar is full of jocular French expats, friends of Jean-Pierre and his wife. 'Old' rooms cost 13,500CFA, new rooms 16,500CFA, and new rooms with cable TV 20,000CFA. All rooms are air conditioned. The Matanda is just around the corner from the Residence Parthénon .

Also good value is **Le Printemps**, which has rooms starting at 17,500CFA. All rooms have air conditioning and television. The staff are very friendly and amenable. The bar downstairs has karaoke on Friday and Saturday nights, as well as regular themed nights with special offers on food and drinks, so don't expect peace and quiet. Round the corner from the Lagon Bleu is **Le Massaï**, a small motel and restaurant. The rooms (20,000CFA) are tiny but well designed, with a television on top of the cupboard and a fold-down desk.

At the **Hotel Abone** (tel: 55 00 59) there are drab, stuffy rooms for 15,000CFA/20,000CFA a single/double. All rooms are en suite, and have air conditioning and television. **Motel Iguri** (tel: 56 52 50) is an even gloomier establishment, although it is clean and all rooms have shower and toilet. Those with air conditioning cost 15,000CFA, and those with fan 13,000CFA.

Where to eat

There are masses of places to eat in Port Gentil, although many have almost interchangeable menus. Old places change hands and names frequently, and new places are continuously springing up. For details of hotel restaurants see under *Where to stay* on pages 121–4. Expect to pay an average of 10,000CFA a main course in the very best restaurants in town, but most places do special menus, at least at midday, which are much better value. A lot of places have an English menu – just ask.

Upper range

The Italian restaurant **San Lorenzo** (tel: 55 11 97, 34 23 69) is considered by many of Port Gentil's expats to be the most delicious restaurant in town, with excellent lobster and fresh pasta and a large choice of desserts. It is certainly very elegant, with starched white tablecloths and napkins. There is an extensive choice of fish and seafood dishes round the corner at **Le Marlou** (tel: 56 23 87). One of the chef's specialities is *langoustes jake*, langoustines flambed in whisky and served with a crème fraiche and saffron sauce.

The **Pacific 2 Restaurant** (tel: 56 07 80) has a good-value French menu for 7,000CFA (three courses with half a bottle of wine and coffee). The food is reasonably good and portions are large. It's possible to play boules outside while you wait for your food. **La Presence** (tel: 56 54 58) has a rotating dish of the day (about 5,000CFA) in addition to its menu; Fridays is couscous and Saturdays is paella. The English-run **La Rotisserie** (tel: 23 21 99) specialises in barbequed fish and meat, pizzas and salads.

Club Sogara (tel: 56 31 79) is very popular with Port Gentil expats, particularly at weekends when the weather is good and eating on the terrace by the beach is a real pleasure. There's a large menu with pizzas, crêpes, pastas, ice creams, fish and meat dishes, and a set midday menu at 10,500CFA (the Sunday buffet is 14,000CFA). There's also a Sunday midday buffet at the **Alizé** (tel: 55 54 29), which is at the end of the bumpy road to the left on the way to Club Sogara. There is a swimming pool here too.

Moderate

A change from the norm, and less pricey than any of the above, is **Byblos**. Here you can enjoy excellent Lebanese food in a relaxed atmosphere. The extensive menu has a good range of choice for vegetarians. **La Marmite** is a nicely decorated little restaurant with a good French menu. The midday *menu du jour* is good value at 7,500CFA for three courses, coffee and a pitcher of wine or a beer. For a lighter lunch, order soup, which is served in such an enormous bowl it constitutes a full meal for most people. **Yababa** (tel: 55 23 25) serves French, Italian and Lebanese dishes. The noodle dishes are plentiful and delicious. Prices start from 3,500CFA for a pizza. Next door to Yababa is French restaurant **Le Retro** (tel: 55 31 77), serving the usual salads, pizzas, pastas, fish and meat. Downstairs is a small café selling ice cream.

The **Café du Wharf** is a large, airy place, but the food can be disappointing. A popular weekend haunt is **Le Petrolier** (tel: 36 48 89, 38 67 62), an open restaurant above the beach at Cape Lopez, where a copious lunch or supper will set you back about 10,000CFA. Sundays at midday there is a buffet. Their specialities are *grillades* and upside-down pineapple cake. To get there follow the Cape Lopez road and turn left down the road at Elf Gabon. It's about a 20-minute drive from the centre of Port Gentil.

Budget
The **Tea Punch**, right outside Score supermarket, is a very popular spot for early-morning coffee. **Tom-Pooce** in the Matanda *quartier* (tel: 55 27 71) is a small, local restaurant serving good food under a *paillotte*. At **Cococabana** the service is very slow but the food – mostly barbequed brochettes – is inexpensive and tasty. Opposite Le Printemps is **Saint Claire**, the only place to find a meal in the middle of the night, serving big portions of chicken and chips, or omelette and chips for 2,500CFA.

Bars and nightspots
There are enough watering holes in Port Gentil to constitute an extensive pub crawl, and of course the hot spots are in constant flux. A safe bet to start with, however, is **The Tube**, which has a terrace overlooking the rusty tubs in the port. They serve a strong and fiery house punch here. Work your way back towards the centre, pausing for a drink on the terrace of **Café du Wharf**, which first opened its doors for custom more than 50 years ago. Then continue to the **Havana Café**, known for its good but expensive cocktails. Opposite is a small alleyway down which are hidden the disco **New Saf** and the bar-club **Bouffetard**, with its predominantly expat clientele.

Other than that, the bar at **Le Printemps** hotel has karaoke on Friday and Saturday nights, and there's the rather pokey **Casino Port Gentil** (Thursday–Sunday 22.00–late), which has blackjack, roulette, poker and the usual machines. **Le Galleon** is a bit of everything: a bar and pool hall, serving food, where people dance. Keep an eye out for posters advertising special nights at any of the above. As usual, the **cinema** is not functional.

Where to shop
As well as the Score supermarket, there are three open-air markets in Port Gentil. On Fridays and Saturdays the **Marché de la Ville**, also called Marché du Port, is open, mostly selling food and clothes. **Marché Balise** – food and wood – is just north of the Léon Mba roundabout. The largest and loudest market is the **Marché du Grand Village**, which lies north of the Tobia

roundabout and south of the Hassan roundabout in the animated *quartier* of the same name. This market sells everything and more.

There are several places to buy souvenirs in Port Gentil. There is an **artisan's shop** called *L'Atelier* in the row of outlets behind the left-hand side of Score, where you can find amongst other things sculptures in Mbigou stone. A Beninese craftsman called **Shola** (Mon–Sat 08.00–18.00; tel: 37 85 18; email: batikshola@yahoo.fr) sells wonderful batiks from his shop in the *quartier* Bac-Aviation. Take the airport road and turn off to Cape Lopez. The shop is on the first small road on the left, next to the small Stécy bar. A lady called **Blanche Masson** (tel: 35 50 02) sells washbags, handbags and beachbags made from patterned Cameroonian material priced 6,000–20,000CFA. Contact her to arrange a viewing at her home in the SBOM *quartier*. In the same area, **Nicole Andorra** (tel: 56 06 55) sells lovely candlesticks, pottery, cushions and paintings from her home-shop. Once again, call to propose a visit. In the afternoons, a craftsmen sells carved wooden objects outside Le Ranch hotel-restaurant.

The little shop **Mine de Rien** (tel: 56 56 88) is a treasury of stylish clothes and shoes at a snip, some of them secondhand. Ask to be directed to a tailor if you need something altered. Next door is **Galeries Orientales**. On the waterfront is a very good **bookshop** selling English papers and magazines, language dictionaries, wallets, hip flasks and more. There are small **jewellery** shops dotted throughout the city.

Unless otherwise specified, the above all operate under standard opening times with long lunchbreaks (see under *Souvenir shopping* in *Chapter 4 Travelling Around*).

Tourist information

The banks, Western Union, the airline and car-hire agencies, the post office, the hospital and the police station are all on Port Gentil's main commercial street, avenue Savorgnan de Brazza. There are two branches of the **BICIG**, just paces from one another, one of which has a Visa-card machine. The travel agency **Mistral Voyages** (tel: 56 25 25) has an office here as well as in Libreville, which means that to book flights with one of the smaller airlines there's no need to go all the way to the counters at the airport. On the street starting just behind the Banque Gabonaise de Développement (BGD), there is a **medical centre** and a gleaming new **cybercafé** (Mon–Sun 08.00–23.00) with more than 20 stations.

What to see and do

One building in the city centre of historical and architectural interest is the **church of Saint Louis**, which dates back to 1927. It's a pretty building, with striking windows, a clocktower and covered arcades down each side. If it's closed, find the Father, who will be happy to open up for you. Services are held Monday–Thursday at 06.10, Fridays and Saturdays at 06.30, and Sundays at 08.30 and 10.00.

Part of the Hotel du Parc complex is a small **zoo** (free admission) founded by the hotel owner, an animal enthusiast. He has landscaped a large area with cages and pens around a pond traversed by a liana bridge. The residents include palm vultures, mandrills, mongooses, chimpanzees, chickens and red river hogs. The zoo has caused some controversy since its creation in 1994, with charges of poor animal care and even meat production.

If you fancy some exercise there are tennis courts at **Club Sogara** (tel: 56 31 79), costing 5,000CFA/hour. If you're going to be sticking around it will prove more economical to join on a monthly basis. The club doesn't charge for the use of the beach here, and the water is calm and warm. The beach at **Cape Lopez** – reached by a sandy track a five-minute drive before Le Petrolier – is popular with picnickers at the weekend, who make use of the open beach shelters here. The water is colder and the currents stronger than at Sogara. Leave behind any valuables as I have heard occasional reports of beach theft.

There is a **golf club** not far out of town. Follow directions to Le Petrolier restaurant, looking out for a small road on the right signposted 'golf club'. There is a good restaurant-bar here with a regularly changing menu.

River Tour

After a period of non-activity, the company River Tour has been reactivated, which is good news for the visitor as this is currently the only reliable way to visit the waterways around Port Gentil (for details of lake excursions from Lambaréné see under *The lakes* in *Chapter 7 The Middle Ogooué*). A series of two- to four-day trips in motorised *pirogue* are on offer, including explorations of the Fernan Vaz lagoon and the lakes near Port Gentil, as well as an Albert Schweitzer themed trip up the Ogooué as far as Lambaréné. Accommodation on the Fernan Vaz lagoon is at the mission Saint Anne (see page 128) and a forestry camp, and overnight stops on the River Ogooué are at a local village.

Prices and booking Trips vary in cost depending on distance and type of accommodation. Prices are between 135,000CFA and 285,000CFA per person per day all-inclusive, plus 35,000CFA per person for drinks for three days. For an extra 55,000CFA visitors can have an organised day in Port Gentil before the trip proper starts. Most trips require six to eight participants. Bookings can be made direct with Patrick Brin (tel: 56 20 81, 34 36 37; email: brin.rivertourgabon@inet.ga).

Ozouri

Under 40km (25 miles) to the south of Port Gentil is a finger of land that stretches between the ocean and the Ozouri lagoon for 25km (15.5 miles). In 1995 Alain Chevrot built the Inguessi camp here with the lagoon in front and the beach behind. There are ten rooms, equipped with fan and mosquito net, and a separate shower block. The camp is popular with fishermen mid October to mid March, but Alain also offers 4WD excursions into the forest in search of birds, monkeys, antelopes and buffaloes. Animal sightings are by no means certain, but the fishing is reliable, with tarpons of 80–120kg being a regular catch. Since the indefinite closure of the fishing camp at Olendé (on the Nkomi lagoon to the south), the camp at Ozouri is now the only camp accessible by car from Port Gentil.

Prices and booking The basic daily tariff for adults covering board and lodging is 45,000CFA. Transport to/from Port Gentil (usually 4WD and a transfer by boat, but possibly by boat all the way) and 4WD safaris are extra, so budget for about 65,000CFA a day. A full-day's fishing on a boat for two to three people is 120,000CFA. There are discounts for children and stays of more than three days. Contact Alain (tel: 28 58 55, 55 58 91) for more details and to book. The camp closes annually between about August 15 and October 1.

Fernan Vaz lagoon

A trip to the Fernan Vaz lagoon is one of the highlights of any exploration of the Coastal Ogooué region. The lagoon takes its name from the Portuguese sailor Fernão Vaz who discovered it at the end of the 15th century but its most famous landmark dates from four centuries later. The church at the **Mission Saint Anne** was built in 1889, the same year as the Eiffel Tower, and, unlikely as it may seem, there's a connection. Look no further than Gustav Eiffel himself, who shipped the plans and materials all the way from Paris at the behest of Mrs Bichet, the mother of Saint Anne's founding priest and a wealthy woman with Paris connections. The church stands tall and elegant, the metal worn to a deep, rusty red over the years. Day or overnight visitors can take guided walks in the surrounding forest or along the beach, and visit local villages or the geodes at Kongo.

Petit Evengue, popularly known as *Ile aux gorilles* (Gorilla Island), is the location of a small project run by Operation Loango to care for gorillas. There are currently three gorillas in the enclosure, either orphaned or born in captivity. The project's end goal is to release them back into the wild. At the moment visitors can either drop in for feeding time or spend the night.

How to visit To get to Fernan Vaz lagoon entails a flight to Omboué from Port Gentil or Libreville, followed by a journey in motorised *pirogue*. Tourism at the mission is very much in the early stages. One of the colonial buildings near the church has been converted into visitors' rooms, with either air conditioning or fan, and there is a restaurant with a terrace overlooking the lagoon. **Mistral Voyages**, for example, offers two-night packages at the mission, with return flights to Omboué. The cost is just under 200,000CFA per person, based on two people sharing. **River Tour** also offers a tour that includes the Fernan Vaz lagoon, also staying overnight at the mission.

Stays at **Gorilla Island** – including forest walks, tours of the lagoon and a visit to the mission – can be organised through the main Operation Loango project, Ye Tsanou (see pages 129–30). There are currently two rooms (each with a double and a single bed). The rate is around 70,000CFA per day, including meals and activities.

LOANGO NATIONAL PARK

The Loango National Park was created in 2002 when the Iguela and Petit Loango Reserves were merged to become one. The Iguela Reserve had covered an area of 230,000 hectares (568,330 acres) surrounding the lagoon alternatively called Iguela or Nkomi. Neighbouring it to the south was the smaller coastal reserve of Petit Loango. Visitors come to Loango National Park to enjoy the irresistible combination of scenery and wildlife – ocean, lagoon, forest and savannah – and the different ways of exploring them: namely by boat, 4WD or on foot. The attractions change depending on the time of year. The whale season begins around mid July and continues through to mid-September, the tarpon fishing season October to mid November, and the turtle season is October to mid January. At all times, you will see at least some of the following: buffaloes, hippos, crocodiles, manatees, elephants, chimpanzees and gorillas.

How to visit

The northern section of Loango National Park (formerly the Iguela Reserve) is normally visited by flying into Omboué and transferring to one of the camps on the Iguela lagoon. The southern section of Loango National Park (formerly Petit Loango) is normally visited by flying into Gamba (see pages 132–3) and transferring to Sette Cama (see pages 130–2). At the moment there is no practicable way to travel between Sette Cama and Iguela. The only possibility is to be taken by boat from Sette Cama northwards along the lagoon as far as Sounga, then to walk 18km (11 miles) until you meet the river Mouna Mouelé. Then it's about a three-hour boat ride to Iguela. The boat would of course need to be waiting there for you. The whole journey would require a degree of collaboration between the different tourists camps that does not exist at the moment. As it stands, visiting both the northern and southern sections of the park means returning to Port Gentil.

Iguela is reached by a flight to Omboué (several times a week from Libreville via Port Gentil), followed by a 1.5-hour transfer in 4WD. The 45km (28-mile) road is fairly arduous at the moment, but there are plans to improve it. (While I wouldn't necessarily suggest a sightseeing trip of **Omboué**, if you happen to be looking for somewhere to eat, ask to be directed to Mama Brigitte, who serves good Gabonese food in her front room.) There is also a runway for light aircraft at Iguela itself, for those who wish to arrive in style. Operation Loango – which owns Ye Tsanou lodge – has a plane that can be hired for ferrying guests. There are no boats operating any kind of service between Port Gentil and Iguela, although in theory this route is possible. The camps overlook the northern end of the lagoon and border the national park. Camp bookings can be made direct or via a travel agent who offer packages that include flights to Omboué (check what excursions are included).

Where to stay

Ye Tsanou (email: Iguela@uuplus.com) is a lodge run by a fantastic Dutch couple, Mireille and Piet, on behalf of **Operation Loango**, a private company committed to conservation and sustainable tourism. The atmosphere is relaxed and friendly, and the chef, Jean-François, is superb. Everything was completely rebuilt in 2002 with a swimming pool, ten new bungalows (complete with air conditioning, fan, hot running water and balconies), including one super-luxurious suite.

Prices for full board at Ye Tsanou lodge (including transfers Omboué-Iguela by car, one game drive a day and one fishing/lagoon outing) are 100,000CFA/150,000CFA room/suite per person per night. Add an extra 20,000CFA per person per day covers all drinks consumed 10.00–22.00. Ask at the time of booking if you want to arrange a half-day trip to Fernan Vaz lagoon – including tours of Saint Anne's mission and Gorilla Island – which is done straight after arriving in Omboué. Visitors are then transported to Ye Tsanou via the River Mpive and 4WD. Whale-watching trips are made on a semi-rigid boat with a 285 horsepower engine and room for seven passengers (usually three researchers, four tourists). There are no seats, and the ride is wet and uncomfortable, but that's all made worthwhile by the fact that the boat gets excitingly close.

From mid 2003 there will also be two satellite bush camps. **Akaka** camp is on the edge of Petit Loango, a 3-hour journey away from Iguela by motorised *pirogue*. Akaka is used as a base from which to explore the river by canoe, not disturbing birds and animals with an engine. A day trip to Akaka costs 35,000CFA per person for four people, or 50,000CFA per person for two people. To stay for a couple of days costs 120,000CFA per person per night. There is an infernal number of tsetse flies on the river, so cover up and wear insect repellent.

The second satellite camp, **Tassi**, is on the beach, a two-hour game drive away from the Iguela on the other side of the lagoon. A day trip to Tassi will set you back 20,000CFA per person, while staying overnight will cost 110,000CFA per person, including game drives and, depending on the season, turtle observations or early-morning walks in search of gorillas.

Next door to Ye Tsanou is **Gavilo**, a camp owned by Dr Ndelia, which also caters for fishermen and wildlife enthusiasts. There are nine small but nicely decorated bungalows (three with air conditioning, six with fan), a restaurant on a platform over the lagoon and a small medical centre for the villagers. The daily rate is 80,000CFA per person based on two people sharing. Book through any travel agent.

Sette Cama

The village of Sette Cama lies directly to the south of Loango National Park. Visitors come to Sette Cama to go walking in the southern section of Loango National Park, to go fishing and to explore the Ndogo Lagoon. Tourist accommodation is very close to Sette Cama, just one of a number of small fishing villages that grace the shores of the expansive Ndogo Lagoon, the ocean directly behind them.

The usual way to reach the village of Sette Cama is to cross the lagoon by boat from Gamba. (It is also in theory possible to drive over sand to Sette Cama from Gamba in a 4WD in little more than 1.5 hours.) The boat option is not much quicker, but less hassle. On the way, it's possible to stop off and see the remains of the late-19th-century **Mission Saint Benoit**, a short walk inland through the forest. Actually there's not much to see, except a statue of Saint Benoit himself, the old bell and a few sections of rotting balustrade. The last few paces are very unsteady as this is the fallen building itself.

It is difficult to believe that in the 16th century Sette Cama village was an important port on the African coast for traders of padouk timber and ivory. The ruins behind the village are those of the house of the last French governor, and there is a small cemetery on the beach near the Brigade des Eaux et Forêts. Visitors are welcome to drop in to the Brigade des Eaux et Forêts to visit the small **museum** filled with skulls, bones, teeth and trap cables found in the forest.

Fishermen and wildlife enthusiasts are unlikely to leave unsatisfied. A typical day might start with an exploration of the Ndogo Lagoon by motorised *pirogue*, keeping an eye out for crocodiles and manatees. Then in the afternoon visitors could be transported to Loango National Park by *pirogue*, for a walk through the forest to the beach in time for sunset, the sound of crashing waves getting louder and louder. It's hard work walking along the beach, but absolutely worth it. To give you an idea, in the five hours of my first walk I was lucky enough to see a small antelope and a group of five gorillas in the forest, followed by a herd of buffalo, a herd of bush pigs and four separate groups of between two and four elephants on the beach.

How to visit

A visit to Sette Cama must be arranged in advance with one of three companies. The adventure starts on arrival at Gamba airport, from where visitors are transported to the camp of their choice by boat departing from Gamba market. (Sette Cama also has a landing strip for those who have hired their own light aircraft.) At present there are three possible options, which are detailed below.

Where to stay

Cecotour (tel: 53 42 76; 07 59 60) is a non-profit venture founded by WWF to promote ecotourism by and for the local population. The Director is Jean-Pierre Baye, an impassioned conservationist and turtle fanatic. He also has a talent for handling crocodiles with his bare hands and will take you out searching for them at night. They accommodate visitors at Sette Cama in one of the houses at the Brigade des Eaux et Forêts, where there are three rooms with shared bathroom facilities (currently no running water). Sometimes use is also made of the beautiful if dusty house of a deceased Gabonese minister at the tiny village of Mougambi. Overnight stays can also be made in the village of Pitongo. The cooking at the Brigade is done by Jean-Pierre's wife, Angelique. Cecotour cannot cater for fewer than three or more than six people at a time. Certain little luxuries may not be available, but it's a bargain at the all-inclusive rate per person per day of 50,000CFA.

Gamba Vacances (tel: 39 80 08, 55 82 56) have built a camp in a superb location with a view of the lagoon on one side and the sea on the other, although admittedly the view of the sea is partially obscured by trees. There are 18 small rooms in a single block, half of which have en-suite facilities. This is primarily a fishing camp, although walks can be arranged on request. The daily rate is 90,000CFA.

The most luxurious accommodation is at **Sette Cama Safaris** (tel: 26 23 09, 24 08 24, 28 67 47), where at present there are three beautiful and spacious chalets. Each chalet has a large double bed, en-suite bathroom, mosquito nets and a small veranda. The restaurant-bar is equally breezy and pretty. The daily rate is 80,000CFA. There is a plaque under the trees in camp commemorating Maurice Patry (1924–98), a legendary guide hunter whose ashes were scattered over the area.

GAMBA

Gamba has an estimated population or around 8,000 people, most of whom came here to work for the oil company Shell. In fact, for most, Gamba has become synonymous with Shell. This is a town that grew quickly after the arrival of Shell in 1963, and its fortunes are inseparable from the company. The Gamba-Ivinga oil field is still producing 10,000 barrels a day, but there's no denying that oil is on the decline and continued production after the year 2007 is highly questionable. Gamba's residents are concerned, as the departure of Shell would surely spell socio-economic disaster and turn Gamba into a ghost town.

There is very little to retain the visitor in Gamba itself, although the lagoon-side location is very pretty. It is a small but structured place divided into five *plaines* or districts. Outside the town proper is Yenzi, a vast Shell compound for '*les Shellois*' (Shell's expat employees), boasting everything from a gym and a hockey pitch, to a swimming pool and an 18-hole golf course. Gamba's primary interest for visitors is its airport, their point of arrival for a trip to Sette Cama (see pages 130–2).

Getting there and away

There are flights several times a week between Libreville and Gamba, stopping in Port Gentil on the way. The total journey takes 1.5 hours. The airport is located 10km (6 miles) out of town. A shared taxi from the airport to town costs 500CFA.

If you want to head south, bear in mind there are no flights from Gamba to Mayumba (although Air Services do run flights from Mayumba to Gamba twice weekly). It is possible to go by road to Mayumba or Tchibanga, although this shouldn't be attempted by those with no experience of driving on sand or through water (sections of the road are flooded in the rainy season). *Taxis-brousse* start looking for customers at Gamba's *gare routière* from about 08.00. The journey to Mayumba takes five to six hours along Route Nationale 6, and costs about 13,000CFA. If there are no vehicles going direct, you may have to travel via Tchibanga. Either way, there are two *bacs* (ferries) for crossing. The first, at Mayonami, is motorised. There is often a queue so you may have to wait. The second *bac*, shortly before the picturesque village of **Panga**, is pulled by hand. (If you have your own transport and supplies and want to camp on a remote, isolated beach, ask the villagers to direct you.) Not far from Panga the road meets the RN6, a smoothish dirt road. Until this point the surface has been sand and the journey adventurous and very dusty.

Above Every village has a *corps de garde*, used for socialising and ceremonies (JT)

Left Nesting leatherback turtle, Pongara (MP)

Below Ekwata beach (JT)

Above, below and below right São Tomé town (PM)
Right Drying fish, São Tomé. Fish are commonly preserved by sun-drying. (PM)

There is a car-hire place in Gamba – EGCA (tel: 55 83 21) – but they do ask people where they are headed as there are many routes they don't like.

Where to stay and eat
The best place to stay in town is the **Motel Herman**, which has rooms at 30,000CFA (or 25,000CFA if you book via Cecotour before or after one of their trips). **Hotel Le Nama** has air-conditioned rooms with en-suite facilities for 15,000CFA. The rooms are a bit grotty but the area is quiet. **L'Auberge Le Petrolier** (tel: 50 03 36) also has rooms for 15,000CFA. The hotel is in quite a noisy part of town, just paces away from the Couloir de la Mort. The best place to eat is **Le Baobab**, located on the town's main commercial street.

MOUKALABA-DOUDOU NATIONAL PARK
Moukalaba is a rugged area of great habitat diversity, combining tropical rainforest and grassy savannahs. West of Moukalaba and east of the Ndogo Lagoon are the Doudou Mountains. This is the largest mountain range in southwestern Gabon, reaching an altitude of approximately 700m. Under the network of national parks established in 2002, this area has become the **Moukalaba-Doudou National Park**. At present there is no infrastructure for visitors, but it is hoped that the park could become an important site for observing gorillas and chimpanzees, as well as birds and insects. This is an important centre of endemism, the full extent of whose biological value is as yet unknown. For example, research in the Doudou Mountains has identified 39 genera of ants and 16 genera of wasps. The park already has a means of access, the Tchibanga-Doussala road. In the 1980s the Doudou mountains were selectively logged but the area is now completely uninhabited. Previous logging means there is a network of old forestry roads that could be turned to tourist use when the time comes.

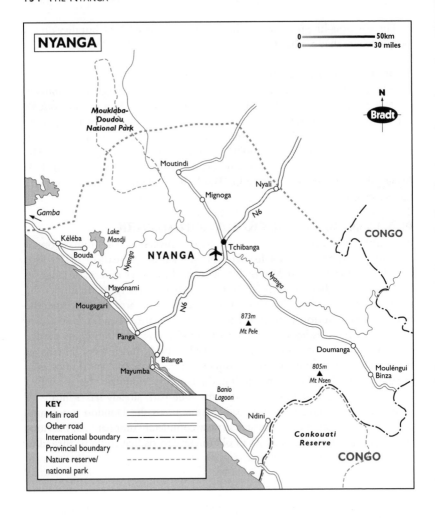

The Nyanga

Nyanga is in the far southwest of Gabon, its limits defined by the ocean to the west and the border with Congo to the south. The provincial capital, Tchibanga, lies beside the River Nyanga in a low-lying corridor between the Mayumba mountains and the Ikoundou mountains, paralleling the Ngounié valley to the east. It is a fairly wealthy region with fertile soil. Its agricultural industry – based largely on rice and some vegetables – is centred around Moabi, and marble is quarried near to Tchibanga. Tourism is an embryonic industry at the coastal town Mayumba, famed for its pristine beach. Talk of building a port on Gabon's southwestern coast has raised fears about the future of Mayumba, but it seems an unlikely choice as long as oil is not found here.

TCHIBANGA

Tchibanga is the capital of the Nyanga province, which explains the number of government buildings. It's a town of about 10,000 residents, surrounded by pretty countryside. When I visited just before Independence Day 2002 it was a frenzy of activity. The town resembled an active construction site round the clock, as there was a mad rush to finish modernising the airport, surfacing roads and erecting new government buildings in honour of the President's 24-hour visit.

This is a nice, relaxed place to stop if you are not pressed for time, but there is little to see or do as such. Approached by road from the north, there is a wonderful view of the town from above, especially in the rainy season when the sky is clear. The market, shops and the *gare routière* are all very close together in the commercial centre, which is at the opposite end of town to the administrative centre. Ignore any signs you see for telephones, faxes or internet access – the town currently has no telephone lines and everyone operates on mobiles.

If you have your own 4WD transport, you could visit the **Ivela Falls**. Take the road to Moabi and stop at the village of Louango (1 hour), where you should ask for a guide to take you to the falls on foot through the forest (about 1.5 hours each way). There is some lovely cycling to be had in the surrounding countryside, but nowhere to hire bikes, unless you are able to convince someone on the street to part with theirs for the day.

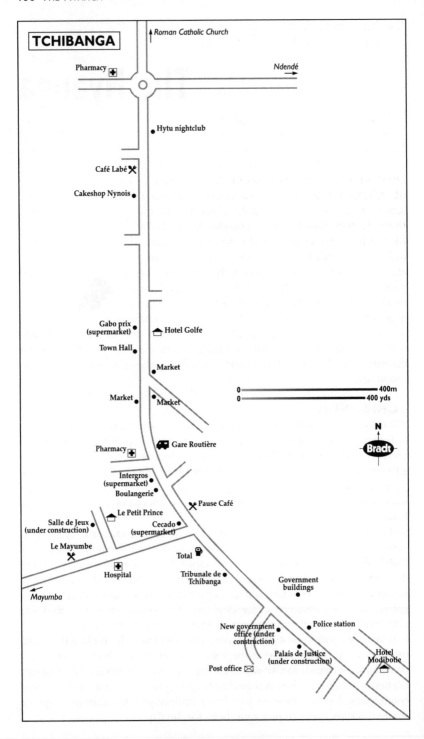

TCHIBANGA

Roman Catholic Church

Pharmacy

Ndendé

Hytu nightclub

Café Labé

Cakeshop Nynois

Gabo prix
(supermarket)

Hotel Golfe

Town Hall

Market

Market

Market

0 ——————— 400m
0 ——————— 400 yds

N

Bradt

Pharmacy

Gare Routière

Intergros
(supermarket)

Boulangerie

Pause Café

Le Petit Prince

Salle de Jeux
(under construction)

Cecado
(supermarket)

Le Mayumbe

Total

Hospital

Tribunale de
Tchibanga

Government
buildings

Mayumba

Police station

New government
office (under
construction)

Palais de Justice
(under construction)

Hotel
Modibolie

Post office

Getting there and away

There are flights to Tchibanga from Libreville twice a week. A *taxi-brousse* to/from Mayumba takes 4–5 hours and costs 5,000CFA. A *taxi-brousse* to/from Mouila takes 3.5 hours and costs 6,000CFA. For a *taxi-brousse* to Mouila, passengers should be at the *gare routière* at 08.00, and for Mayumba even earlier.

Where to stay, eat and go out

There is not a great number of places to stay in town. Traditionally the **Hotel Nyanga** (tel: 82 00 06) was the top hotel in town – it certainly has a great view over the river Nyanga – but it has been closed for a long time for refurbishment, which includes the addition of a tennis court. The **Hotel Modibotie** is a newish establishment with ordinary rooms at 20,000CFA and larger VIP rooms at 30,000CFA. All rooms have TV, air conditioning and fridge. Unfortunately, this area of town quite often has its water cut. The hotel has the best, and most expensive, restaurant in town, serving *grillades*, pizzas and African dishes, though you may have to place pizza orders in the afternoon. It also has a mediocre nightclub – **Le Nambe** – open Fridays and Saturdays (3,000CFA entrance for non-residents of the hotel). More fun is the **Hytu** nightclub in the heart of the *quartier commercial*, which doubles as something of a nightspot after dark.

The **Hotel Golfe** (tel: 82 01 82) is clean and good value. As a bonus, the owner, Mr Hamed, is very helpful and friendly. Rooms with fan/air conditioning cost 13,500CFA/17,000CFA. All rooms have TV and en-suite facilities, although there's no restaurant. **Le Petit Prince** have slightly shabby, air-conditioned rooms with TV for 15,000CFA. They also have six small rooms with fans at 5,000CFA, all sharing one shower and toilet. The food in the restaurant-bar is good.

Just around the corner from Le Petit Prince is **Le Mayumbe**, a restaurant serving good African dishes for around 3,000CFA. They also do pizzas, although you may have to place pizza orders in the afternoon. For cheaper eats try **Café Labé**, a small Senegalese restaurant with just four tables, where you can eat *riz Senegalais* and *lait caillé* for 2,000CFA. Otherwise there is the **Pause Café**, whose tiny terrace is a popular place to oversee what's going on in the street.

MAYUMBA

The small town of Mayumba is divided into two parts, straddling the Banio lagoon. The town centre is located on the peninsula between the lagoon and the ocean. There is a great view of the ocean from the hospital on the hill. The Gabonese will tell you that Mayumba has the best beach in the world. It's almost certainly the best in Gabon. The beach stretches for kilometres into the distance, a curve of silky sand fringed with palm trees. Best of all, it is virtually deserted, no doubt an important factor in determining its popularity with nesting turtles. The NGO Aventures Sans Frontières (see page 59) has conducted turtle surveys on Mayumba beach throughout the turtle season for several years. Their research, which shows Mayumba has the largest concentration of nesting leatherback turtles on earth, was highly instrumental in the establishment of **Mayumba National Park** and has also resulted in Mayumba being proposed as a World Heritage Site. There are currently no organised tourist activities in Mayumba – this is of course part of its charm – although the potential for whalewatching and fishing is there. The waves can be strong so take care, and you should bring your own picnic.

During the hours of daylight it is possible to cross the lagoon from one part of town to the other, either by taking the *bac* (ferry) if you are in a vehicle (5,000CFA), or jumping aboard a *pirogue* if you are on foot (500CFA). Those wanting to make a longer *pirogue* trip on the lagoon or one of the rivers that feeds it should ask around for a willing *piroguier*, starting at the lagoon landing stage below the market.

Getting there and away

There are flights about three times weekly with Libreville and once a week with Port Gentil. The latter stop at Gamba on the return leg. The easiest is to buy an airline ticket at the airport. There are *taxis-brousse* to/from Tchibanga (4–5 hours/5,000CFA) and Gamba (5–6 hours/13,000CFA). See under *Gamba* in *Chapter 9* for more details of this journey. Vehicles for Tchibanga start filling up at the market at about 10.00 every day.

Where to stay and eat

There are two *cases de passage* in the Bana section of town, one called **Bissona Bisso**, the other **Tsona Stella**. Both have ventilated rooms for 5,000CFA. Some of the rooms have a wash area with a bucket of water. The WCs are communal and strong smelling. There is also the **Hotel du Bac** (clean, air-conditioned rooms for 12,000CFA), next to where the *bac* (ferry) comes in to pick up and drop off vehicles. The hotel has a bar, but does not serve food. There is a handful of small and cheap bar-restaurants in the centre, as well as a good bakery. The **Caféteria Solidarité** is a bit gloomy but serves passable food. The **Restaurant Africain** is a bit more cheery. Both serve main meals for 1,000-1,500CFA. The usual snack food is available at the market.

On the other side of the lagoon are the **Catholic mission** and the **Safari Hotel**, both of which have great views over the lagoon. Of all Mayumba's accommodation options, the Safari is definitely the best bet, with nicely decorated, inviting rooms.

Woleu-Ntem

This region takes its name from two large rivers, the Woleu and the Ntem. It is a frontier region, separated from Cameroon to the north by the River Ntem, and butting up to Equatorial Guinea to the west, and around the Crystal Mountains to the south (see pages 103–4). The regionalboundaries were created by the French in the early 20th century. Woleu-Ntem fell under Germancolonial control in 1912–15 – the German legacy liveson in the cocoa they planted – but the factor to impact on the region today is the influx of immigrants from these neighbouring countries.

Woleu-Ntem has an estimated population of 220,000 people, making it second only to the estuary in terms of population density. The majority of its inhabitants are Fang, who are known for the *Mvet*, the name of a Fang stringed instrument and musical tradition. There are also villages of Baka pygmies near the Cameroonian border. As well as being one of the country's most densely populated regions, Woleu-Ntem is one of the most wealthy. An immediate indicator of its importance is the beautifully surfaced main road, which allows produce from Cameroon to be easily transported south through Bitam, Oyem, Mitzic to eventually join the road to Libreville.

The region's wealth is based in agriculture, and specifically on the company Hévégab, which carved massive hevea plantations totalling thousands of hectares into the forest here in the early 1990s. These work opportunities not only meant less of an exodus of the young from Woleu-Ntem compared to other, less-wealthy regions, but also acted as a magnet for jobless young men from across the borders. Unfortunately, Hévégab is now experiencing difficulties. Jobs can no longer be taken for granted and unemployment is rising.

Because of the region's higher altitude, the weather tends to be colder than most of the rest of the country, with a longer rainy season. Seen from the sky, the region's overwhelming feature is the dense and breathtaking forest, broken only by the dramatic inselbergs that give shape to the landscape, and the occasional roads with their pretty villages dotted with avocado, mango and banana trees. The far northeastern corner of the region, and the country, is uninhabited impenetrable forest broken only by massive granite outcrops.

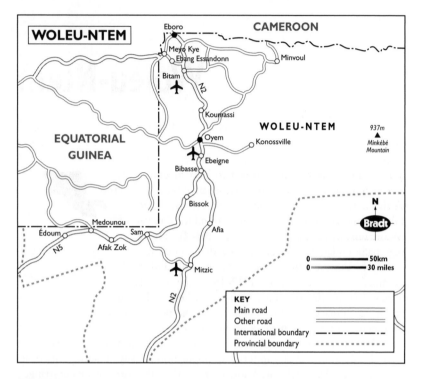

OYEM

The population of the capital of Woleu-Ntem is a well-integrated mixture of people from Gabon, Cameroon and Equatorial Guinea. While the town centre is manageable on foot, the town as a whole is quite spread out and taxis come in very welcome. It's possible to negotiate with taxi drivers to take you visiting out of town too, although this is obviously easier if you have your own transport. Just out of town, on the road to Bitam, is the Catholic mission of Angone, a beautiful red-brick church surrounded by dense forest. About 25km (15.5 miles) further on is the village of **Koumassi**. The village is impossible to miss, or rather its inselberg with its iron cross on top is (*Koum* in Fang means mountain). Stop at the village and ask the chief to provide you with a guide. It's easily less than an hour to the top and the views are more than worth the effort.

Getting there and away

There are four flights a week from Libreville. A taxi from the airport to the centre of town costs 2,000CFA for *une course*. The RN2 runs from Eboro down through the region past Mitzic and into the Moyen Ogooué. It's a beautifully surfaced road, making travel a quick and painless exercise. The state of the roads means that normal taxis taking just four to five passengers shuttle between towns. Taxis leave Oyem's *gare routière* intermittently throughout the day until about 17.00, for Bitam (2,000CFA) in the north and Mitzic

(3,000CFA) in the south. All travellers in the region will find themselves disembarking at Oyem at some point, however briefly, as travellers between Bitam and Mitzic have to change vehicles here. If you are travelling between Oyem and Mitzic under your own steam, you might want to stop at the leprosy village of **Ebeigne** to buy raffia baskets, chairs, lamps and so on.

Where to stay and eat
To be honest, none of the places to stay in Oyem is really up to much, but then tourism is not exactly a flourishing business here. The town's one supposedly upmarket hotel is the **Mvet Palace Novotel** (tel: 98 65 52), which is in need of renovation but at least has character, a bar-restaurant and a souvenir shop. The setting's not bad, as many of the hotel rooms overlook gardens and a lake. The basic en-suite room costs 12,500CFA, or 17,500CFA with television. A suite will set you back 25,000CFA. All rooms have air conditioning.

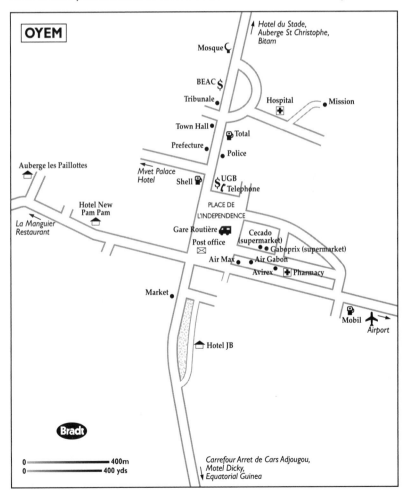

Hotel New Pam Pam (tel: 21 47 27), which backs onto the Mvet lake, has en-suite rooms for 8,000CFA/15,000-18,000CFA with fan/air conditioning. There's no restaurant, but there is the **New Pam club**, open Thursdays through Saturdays from 23.00. Further along the same road and down a track to the right is the **Auberge les Paillottes**, which has quite a good bar-restaurant under a *paillotte* serving avocado salad (1,500CFA) and steak in cream (3,000CFA). There are rooms with fan and shared WC/shower for 5,000CFA. Also at this end of town is **La Manguier**, a bit more expensive but generally considered to be the best restaurant in town.

Heading towards the outskirts of town on the Bitam road are the **Hotel de Stade** (tel: 98 64 29) and the **Auberge Saint Christophe** (tel: 98 66 97). There's not much to choose between them – the Hotel de Stade might just have the edge – as both have rooms with fan for about 6,000CFA and a small bar. At the other end of town is the **Motel Dicky** (tel: 98 62 21, 06 20 26), which has air-conditioned rooms for 8,300CFA/10,300CFA for a single/double, and rooms with fan for 5,300CFA/8,000CFA for a single/double. There is a restaurant serving meals for about 2,500CFA.

The most central of all the options is **Hotel JB** (tel: 98 67 89) from where you can easily walk around the centre. Rooms start at 10,000CFA for a basic room without WC, and rise to 12,000CFA for a room with en-suite facilities and 20,000CFA for the same only larger. There is in theory a restaurant – a room with a few tables – although it won't open unless guests indicate that they actually want to eat there. Opposite the hotel is a small Malian *maquis* serving passable food.

A few kilometres out of town, behind the hospital, is the large church of Saint Charles Lwanga. Behind the church is a **mission**, where passers-by are always welcome to drop in for a chat, or to stay if it's during the long summer holidays (end of June to September 15). They have a dormitory of six beds, one double room and a little kitchen. The mission's patch of lawn will be of particular interest to travellers with vehicles and/or tents, as there is room for both, and access to hot water. The price is around 5,000CFA per bed, and 3,000CFA per person in a tent or camper van, but these rates are negotiable for those without means. There is a small workshop where the artistic creations of the female students can be bought, mostly pottery. The standard is very good.

BITAM

This is the northernmost town in Gabon, just 30km (19 miles) south of the border with Cameroon. Everything is concentrated in a small central area – the market, the hotels, the post office, the petrol station, the bank, the pharmacy, even the airport are all within easy walking distance. Given its size proportional to the number of visitors and the number of hotel rooms, you can't help asking yourself how often they are occupied. About 4km (2.5 miles) out of town in a northerly direction is the Sacre Coeur church, where there is a small museum of religious art and Fang traditions.

The border village, **Eboro**, is just a short *pirogue* ride across the Ntem from Cameroon. On Wednesdays and Saturdays there is a massive market on the

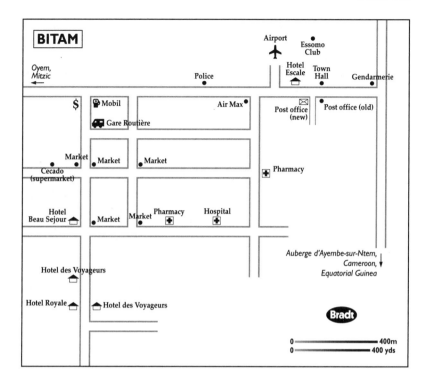

Cameroonian side, 5km (3 miles) beyond the border. To get to **Minvoul** – the most remote settlement in the region right in the heart of the forest – entails a much longer, more arduous journey. Once you turn off the RN2, the road is not tarred, which makes it very difficult in the rainy season. The pygmy villages in the area are places of pilgrimage for people from all over Gabon who wish to be treated with pygmy traditional medicines.

Getting there and away
There are several flights a week from Libreville. The airport is right in town, 500m from the market, from where taxis heading north and south leave regularly. It is not possible to take a taxi direct from Bitam to Mitzic; passengers must change vehicles at Oyem.

Where to stay and eat
Those arriving by plane will see the **Hotel Escale** (tel: 96 81 12; fax: 96 83 68) as they disembark. This is Bitam's newest and most luxurious establishment with an inviting restaurant. Room rates start at 16,000CFA and rise to as much as 45,000CFA. All 20 rooms are en suite and have air conditioning.

Bitam's other three hotels are grouped together below the market. The **Hotel Beau Sejour** (tel: 96 82 40) is the least salubrious. Management is awaiting funds to finish the building works above the bar, but there are still rooms available (5,000CFA with fan). There is stiff competition for custom between the newer Royal Hotel and the older L'Auberge des Voyageurs, and the rates tend to mirror one another. The **Royal Hotel** is the rather grand building that could pass for a Mediterranean villa. Rooms with fan cost 10,000CFA, while rooms with air conditioning are 14,000CFA/18,000CFA. There is no restaurant, but there is a bar, as well as a beauty salon.

L'Auberge des Voyageurs (tel: 96 80 20) spreads across two buildings, one on either side of the road. It has rooms at many different rates. The cheapest is a room with fan and shared bathroom at 5,000CFA, and the most expensive is a large en-suite room with air conditioning at 16,000CFA. Meals can be cooked by arrangement, and there is a nightclub that opens very occasionally. The hotel is owned by a friendly and helpful couple, Mr and Mrs Hauger, who are committed to developing tourism in their little visited region.

The Haugers also own the **Auberge d'Ayembe-sur-Ntem**, a single wooden building on the bank of the River Ntem, about 30km (19 miles) out of town. The hotel is nothing fancy – just a handful of en-suite rooms and two dormitories that are often used by local football teams – but the pretty location makes it a popular local getaway for fishermen and walkers. Rates are 5,000CFA per room; meals to be arranged on request. Cover up and wear thick socks to protect against ferocious biting insects. It's normally possible to arrange transport from Bitam with the Haugers. To get there with your own vehicle take the road from Bitam to Eboro, turning right at the petrol station as if heading to Minvoul. After about 10km, there is a turn-off to the left. In the rainy season a *pirogue* must be taken the final leg of the journey, as the road is submerged. The best time to go is the end of July to the beginning of August, when it's apparently dry enough to walk to Cameroon.

MITZIC

This is essentially a one-road town with an estimated 3,000 residents, although the number of unofficial immigrants make it hard to be sure. Visitors are greeted with great curiosity. There are no taxis and no need for them either, as it's possible to walk from one end of the town to the other in a leisurely ten minutes, barring impromptu conversations of course. Travelling around Woleu-Ntem might entail the need to stop here for the night and change vehicles.

Getting there and away

Taxis do the run between Mitzic and Oyem several times a day if there's the demand. Passengers for Bitam must change at Oyem. There should be a *taxi-brousse* for Libreville (9 hours/10,000CFA) every day, especially during the holidays. Loading normally kicks off at around 10.00 in front of the market, but the journey proper might only start several hours later. Reserve your seat early on and arrange to be picked up on departure. Vehicles from Booué arrive in Mitzic about 09.00, and depart again around 14.00.

Where to stay and eat

The choice is very limited, but everyone will tell you that the best place to stay in town is **Hotel Ngue**, one of the last buildings on the left as you head south out of town. This may surprise you once you see the dark and gloomy rooms (5,300CFA, or 8,300CFA for the luxury of a fan and bucket-flush WC). The rooms aren't great, but the staff are, and there is a small, friendly bar. Good food is served at the Cameroonian restaurant **Bam's** at the Oyem end of the main street, on the same side of the road. In between the hotel and the restaurant are JB's nightclub, the post office (there are phones here but they rarely work), the market and shops.

Travellers with their own transport could avoid staying in Mitzic and stop off at the **Hotel-Restaurant Le Chalet** instead – 12km (7.5 miles) out of town on the Oyem road – which is run by Mr Balloche. Here there are air-conditioned rooms (about 17,000CFA), good food and a small animal park with a few antelopes.

Africa Geographic
and
Africa – Birds & Birding

Award-winning magazines
about a continent
worth saving

For subscription details contact:
Africa Geographic/Africa – Birds & Birding
P O Box 44223, Claremont 7735,
Cape Town, South Africa.
Tel: (+27-21) 686 9001. Fax: (+27-21) 686 4500.
E-mail: *wildmags@blackeaglemedia.co.za*
Website: *www.africa-geographic.com*

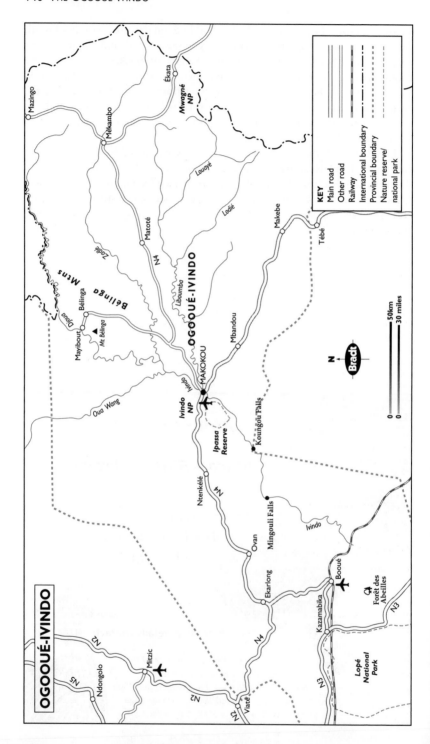

The Ogooué-Ivindo

The Ogooué-Ivindo is one of the least populated regions in Gabon. It is traversed by the Ogooué and Ivindo rivers, and the RN3 and the RN4 main roads. The regional capital is the small town of Makokou. East of Makokou the RN4 passes through some villages before arriving in Mékambo, the furthest town before the road splits and crosses the frontier into Congo in two different places. Away from the roads, this region is inaccessible and uninhabited, except for the Pygmies living along the length of the River Ivindo and the gold panners sifting through the small streams around the River Nouna. The other peoples living here are mostly Fang, Kwélé and Kota. They are eking out a subsistence existence, growing, fishing and hunting their food. There are iron deposits around Mount Bélinga that were once a source of great hope, but the quality is simply not good enough to justify the expense of mining it and transporting it to the coast. Now the government, in conjunction with environmental organisations such as WWF, hopes that ecotourism will provide a boost to the economy in a region that is after all one of Gabon's richest in terms of flora and fauna. Until now, Lopé has been the only real option for tourists, from those in search of the little-known Dja River Warbler or a rare species of orchid, to those interested primarily in a 'gorilla experience'. The formation of three new national parks (Minkébé, Ivindo and Mwagné) means an explosion in tourist possibilities is imminent.

LOPÉ NATIONAL PARK

Lopé National Park is a vast expanse totalling 5,360km² (2,069 square miles). It is bordered by the Ogooué to the north, the Offoué to the east, the du Chaillu mountains in the south and the River Mingoué to the west. Lopé was created as a national park in 2002 (prior to this it had been a reserve since 1946). More than 1,500 plant species have been recorded here, of which 40 represent new species for Gabon. Lopé is also home to 400 of the 680 species of bird recorded in Gabon, and according to ECOFAC there are 60 different species of mammal within the reserve. Little wonder Lopé is the chosen research centre for long-term studies on gorillas and mandrills. In the region of 1,350 mandrills are thought to inhabit the reserve and the surrounding area. They are particularly visible in the dry season (July–August), when they hang around in supergroups numbering hundreds in the north of the reserve for up to two weeks at a time. There are an estimated 3,000–5,000 western lowland gorillas roaming within the reserve.

The first thing to strike you as you arrive at Lopé is the dramatic patchwork landscape of open savannah and dense rainforest. The explanation for this landscape lies in the last icecap in northern Europe, 18,000 years ago (see pages 17–18), when the cooler, drier climate caused great stretches of tropical rainforest to disappear. When the Ice Age ended about 12,000 years ago, the forest recolonised the open savannah. The forest that you find in Lopé, therefore, is relatively young compared to the really ancient forest. There are still areas of savannah along the northern and eastern borders of the reserve, which have survived because here the average annual rainfall is just 1,500mm, insufficient rain for the forest. The Lopé region has one of the driest climates in Gabon and therefore the most fragile rainforest.

Another reason for the survival of La Lopé's savannah areas is down to humans. Archaeological findings from Otoumbi (just outside the western border of the reserve) indicate that people have been present in the Ogooué valley for 400,000 years. Numerous other local findings suggest humans may even have been a continuous inhabitant of this region for the last 60,000 years. It is likely that for these early inhabitants fire was the most usual device for controlling their environment and that by regularly burning the savannah areas, the encroachment of the forest was stalled. Burning is still used each dry season by the Ministère des Eaux et Forêts to ensure that the limits between forest and savannah are maintained.

Granting La Lopé national park status represents the logical and desirable culmination of Lopé's evolving status over the years, and the successful outcome of all the work ECOFAC (see page 31) has put in since its first involvement in 1992. Not only has ECOFAC conducted much research, but it has developed and maintained 40km (25 miles) of trails and six bridges, financed an anti-poaching brigade, built positive relations with logging companies in the fight against poaching and introduced a tourism designed to finance conservation.

Choosing and booking your safari

This is probably simpler than you may imagine. The choice is not so much where to stay – the Lopé Hotel and the satellite camps of Mikongo and Ololo are the only safari camps – but for how long to stay in each place. My recommended minimum length of stay would be five days, with an overnight stop at the beginning and end at the Lopé Hotel, including one full day of excursions from the hotel. Ideally you should have one night and one full day of activities in both Mikongo and Ololo, but obviously to maximise your chances of seeing certain primates or birds, it would be preferable to have two days and two nights in each place. Bookings for all three should be made through any of the main travel agents in Libreville. It is not viable to book with the Lopé Hotel direct as there is no telephone line and, anyway, tracking permits have to be issued in Libreville.

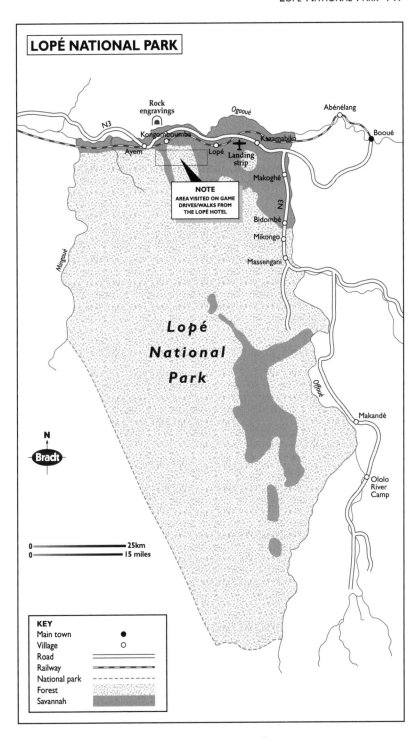

LOPÉ NATIONAL PARK

NOTE
AREA VISITED ON GAME
DRIVES/WALKS FROM
THE LOPÉ HOTEL

Rock
engravings

Ogooué

Abénélang

Booué

N3

Kongomboumba

Ayem

Lopé

Kazamabika

Landing
strip

Makoghé

N3

Bidombé

Mikongo

Massengani

Mingoué

Lopé
National
Park

Offoué

Makandé

N

Bradt

Ololo
River
Camp

0 ——— 25km
0 ——— 15 miles

KEY
Main town ●
Village ○
Road
Railway
National park ---
Forest
Savannah

If there is a downside to visiting the park it's that there's no obvious way to do it on a budget. Camping is not allowed, nor is going it alone in the park. The consolation is that your money is helping to protect a key part of Gabon's natural heritage, although just how much of it is not clear. Given that the owner of the Lopé Hotel is also the Ministère des Eaux et Forêts there is evidently something of a conflict of interests. While the Lopé Hotel is private, the camps of Mikongo and Ololo were built by, and the guides and trackers are employed by, ECOFAC. The Lopé Hotel pays for the right to use the camps and profits are fed back into park projects, such as anti-poaching patrols. When the camps are up and running smoothly, they too will be privatised, most probably to the Ministère as well.

Lopé Hotel

The Lopé Hotel is perched on a bend of the Ogooué River. It's a beautiful location, best enjoyed from the swimming pool terrace and chalets 9b and 10b. All the chalets have air conditioning, and electricity and hot water mornings and evenings. There are also family chalets. Meals are served in an open-sided restaurant-bar overlooking the water. The food is generally good, and the French-trained chef will make an effort with any special meal requests you may have. Board games such as Scrabble and chess are kept behind the bar. At reception T-shirts and ECOFAC's excellent field guides on the reserve are on sale. It's worth noting that they're not cheap and the hotel does not accept credit cards, only cash (CFAs and euros).

On the grass in front of the bar-restaurant is a varnished elephant skull, from the largest of five elephants ploughed into and killed by a manganese train one night. Not far from the swimming pool is a simple memorial to a French army officer who went swimming in the waters in front of the hotel and drowned. His body was never found.

A standard room at the Lopé Hotel is 27,500CFA. Breakfast is 5,000CFA and a three-course lunch or dinner 14,000CFA. Drinks have to be paid for on top. Try asking for a reduction if you are booking direct for several days. Half-board is 46,000CFA per person based on two people sharing a room.

Excursions from the Lopé Hotel

The excursions on offer include a half-day game drive through the park. The turn-off to the park entrance is just a few minutes' drive from the hotel. The wooden houses immediately to the right are lived in by the employees of the Ministère des Eaux et Forêts and their families, who are responsible for protecting the park against poachers. At last count there were just six of them responsible for 500,000 hectares. Just beyond on the left are some beds of orchids and a red-tiled building, which will at some point open as the Lopé Museum, exhibiting findings from the prehistoric sites and information about the flora and fauna. The next and last building you will see on the drive is the house of the Lopé ECOFAC representative.

Only a small portion of the park is open to tourists. The designated safari route largely sticks to the savannah, with brief forays into patches of forest.

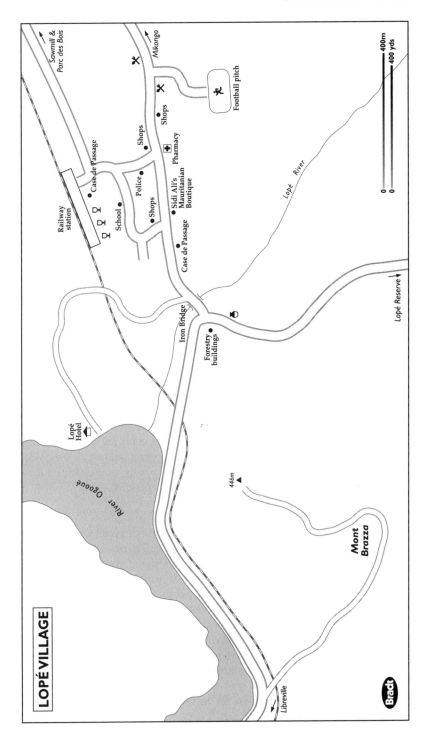

LOPÉ VILLAGE

Sawmill & Parc des Bois

Mikongo

Football pitch

Shops

Shops

Case de Passage

Railway station

School

Police

Pharmacy

Shops

Sidi Ali's Mauritanian Boutique

Case de Passage

Lopé River

Iron Bridge

Forestry buildings

Lopé Reserve

Lopé Hotel

River Ogooué

446m

Mont Brazza

Libreville

400m
400 yds

Bradt

The horizon backdrop alternates between mountains and forest. August and September is the time when elephant, buffalo, sitatunga, monkeys and gorillas are most visible. Take some binoculars so that you can identify between the groups of mangebeys, putty-nosed monkeys and moustached monkeys that you will no doubt see crashing through the treetops.

Lopé is the location of Gabon's most important archaeological site. About 40 minutes by motorised *pirogue* from the Lopé Hotel is the landing point for a walking tour of rock engravings that attest to man's presence here in the Iron Age (2200–1800BC). Found in a small savannah area of great beauty on the banks of the Ogooué, the reason for the engravings is difficult to guess at, although it's possible that they, and the hollows carved in some of the rocks, have a sacred significance. Of the 1,500 rock engravings discovered in the reserve between 1987 and 1993, three-quarters are abstract and symbolic designs. The concentric circular designs in particular, also found elsewhere in Africa, are typically Bantu. Animal representations account for 8% of the engravings. Interestingly, none is of the large mammals, such as elephants and buffalo, which feature so prominently in the archaeological finds of southern Africa. Engravings of drying civet hides probably point to their importance in the *Bwiti* initiation ceremony, while the significance of lizards is less clear, but probably is somehow linked to mystical beliefs. Weapons and tools account for 6% of the engravings.

An outing you can do independently is to climb Mount Brazza, named after the explorer Savorgnan de Brazza whose expedition arrived here in 1875, after protracted negotiations with the local Okandé people. Just follow RN1 to the base of the mountain or ask the hotel to take you by car. The actual ascent is about an hour to the antenna at the top. The climb is best done in the afternoon as in the morning the summit is often shrouded in mist and as a result the view is not up to much. The pond at the foot of Mount Brazza attracts numerous birds. It is also possible to arrange guided walks in the forest with the hotel. You can discuss the route and level of difficulty with the guide.

The hotel charges 16,000CFA for each half-day outing, or 26,000CFA for a full day (which can be made up of two half-day excursions).

Where to stay and eat in Lopé village

Contrary to what they would have you believe, the Lopé Hotel is not the only place to stay, although it is without doubt the best. There are two alternative accommodation options in the village itself, although if you are intending to visit the park in whatever capacity (and this is really the only reason for coming here) then you still have to organise and pay for this at the Lopé Hotel.

The first *case de passage* is at the train station, the second is in the heart of Lopé village. There is not much to choose between them. Both have rooms for 5,000CFA with a mosquito net, or for 10,000CFA with a fan but no mosquito net. Take your pick. There is a third *case de passage* just inside the entrance to the park, but this is currently open only to people in some way associated with work in the park.

There are a couple of restaurants on the village's main drag, and some small bars at the train station.

Mikongo

Mikongo functions as a satellite camp for the Lopé Hotel, and a research station for the study and habituation of La Lopé's gorillas. Small groups of two or three tourists are taken in to the forest for walks averaging 10km (6 miles), about 8 hours, in the hope of seeing primates, forest elephants and birds. The wildlife is exactly that, wild, so don't count on being able to see everything. A lot of the tourists who come here are primarily interested in gorillas, but Mikongo's researchers stress the broader appeal of the forest. For the time being there is no off-trail gorilla tracking, but gorilla sightings may increase as the habituation process makes headway.

Visits must be arranged in advance, preferably before you arrive at Lopé, as time is needed to issue the tracking permits in Libreville. The Lopé Hotel will transfer you to Mikongo in a 4WD, a journey that takes about two hours, and potentially a lot longer during or after heavy rain. The route takes you through the villages of Matégé and Badongé, where banana and manioc plantations can be seen alongside the road. The terracotta-red laterite road snaking through the grassy savannah makes this a really scenic drive. After crossing the Obidi River you'll take a right into the bush for a bumpy and slippery 12km (7.5-mile) drive on an old forestry road. If the vegetation hasn't been cut back for a while – it needs to be cropped about twice a month – then you'll be crashing through the undergrowth, a fitting beginning to your arrival deep in the forest.

Mikongo was established as both a gorilla research station and a tourist camp, the long-term idea being that the money from tourism would support the research. The first tourists visited in October 2000, but even now the habituation process is still very much in its infancy. Trekking is done in an area of about 100km^2 (39 square miles) around the camp. This area spans a variety of habitats and is criss-crossed by approximately 220km (137 miles) of *pistes* or trails, either former forest roads and logging trails, elephant trails or new secateur trails. There are an estimated 80–100 gorillas in this area, although the gorillas' range and the lack of surveys at present means it is difficult to say with absolute certainty. There are lots of small groups of three to four members and quite a few solitary males. The largest group identified so far is Group D, with 18 members, including one silverback and a younger male.

Usually the trackers have a good idea of where the different groups spent the night or in which direction they were heading the previous day, but sightings are far from guaranteed. These gorillas are unaccustomed to human contact and the first step in the long process of habituation is for the gorillas to recognise and accept the presence of humans. The researchers alert the gorillas to their presence by making a clucking noise, a sound chosen because it is completely unrelated to gorilla communication. Simply by virtue of their being there, tourists themselves are assisting in habituation every time there is a successful encounter. Any sightings seek to identify the group and the individuals within it, noting gender, age, size and facial features, such as nose shape and possible scarring. Even old gorilla traces, such as faeces or tracks, are fully recorded with GPS coordinates.

GORILLA ETIQUETTE

If you are lucky enough to have the opportunity to observe gorillas, here are some common-sense reminders to help ensure it is a positive and safe experience for both parties.

- Don't point – it's rude! Plus, raised arms can be mistaken as threatening.
- Don't stare – this is also rude, and direct eye contact can be mistaken as a challenge.
- Don't use camera flashes. If you have an automatic flash, cover it with opaque tape.
- Don't run! If you are charged, fight the urge to flee and instead crouch down in a submissive pose.
- Don't make noise – talking or crashing through the undergrowth will alert wildlife to your presence and greatly reduce your chances of seeing anything.

At this point it is worth stressing that any 'gorilla experience' here is not going to be of the cuddly, playful kind tourists might encounter elsewhere, in Rwanda for example. It takes up to five years for gorillas to become 'habituated' and, besides, the kind of habituation intended for Mikongo is one of minimal cross-species contact. This way human contact will not be affecting natural gorilla behaviour, just monitoring it. In addition, it is hoped that by keeping a proper distance, the exchange of diseases will be averted. In order to keep an eye on gorilla health, and the effects of possible stress on the gorilla immune system, the research team is conducting a programme of faeces data collection alongside the habituation process.

The team – three expat researchers and seven local guides and trackers – is enthusiastic and knowledgeable. Enormous time and effort was invested in finding and training trackers who were really familiar with the forest, who can find and follow animal trails, judge the age of faecal deposits, look at a half-eaten fruit and tell you who the diner was, and read broken vegetation to give the direction of travel. Most of them come from villages in the Makokou area and were taught to hunt in the traditional way by their fathers. The more French you can speak, the more you will learn (of the guides and trackers only one speaks English), and given that seeing gorillas is not a certainty the camp staff will try to interest gorilla-obsessed tourists in other aspects of the forest, usually with some success. The guides can wax lyrical about the flowers and fruits of the forest, and describe how the bark, leaves and roots of various plants are prepared for use in traditional medicines. Keen birdwatchers will no doubt be interested to know that there are seven known nesting sites for the rare Picatharte rock-fowl within reach of camp. This gawky, timid bird is very habitat specific, favouring large, leaning rocks near small rivers.

If you have time for only one full day's trekking and want to make the most of every minute, you can arrange for a guide to meet the car just before you arrive at the camp the day before. You'll end up approaching the camp on foot after an easy introductory walk of about 1.5 hours through fairly light and open marantatia forest. A perfect ending to a sweaty trek is to bathe in the river below camp (black panther are sometimes seen here).

At present the camp has just three chalets sleeping two tourists each. The chalets – built in wood with palm-frond roofs – each has its own bathroom, mosquito nets and view directly into the forest. Sitting on the veranda looking up into the trees, you might be rewarded with a sighting of Emmanuel, a solitary male putty-nosed monkey – named after the camp's founder – who hangs around camp for company. There will eventually be another couple of tourist chalets, and there are exciting plans to set up several basic tented camps on the far reaches of the Mikongo catchment area. This would make tracking gorilla groups on successive days that much easier when they are far from the main camp.

Prices per day (inclusive of tracking permit, guides, packed lunch and three-course dinner) are 105,000CFA. There is a box for tips – estimate about 5,000–10,000CFA for each day you are there – which are later split between all the staff, not just the more visible ones.

Ololo River Camp

At the time of writing, the Ololo River Camp had just finished being built and was beginning to receive the first trickle of visitors, sent up from the Lopé Hotel with their own kitchen staff. Even more so than Mikongo, Ololo is located in the heart of the forest, and because of this you needn't even leave camp to see a fair amount of animal and bird life (or be eaten alive by insects). Trees tower over the tented huts and the noises of the jungle are louder than ever. The camp is surrounded on three sides by rivers and as such is a haven for river birds. The camp is centred around a raised wooden walkway with the eating area at one end and the bar at the other. The bar overlooks a beautiful lake fringed by misty forest, or at least will do once some bushes have been cleared. A salt lick has been created at the lake's edge to encourage animals to drop by, nicely in view of those enjoying their sundowners at the bar.

Ololo first opened to visitors in 2002, and improvements are being made all the time. At some point these might include canopy platforms perfect for birdwatchers and photographers, a cable bridge and viewing platforms on the Ofooué River, and medicinal plant trails and gardens. There are already several small walking trails leading away from camp, including a nice walk up the hill southwest of camp, and the intention is to develop some of the elephant trails leading away from the Ofooué to make part-*pirogue*, part-trekking excursions possible. Fishing using traditional methods will be another possibility.

There are six tented huts for tourists, with two single beds in each. Just in case you were tempted, don't drink the water from the taps in the huts. It is pumped straight out of the Magangé River, and therefore of questionable nutritional value. There is no electricity in the tented huts, just paraffin lamps. There is road access to the camp, but usually visitors arrive by motorised

ON FOOT IN THE FOREST
- Always follow the instructions of your guides and trackers.
- Dress appropriately – lightweight, long-sleeved trousers and shirts are preferable, despite the heat, as these provide proper protection against scratches and bites. Try to avoid bright colours, such as blues and whites, that aren't normally found in the jungle. Blue also attracts biting tsetse flies. Waterproof boots are preferable, though expect to get wet feet anyway. Guides and trackers may be wearing wellington boots, but many people find these uncomfortable for a long walk. Gaiters are not only good for keeping water out, but also biting ants and ticks. If you intend to try to keep dry you should take a waterproof, but anything other than the best quality will not withstand the weight of a rainforest deluge.
- Drink plenty – for a walk of about 9 hours you should carry at least 1 litre of water with you. The guides and trackers know which streams are safe to drink from, or even which rattans and lianas contain water, so you can always rehydrate en route.
- Aim to leave about 1.5m between walkers to avoid bumping into one another.
- Wear insect repellent (except if you are tracking elephants, who are sensitive to the smell).
- Always look carefully before leaning against anything or you might get a nasty surprise. Some stinging caterpillars are camouflaged against bark.

pirogue along the River Ofooué from the small and dusty village of Massengani. This three-hour trip is all part of the adventure, and a good opportunity for spotting wildlife – elephants, crocodiles, monkeys, monitor lizards and birds. As for Mikongo, the all-inclusive daily rate for Ololo is 105,000CFA per person.

When to visit
The park and the Lopé Hotel are open all year, but the best time to visit to see wildlife and plants in flower is during the rainy season. At this time of year animals are easier to track if you are on foot in the forest and there is more to see on a game drive in the savannah.

Getting around
It is not permitted to drive or walk in the park unguided. All treks, game drives and *pirogue* trips must be arranged and paid for at the Lopé Hotel, or in advance via a travel agent.

Getting there and away
Lopé National Park is without doubt the easiest park in Gabon to get to. Not only is it on the *Transgabonais* railway line, but if you have your own 4WD it's a mere 200km (125 miles) from Libreville along mostly surfaced road.

- Do not leave anything behind in the forest – any rubbish, including toilet paper, should be put in a plastic bag and brought back to camp with you for disposal.
- Do not pick any flowers or remove anything from the forest.
- Never touch a wild animal, dead or alive (see box on *Ebola*, pages 74–5).
- Under certain circumstances, you should stand your ground if you find yourself being charged by a wild animal. This is not the case with elephants! Follow the guide's instructions and stay calm, but be prepared to run. You probably won't need to run for very long as elephants tend to lose interest quite quickly once they've made their point.
- If you find yourself dangerously close to a snake, back away very slowly, taking care to avoid making any sudden, aggressive movements.
- If you are going to be camping you will also need camping equipment, a medical kit and a second set of dry clothes to be worn after each day's walk. If it is the rainy season and there is to be any hope of a dry bed, it is a good idea to cover the tents with a tarp. Always choose a campsite with great care, bearing in mind the dangers of animals, snakes and falling trees.
- Finally, and most importantly, don't get lost! This may seem an obvious piece of advice but it has happened, with tragic consequences. On no account and under no circumstances should you wander off on your own in the forest – a trail may look easy to follow when a tracker is leading the way but alone the forest can be very disorientating and dangerous.

By train

Trains from Libreville to La Lopé traditionally leave at 09.00 or 21.00 (see *Chapter 4* for train times). You should buy tickets from Libreville at least three days in advance. The Lopé Hotel can buy your onward ticket for you if necessary. Ask at least the day before you hope to travel. Sometimes you are not able to buy a ticket for Booué in advance, but must go to the train station an hour before the train is due to arrive from Libreville. This is because they need to know how many tickets have already been sold.

By road

The drive from Libreville to Lopé takes over five hours in a 4WD. The road is currently surfaced as far as Alembé, although there is a blip of rough road just after Ndjolé. Be careful on this stretch, particularly after dark. The twisting, turning road and the impatience of logging trucks heading for an overnight stop at Ndjolé accounts for a high number of vehicles run off the road. From Ayem to Lopé, a distance of about 30km (19 miles), the road is very poor and the going is slow. Before reaching Bifoun, the road passes numerous villages. Makeshift stalls of old oil drums display coconuts, bananas and palm wine, and dead monkeys are suspended from poles by their tails. There are occasional restaurants en route, for example on the left-hand side of the road as you drive through Ekouk, but probably the best place to stop for a breather is the half-

A SLICE OF LIFE AT MIKONGO: MONDAY SEPTEMBER 23 2002

James Porteous

There is never a mundane day on this project, but right now, things seem to be particularly positively charged. Nerissa, Raoul and Eme have had a second, excellent contact with gorillas today and we're all on a high, feeling it's a sign of some solid progress with habituation. After most of the day tracking the group of eight or so individuals, they spent three hours with them this afternoon, at less than forty metres, recording some great data. Back at camp they are soaked and tired after ten hours in the forest.

Eme, and Roland, the two new Baka trackers from the remote forest near Makokou, are proving their pygmy heritage and showing uncanny skills, tracking us regularly to gorillas from the faintest traces. They are making the difference. Their acute senses seem other-worldly and make the rest of us quietly consider that perhaps we've lost something.

It's not *all* so good though; the rest of the Mikongo tracking team have refused to work tomorrow. They want more compensation for the dangers and long hours they face in the forest – working conditions and contracts are continuous issues. The forest is majestic and beautiful, but it becomes a hot green slog if you have to go out in it for eight hours every day – especially in the draining humidity of wet season. Enough time out there and one becomes curiously blasé about the elephant, buffalo, gorilla, leopard, snakes and ticks that move in it but ultimately command unconditional respect.

Project leader, Jonathan, back just a day from his month break in Canada, has had to hit the ground running as usual. The tracking team is pivotal to the success of the project and needs to be in the forest every day – gorilla habituation underlies our conservation research and, above all, the ecotourism product that we're building as the financial self-sufficiency generator for conservation effort. No team means no progress, and no data collection. The project can't afford blank days. Some diplomatic motivation and, probably, a hard line, are needed.

Habituating lowland gorillas is enormously challenging because the animals move great distances each day, are very elusive, and must be continually located in difficult forest. Our small combined teams of ex-hunter-trackers and research volunteers are in the forest at first light every morning, for eight hours straight, working towards a five-year horizon. Habituation takes years of effort.

The trackers, ahead, attempt the 'follow' from gorilla clues: fresh dung, recent chews, imprints or, best of all, 'nests' of leaves where the night was spent. These guys are good, very skilled at then staying on the trail through closed forest, right to the feeding group, often pin-pointed by grunts or bellows.

It's at this point that the approach is critical; if the group doesn't flee with the silverbacks' deafening charge, the team must carefully try to make itself obvious at a distance of 40m and attempt to stay with them for as long as possible, ideally until they nest for the night at dusk so they can be easily located the next morning. The team will also use the habituation noise – a 'cluck cluck' – which, by association, conditions the group to the presence of non-threatening humans.

Two years in, and the habituation process is beginning to require a more concentrated effort. We're at a point where the success of the project needs us to better identify groups and put in full days. We have to keep on it and need more good contacts. The habituation work must be delicately balanced with the other project priorities; to increasingly weave tourist clients into our daily routine without interruption, and to push on with the development of the conservation research.

We all have to pitch in here – plans change rapidly. There's a steady stream of tourists beginning two weeks away, but there are a few more immediately important things to think about today. The water pumps at both Mikongo and Ololo camps have broken down, and the wrong replacements have been ordered. Everyone's been using buckets from the river to get by for the last month now, and we're used to the long-distance communication mix-ups. There is also the usual budget problem. We'll guts it out.

The one running project vehicle needs attention too; its 4WD gearing has given up to the severe roads, and a puncture on the last sortie has left us with no spare tyre. It's the first thing on the list.

Otherwise, there are sub-projects to follow up today also. The new research-site construction team needs more cement as soon as possible and it appears that, despite the plans, the new huts have been incorrectly built. The floor planks expected yesterday still haven't arrived and there hasn't been any word on them today. Also, the freshly graded 12km track into camp needs gravel on it, fast. The rains have started and the clay base will reduce to bog unless we get a surface on it.

And, two hours away to the south, at Ololo, the second project camp, there are new *pirogues* for the tourists due in the water this week. A large truck has to come from somewhere to transport them the 50km or so to the Ofooué River. We'll have to call on NSG, the local logging company, again and try to swing their front-end log loader and truck. They are usually happy to help. Also needed are ten local lads with grunt to move, load and unload the dugouts. That should be easy enough; everyone around here is looking for a bit of extra cash, and they like what we're doing.

James Porteous was working in 2002 with the gorilla research team at Kimongo (see page 153) and helping to set up Olol River Camp (see page 155).

way point, Ndjolé (see pages 111–12). From here to Lopé there are occasionally stunning views of the river.

By air

There are no public flights going to Lopé, but there is a small landing strip just across from the hotel. If you are pushed for time but not for funds, then why not charter an aircraft? (See the *Getting around* section in *Chapter 4* for details on how to charter your own aircraft.) Lopé is about an hour and twenty minutes by air from Libreville. Weather permitting, this flight is an excellent sightseeing trip over the sprawl of the city, then the marshy lowlands and finally the dense rainforest, which from above looks like never-ending fields of broccoli. Other than the very occasional logging town or vehicle along RN1, there are no signs of human habitation, a stark reminder of Gabon's underpopulation.

MAKOKOU

Makokou is a small town on the banks of the River Ivindo, and the smallest of all nine of Gabon's regional capitals. After remaining unchanged for years, the city underwent a facelift in honour of the president's proposed visit for the 2002 Independence Day celebrations. There's not much in the way of an established tourist infrastructure, but it's worth a stop of a couple of days at least. As you would expect, there's a bank, petrol stations, post office and several nightclubs near the market, but the real attractions lie outside town.

Getting there and away

There are flights between Libreville and Makokou about once a week. To drive the 600km (373 miles) from Libreville to Makokou – at least 8 hours – requires a 4WD. It's a poor, even dangerous, dirt road after Ovan. Take particular care crossing the bridges. Building a second train line linking the capital to northeast Gabon is no longer a likely future project (the iron is just not lucrative enough), but it is possible to take the train from Libreville to Booué, and from there to take a *taxi-brousse* the 220km (137 miles) to Makokou. Booué is a connection point for travellers to Makokou, who are often required to change *taxi-brousse* here when coming from Libreville, Lambaréné and Lastoursville. Travellers from Franceville should head north via Okandja (ask for the mission here if you need to spend the night). This is a beautiful forest route taking about 8 hours.

Where to stay and eat

There's never been much choice of accommodation in Makokou, and what there has been has not been up to much, so the recent improvements in this area are very welcome. A brand new hotel is being built. Other than that, the **Relais de L'Ivindo** (tel: 90 30 04) is finally being refurbished. This hotel-restaurant in a lovely setting on the edge of the river has operated in a sorry state for years. As in other places where guests are the exception rather than the rule, it is a good idea to order any meals well in advance. **L'Auberge de** l'Assemblée (tel: 50 32 05), in the Mbolo *quartier*, has ten air-conditioned rooms at 12,000CFA. The **Residence Kaczmarek** (tel: 90 30 71, 53 52 52) has popular air-conditioned rooms at 18,000CFA, but it is advisable to book in advance. There are visitors' rooms at the **Catholic Mission**, located in the centre of town not far from Independence Square.

What to see and do

Makokou has not traditionally been a tourist haunt. This is set to change following the creation of Ivindo National Park and Minkébé National Park (see under the relevant parks below for more information). In addition to the parks, a nice thing to do is to spend a day on the river. Despite the fact that there is a road parallel to the river, it is relatively easy to find a *pirogue* in Makokou willing to head upriver (easier in fact than it is to head downriver). The river is wide and calm to the north – there are no rapids – and the chief of the fishing village of Mayibout, for example, is happy for visitors to set up camp here and go walking in the surrounding forest. To the east of Makokou, between the rivers Lodié and Louayé, is the **Mwagné National Park**, known for its massive *bai*, perhaps the largest in the country. This area has sizeable elephant and bongo populations. There are long-term plans to clear the upper River Lodié and construct a route to the *bai*, as well as a tourist camp. Until then the park is inaccessible to tourists.

IVINDO NATIONAL PARK

Southwest of Makokou is the Ivindo National Park. The highlights of the park include its two waterfalls, the Koungou and the Mingouli. By far the greatest are the **Mingouli falls** – a magnificent series of falls that crash down into the river from every direction. A *pirogue* trip through the forest to the falls provides plenty of opportunities to glimpse birds, monkeys and hippos. The dry season is not the best time to go, as the river can get dangerously low and it will be necessary to drag the *pirogue* over the rocks in places.

The park includes the 10,000-hectare (24,710-acre) **Ipassa Reserve**, one of Africa's first protected areas, located directly southwest of Makokou. Incredibly, logging has never been allowed in the Ipassa Reserve (unfortunately that doesn't mean that hunting isn't a problem). A research station has been here since the early 1970s, and at its peak there have been 100 researchers here. Research still continues, but on a much smaller scale. There are currently no guides or facilities for tourists, but there are plans, which would eventually enable tourists to walk researcher trails in search of elephants, buffaloes, gorillas and monkeys. More than 430 species of bird are recorded as living in the Ivindo Basin, making it one of the most rewarding bird-spotting regions in Africa.

Further south in the Ivindo National Park is **Langoué Bai**, a place of unparalleled beauty. The *bai*, which is the pygmy word for forest clearing, is approximately 1km by 300m (3,280ft by 985ft) wide. Its mineral waters lure animals, but above all elephants, out from under the cover of the forest to feed on the nourishing saline soil. The *bai* has been observed by researchers and gradually a database of individual elephants is being compiled to see how regularly they visit and in groups of what size and composition. For example, in the nine months preceding February 2002, there were 2,600 visits to the clearing. The findings provide little known information about the forest elephant, which is much less understood that the savannah elephant. Interestingly, the research suggests that *bai* visits fulfil a social function as well as a nutritional one, by providing a place where the elephants have the space to regroup.

How to visit

Getting to the Mingouli and Koungou waterfalls has traditionally been very difficult, largely because of the absence of motorised *pirogues* waiting to ferry visitors around. There simply hasn't been the demand. Finding a trustworthy *piroguier* was also a concern, and I have heard reports of men who have proved less than reliable. It is hoped that with the creation of the Ivindo National Park such problems will be a thing of the past. WCS is in the process of building a visitors' lodge and viewing platforms at Langoué Bai. A road is under construction south of the *bai*, to facilitate access from the Ivingo train station, southeast of Booué. The Ipassa Research Station has received funds from the European Union for renovation, and the extensive network of paths hitherto used by researchers should be opened up to tourists. A possible future tourist circuit could be to *pirogue* from the bubbling Loa-Loa rapids near the research station to the Koungou falls, then walk some 15km (9 miles) to Langoué Bai (perhaps later taking a 4WD along a forestry road to the pretty Dilo waterfall).

Michael Moussa (tel: 90 30 71, 26 73 61, 53 52 52; email: mmadamo@ yahoo.com) is a politician and businessman who theoretically organises trips to the Mingouli falls. (He even claims he is going to build a mini-camp there.) I say theoretically because in reality he is impossible to get hold of. The cost is about 30,000CFA per person per day for five people. Food and camping gear can be arranged on request. Trips usually take two days, with five hours down river in *pirogue* on day one, and six hours upriver to Makokou on day two.

MINKÉBÉ NATIONAL PARK

The area north of the RN4 and east of the RN2 – encompassing parts of both the Ogooué-Ivindo and Woleu-Ntem – is known as the Massif Forestier de Minkébé. It is an uninhabited area covering 32,000km^2 of dense rainforest, broken only by marshy clearings and impressive grassy inselbergs that pierce the canopy. An estimated 20,000 elephants live here, and there are also sizeable populations of bongos, panthers, giant pangolins, gorillas, chimps, mandrills and buffaloes. In the year 2000, 17% of this total area was established as the Minkébé Reserve. The same 600,000 hectares (1,482,600 acres) in the extreme northeast of Woleu-Ntem were converted into the Minkébé National Park in 2002. Forestry concessions operate in much of the rest, which has inevitably opened up the forest to poachers. The park is rich in tourist possibilities. It is accessible by *pirogue* as well as via hundreds of elephant paths.

The High Ogooué

Historically, the High (Haut) Ogooué region as it stands today has been very cut off from the rest of the country. It even became a Congolese territory (the Niari-Ogooué) in 1925 – because of the building of the railway from Brazzaville to the ocean – and was only reunited with Gabon in 1946. Even then, it was to remain isolated from the other regions until the roads to Libreville and the airport (capable of taking jumbo jets) were built in the 1970s, followed by the *Transgabonais* railway and the Intercontinental Hotel in the 1980s.

The rich resources in the mining towns of Mounana and Moanda in the west of the region played an important role in ensuring that Franceville be brought closer to the capital, but arguably the most important factor was President Omar Bongo himself. Of all the peoples in the High Ogooué – Ombaba, Bawoumbou, Banjabi and so on – the dominant people are the Bateké, the president's people. Bongo hails from Bongoville (originally named Lewai), a village lying between Franceville and Léconi. He has been unceasingly committed to developing his region, but has not yet succeeded in fulfilling his dream to transform it into an important place on the international stage. The airport never handles international flights, and the Intercontinental is never full.

That said, tourists are just beginning to discover the High Ogooué. Admittedly, the tourists are mostly expats already living in Gabon and the attractions are unlikely to lure an international clientele specifically, but the region is beautiful so who knows what lies just around the corner. Poubara's liana bridge and waterfall are a great source of pride to inhabitants of the High Ogooué. The open Bateké Plateaux in the southeast are a wonderful sight for forest-saturated eyes, and the Parks of Lékédi and Léconi mark an innovative move toward South-African style ranching, where tourist safaris and sports hunting can be accommodated on breeding farms.

FRANCEVILLE

Franceville is the capital of the High Ogooué and the third-largest town in the country, with a population of 22,000 people. It began life as Masuku (meaning waterfall), but its name was changed to Francheville by Savorgnan de Brazza in 1880 when he chose the site as a refuge for freed slaves. The French

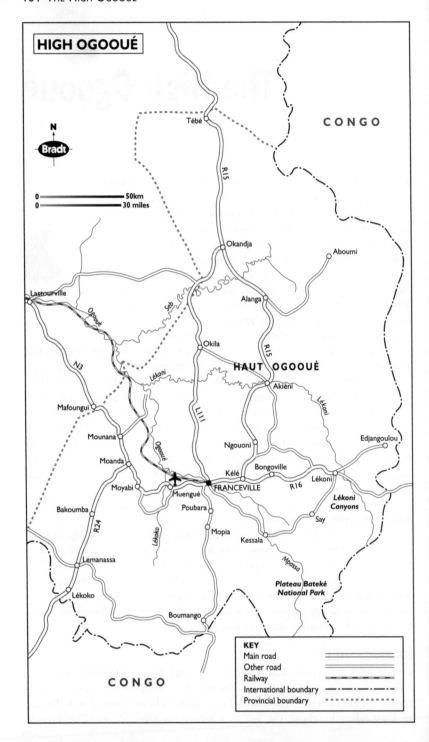

HIGH OGOOUÉ

N

Bradt

0 ——— 50km
0 ——— 30 miles

CONGO

Tébé

R15

Okandja

Aboumi

Lastourville

Ogooué

Alanga

Seb

Okila

HAUT OGOOUÉ

N3

Lékoni

Akiéni

Lékoni

Mafoungui

L111

Mounana

Ngouoni

Edjangoulou

Moanda

Ogooué

Kélé

Bongoville

Moyabi

Muengué

FRANCEVILLE

R16

Lékoni

Lékoni Canyons

Bakoumba

R24

Poubara

Say

Lékoko

Mopia

Kessala

Lemanassa

Mpassa

Plateau Bateké National Park

Lékoko

Boumango

CONGO

KEY
Main road
Other road
Railway
International boundary
Provincial boundary

authorities wasted no time in amending this to Franceville, supposedly because of the region's likeness to certain parts of France.

It's quite difficult to get one's bearings, although it helps to know that the River Mpassa circumvents the town's northeastern shoulder. The town spreads across several hills, with the closest thing to a town centre being the hustle and bustle of the Carrefour Poto-Poto or Carrefour Potos (the streetsellers' roundabout) in the Mpassa valley. The administrative centre (banks, airline agencies and post office) is on a hill to the south. The town has recently undergone an extensive programme of works on the roads, pavements and plumbing. The combination of green spaces between *quartiers*, pleasant hill views and friendly residents makes Franceville a relaxed place to be.

Franceville's landmarks must include the statue of Omar Bongo that stands in Independence Square, also the location of the police station and government offices. There is a commemorative bust of Savorgnan de Brazza just after the mosque as you leave Independence Square behind you and head down the hill to the Carrefour Poto-Poto. The town's most interesting building is the church of **Saint Hilaire**, which was founded in 1899. It's a vast red-tiled building with an improvised football pitch in front. Also of interest is the **Centre International de Recherche Médicale** (CIRMF), although it is closed to the public. This centre of primatology accounts for the sizeable expat community in Franceville, for the most part French scientists. It opened in 1979 to study primates and apply these findings to help man's fight against diseases such as AIDS, Ebola and malaria.

Getting there and away
There are daily flights between Libreville and Mvengué, which is 20km (12.5 miles) west of town. A taxi between the airport and the centre of town costs 5,000CFA. The fast train runs three times a week between Owendo and Franceville. Franceville is 770km (479 miles) from Libreville by road, via Ndjolé and Lastoursville.

Getting around
The usual taxi rates apply: 1,000CFA *course*, 500CFA *demi-course* and 100CFA shared taxi. The town's commercial centre around the Carrefour Poto-Poto is manageable, and best appreciated, on foot.

Where to stay
Léconi Palace Intercontinental Hotel Tel: 67 74 16/17/18; fax: 67 74 19. This is the most luxurious place to stay in Franceville by a long stretch. The rooms are cosy and comfortable, with cable TV and large baths. All 96 rooms have balconies, either overlooking the landscaped pool or Lake Angoubou. Standard rooms are 45,000CFA a night, or 31,500CFA on Fridays, Saturdays and Sundays. Junior suites are 75,000CFA and the presidential suites are 125,000CFA.

Beverley Hills Hotel tel: 67 06 18. This hotel is owned by the ex-wife of the president, the singer Patience Dabiny. Properly maintained, it could be very nice, but

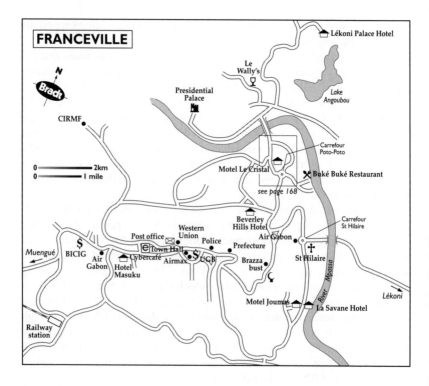

FRANCEVILLE

the pool is dirty and the restaurant smells musty. The rooms, however, are comfortable and large, with thick carpets, cable TV and air conditioning. The best part is the swanky 1970s-style reception area, with its squashy, leather armchairs and coffee tables. Room rates are 35,000CFA, or 25,000CFA at the weekend.

Hotel Masuku Tel: 67 73 51. The Masuku is not a bad option. There is a pool, surrounded by *paillottes* and overlooked by the terrace restaurant. There are 30 rooms at 18,500CFA and five suites at 35,500CFA.

Le Crystal This is definitely the best-value budget hotel in town at 13,000CFA per night for a large double bedroom with en-suite shower and toilet. For 15,000CFA you can have a whole apartment, comprising double bedroom, bathroom with bath, and a huge sitting room with table and armchairs. Some of the apartments also have a TV. The staff are friendly and the rooms are clean and air conditioned. The location – a 3-minute walk from the Carrefour Poto-Poto – is great for those who want to be able to walk to the market and to restaurant-bars.

Hotel La Savane Tel: 23 01 61. There is an unfinished feel to La Savane, as if the builders left before the job was done. The bar-restaurant *paillotte* is right on the river, which means a good view but lots of mosquitoes. There are four small, stuffy rooms with fan and tiny bathroom for 10,000CFA. The three rooms with air conditioning (15,000CFA) are larger and better decorated. A full breakfast with eggs and ham will set you back 2,500CFA.

Motel P. Joumas Tel: 67 04 44. There is a quiet, villagey feel to the location of the Motel Joumas, but the rooms are small, dark and drab, and no bargain either at

12,000CFA a night. One attraction of the hotel was the good Chinese restaurant opposite, but this has now closed (it is expected to reopen as an African restaurant). **Auberge Apily** Tel: 67 72 84. Another small hotel in a quiet location. There are 13 rooms in total: 7 at 12,000CFA with air conditioning and a small partitioned corner for the shower and toilet, and 6 at 8,000CFA with a fan. There is a tiny bar-restaurant.

Where to eat and drink

The **Buké Buké** (tel: 67 70 71) is the best restaurant in town, serving excellent fish, gambas or steak, with fried bananas, French fries, papaya gratin or courgette gratin. Choose three courses for 7,500CFA or a main course for 5,000CFA. Sunday lunchtimes the tables are full of Franceville's expats. It is right on the river Mpassa; to get there, turn left 500m after Le Garage restaurant and continue straight to the bottom of the hill. **Le Garage** (tel: 07 23 03) is a relaxing place to have a beer, a snack (sandwiches, hamburgers), or a proper meal. It serves both local and European dishes, and does *grillades* in the evening. The tables on the small terrace look onto the hustle and bustle of the street.

The everyday food at the **Léconi Palace Hotel** restaurant is unfortunately nothing special, although it has a pleasant location at the poolside. That said, the buffet on Sundays at midday is really quite good (12,000CFA), and the Saturday night *grillades* are also worthwhile. Check the prices of the wines before ordering, as they are hugely overpriced. The hotel also has a bar and nightclub, which is popular on Friday and Saturday nights. Other nightclubs are at **Le Crystal** hotel and the large bar-club called **Le Wally's**.

There is a variety of places to eat in the Quartier Poto-Poto. **Espace Geo Pub** (tel: 04 04 00) is part pizzeria, part arcade (video games and table football). As you'd expect, it is very popular with young Francevillois. The pizzeria also does a takeaway service. Prices start at 3,500CFA for a margherita. **Bord du Mer** is primarily a lively bar playing a mixture of loud and popular African and Western music. It also serves reasonably priced food, although service is very slow. The restaurant **Fast Food 5ième Dimension** (tel: 21 65 72, 21 98 66) may look a bit ramshackle from the street, but the food is reliable and the restaurant is open everyday 08.00–13.00. It serves a bit of everything – salads, fish, steaks – but specialises in local dishes that include smoked chicken and saltfish. If what you want is not on the menu, the owner Daniee will try to accommodate your request. A bit further along the same street is **La Muguet**, which does mediocre *grillades*.

The **Boulangerie Patisserie Poto-Poto** has a coffee shop attached. It's a great place to have coffee and pastries in the morning while watching the TV. There is also the **Boulangerie de la Paix** in the market. Past the market are *les maquis*, small bars that look like nothing during the day but are transformed by night. **Chez Ogoula** is one of the most popular for dancing. There's no sign, but it's diagonally opposite the **Exodus Bar**. The music is good and the atmosphere friendly. Street stalls selling meat brochettes for 100CFA a piece keep dancers sustained throughout the night.

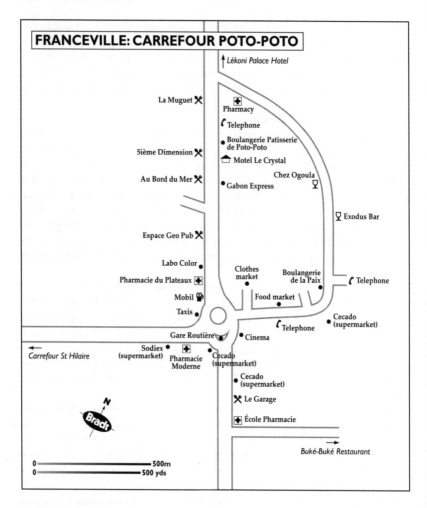

FRANCEVILLE: CARREFOUR POTO-POTO

Useful information

The best place to go shopping in town, whether for fresh produce or clothes, is the **market**, where West African and Lebanese sellers are in the majority. There is also a massive **CECADO** supermarket here. The best pharmacy in town is **La Pharmacie Moderne**, on the Carrefour Poto-Poto. If you are looking for a Visa-card machine, there is one at the **BICIG** bank. Franceville has quite reliable internet connection. The **Cybercafé** near the BICIG bank is open Monday–Friday 07.30–12.00, 15.00–20.00 and Saturday–Sunday 08.00–22.00. The price is 900CFA/hour.

What to see and do

There is a golf club 10km out of the city centre heading towards Léconi, or it's possible to use the swimming pool at the Léconi Palace Hotel for a small charge or the cost of a meal. Essentially though, after a couple of good nights on the town, there is little to keep the visitor in Franceville. This is the most usual entry point for visitors to the High Ogooué, not a place to be visited for its own sake.

Patrick Mennesson is a Frenchman who has lived in the region for over a decade. He organises trips to Poubara (half day/25,000CFA per person), the canyons of the Batéké Plateau (full day/80,000CFA per person) and Kissala for elephant trekking (half day/55,000CFA per person). He also runs motorised *pirogue* trips to the Djoumou Falls from the Buké Buké restaurant. This is a very relaxing way to pass a couple of hours. The price of the trip is 6,000CFA per person, or a minimum of 15,000CFA. Patrick has a three-person minimum rule for most of his trips. If you intend going to Franceville for a jam-packed couple of days, he will do you a special deal on trips and can also get his clients 30% reduction on the rates at the Léconi Palace Hotel. Drop in to see him at the Pharmacie Moderne, which he runs, or telephone him (tel: 67 70 71). He should be given at least one day's notice.

Those with their own means of 4WD transport can obviously access these places – except for Djoumou – by themselves. In the case of the elephant trekking, drive to **Kissala** (about an hour from Franceville) and ask for the guide Hilaire. He charges 6,000CFA per person, or a minimum of 15,000CFA. If you want to be sure he will be around, you can get a message to him via his sister Romaine, who works at the Hotel Masuku. Hilaire will take you on a wet and muddy walk through the forest alongside the Mpassa river. If you're lucky you'll find elephants after about an hour and a half's walk. The best time to go is in the rainy season, either very early in the morning or late in the afternoon.

POUBARA

The Poubara waterfall and liana bridge are essentially the emblem of the High Ogooué region. When Savorgnan de Brazza arrived in the High Ogooué in the late 1970s, he and his companions were amazed at how developed the societies were, in particular in the spheres of agriculture and the building of liana bridges. Poubara's bridge and falls are possibly the most commercially advanced tourist attraction in the country, by which I mean there is a long and complex printed list of tariffs. For visitors to cross the bridge – naturally it's free for the villagers – costs 1,000CFA per person, and to continue on to see the falls is another 2,000CFA. To take photographs is an extra 1,000CFA, to have a picnic an extra 2,000CFA and to camp overnight an extra 4,000CFA. To get to the falls, turn right after the bridge, walk through the little village and follow the road up the hill. About half-way up there is a small track leading off to the right into the forest. From here it takes about 15 minutes to walk to the falls. If you want the security of a guide to show you the way, it will cost you another 2,000CFA.

In my opinion both the bridge and the falls are well worth the entrance fee. The bridge is 52.5m long and hangs 6m above fast-flowing water. It has to be replaced every year, a process that takes three months. The new bridge is built above the existing bridge, which is only cut down when it's time to start the whole process again. The result is that there are in fact two bridges, and crossing while the new bridge is in the early stages of construction can feel a bit precarious. The falls crash down from a height of some 70m; expect to get sprayed at the viewpoint.

Getting there and away

Excursions to Poubara can be organised by Patrick Mennesson, the Parc de la Lékédi or the Léconi Palace Hotel in Franceville. If you are driving yourself, you have two possibilities. There is a right turn to the falls off the Franceville to Moanda road, just before Mvengué airport. The road is signposted for the Yugoslavian road construction company SOCO BTP, and is sandwiched between an old brewery and an electricity plant. A 4WD is not absolutely essential although the road is fairly rough in parts. From the main road to the falls is about a 30-minute drive. Alternatively, leave Franceville by the train-station road. Go straight for 15km and then take the right *piste* for a further 5km to reach the falls.

MOANDA

Nestled between two mountains, Mount Boudinga and Mount Moanda, is the bustling modern town of Moanda, with a population of about 23,000 people. This is not a tourist town, but it is an important town, nothing short of the manganese capital of Gabon and the third-biggest manganese producer in the world. The company that made it all happen is the Compagnie Minière de l'Ogooué (COMILOG), whose offices perch on a hill above the town centre.

COMILOG have been mining manganese in the area since 1957. By 1959 the company had started work on the construction of a 76km (47-mile) cable car linking Moanda to M'binda in the Congo. From M'binda a train carried the manganese to waiting boats at Point Noire. But after just 30 years of operation the cable car became redundant, and so did hundreds of workers. With the arrival of the Transgabonnais railway in 1986 the manganese could now be directly transported to the Gabonese coast, which was obviously preferable. In the year 2001, more than 1.7 million tonnes of manganese were transported via the railroad.

Moanda's twin mining town is **Mounana**, a smaller place of just 8,000 inhabitants. It lies 25km (15.5 miles) to the northwest on RN3. Mounana's equivalent of COMILOG was the Compagnie des Mines d'Uranium de Franceville (COMUF), who were founded in 1958 to mine the local uranium deposits. They did so until a combination of factors – a decline in world demand, increased competition and, ultimately, much smaller yields – forced them to close in the late 1990s. Ever since the town's conundrum has been to provide alternative sources of employment. The land around Mounana and Moanda is dotted with agricultural projects on a larger scale (sugar cane, fruit and vegetables). In 1997 the quality **Auberge du Lac** (tel: 62 03 14, 62 03 15/16/17) opened, with clean and attractive rooms starting at 25,000CFA. There is also a panoramic restaurant overlooking Mounana's artificial lake, and an ultra-modern leisure complex with a boat-style nightclub and billiard bar.

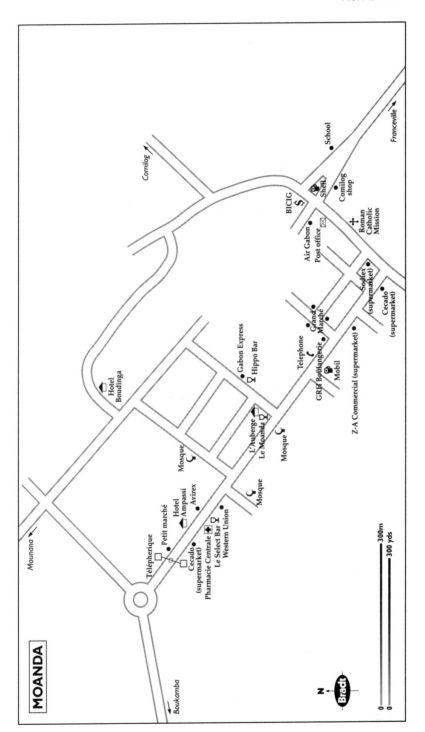

MOANDA

172 THE HIGH OGOOUÉ

Getting there and away

There are flights about three times a week from Libreville to Moanda. Moanda is also the penultimate stop on fast trains from Libreville to Franceville, which run three times a week. Libreville to Moanda is scheduled to take about 8 hours, but 9–10 is a more usual minimum. To get from Moanda to Franceville requires a short journey of just 50km (31 miles) along the surfaced RN3. Lastoursville is 120km (75 miles) northwards on the RN3, passing Mounana on the way. There are *taxis-brousse* leaving Moanda regularly in both directions.

Where to stay and eat

The **Hotel du Mont Boudinga** (tel: 66 15 72) is the largest and most luxurious option, with en-suite facilities and air conditioning as standard. Rooms cost 17,000CFA/21,000CFA/23,000CFA for a single/double/suite. Non-residents can use the swimming pool at a charge of 1,500CFA. The restaurant has a daily set menu for 7,500CFA. The hotel also has a nightclub. The **Hotel Ampassi** and **L'Auberge** both have rooms for 10,000CFA. It is also possible to stay cheaply in air-conditioned rooms at the **Catholic Mission**, which is right in the centre of town. There are plenty of shops (Cecado, Sodiex, Z-A Commercial) and bar-clubs (Hippo Bar, Bar L'Escalier, Le Select Bar, Le Moanda). CAMILOG's input into Moanda has even stretched to a nice, nine-hole golf course.

LÉKÉDI PARK

Like everything else in the small town of **Bakoumba** (population 2,500), Lékédi Park owes its conception and creation to the mining company COMILOG (see under *Moanda* on page 170), who decided to create it in 1990. As Station F of the cable car and the location of the command and maintenance stations, Bakoumba was hit hard by the cable-car closure. The impetus behind the founding of the Societe d'Exploitation du Parc de la Lékédi (SODEPAL) was threefold.

The first aim was to provide work for former COMILOG cable-car employees, albeit at a reduced wage. The second was to breed animals for consumption, notably fish, antelope, buffalo and bush pigs. As part of this process, impala and ostriches were flown in from Namibia and three fisheries were set up. Fish production now stands at 100 tonnes of Nile perch a year, which is sold in the local markets of Bakoumba, Moanda and Franceville. Aside from the fish, organised sale of meat is not yet in place.

The third aim was to create a park where tourists could see animals such as primates in a protected environment, and where at some point sports hunters could shoot animals on foot (buffaloes and antelope primarily). The park is divided into three separately fenced modules (access is through 18 gates), which correspond to the three stages of its expansion between 1990 and 1995. Module 1 is 650 hectares, Module 2 is 1,750 hectares and Module 3 is a massive 11,600 hectares.

Getting there and away

There are a number of ways to get to Bakoumba, the base from which to visit Lékédi Park. Moanda (see page 170) has an airport and a train station and is

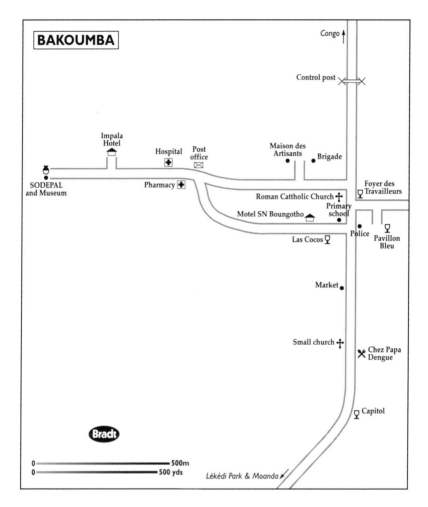

just over an hour's drive north of the park. There are more regular flights to Mvengué (1.5 hours to Bakoumba). The Hotel Impala offers transfers of 15,000CFA (Moanda) and 20,000CFA (Mvengué) per person (minimum two people).

The park is about 110km (68 miles) from Franceville along mostly surfaced road, but a 4WD is advisable. In the dry season the drive from Libreville can be done in 10 hours, but a 4WD is essential. The tarmac runs out past Moanda. Work on the Bakoumba road was started in the 1998 elections but never completed. The population is eagerly awaiting the lead-up to the next elections in 2005 when it is hoped the road will be finished.

Getting around

It is not permitted to drive or walk in the park unguided. All excursions must be arranged and paid for at the Impala Hotel.

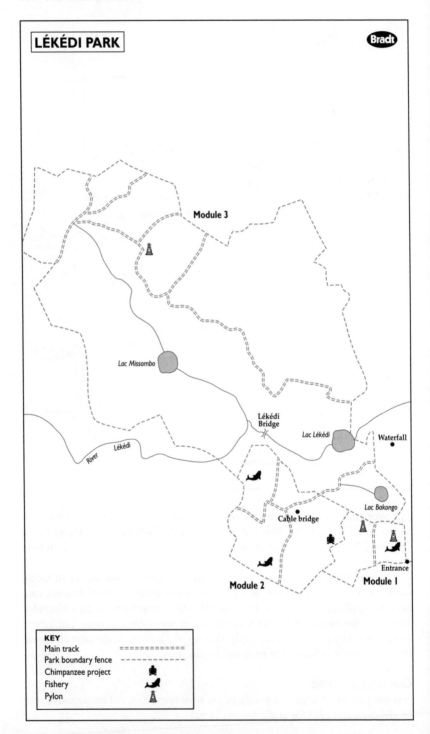

Where to stay and eat

The Lékédi Park (www.sodepal.com) is just a 15-minute drive from Bakoumba, which is where visitors will stay. The **Impala Hotel** is the Lékédi Park's official hotel. The hotel occupies buildings that were once the largest of CAMILOG's maintenance and command stations. The buildings have changed very little, which accounts for the hotel's dilapidated charm. There are six double rooms at 18,000CFA and ten villas sleeping four to six adults plus children (36,000–50,000CFA). Rooms are calm, spacious, air conditioned and sparsely furnished. Meals at the hotel are served under a *paillotte* overlooking the swimming pool and tennis court. Portions are generous, but the menu is not very varied (Nile perch is the chef's speciality). Breakfast is 3,000CFA, lunch or dinner 7,000CFA. There is a huge colonial-style bar.

There are two basic *cases de passage* in Bakoumba each costing 5,000CFA a night. One is in the market, the other is called Motel S N Boungotho and is in the little street behind the main church.

There is a number of bars in town. They include the **Foyer des Travailleurs**, which was founded for COMILOG workers, and the small but happening **Les Cocos**. There is a restaurant called **Chez Papa Dengue** on the left-hand side beyond the main commercial strip as you head towards the park. Papa Dengue is a retired COMILOG worker turned restaurant-owner. The '*menu du jour*', invariably bushmeat, is chalked on a blackboard outside the restaurant. If you are tempted, please read the box on Ebola (pages 74–5).

Excursions from the Impala Hotel

In two full days visitors can make four excursions, which is about the right amount for really getting the measure of the park. Excursions are made on foot in the forest, by boat on one of the lakes, or in 4WD across the savannah. Excursions cost on average 8,000CFA. The usual introductory excursion traverses Modules 1 and 2, taking in the fisheries, the chimpanzee project, the ostriches and the thrilling cable bridge, which stretches for 365m (1,198ft) above the forest canopy of the Mioula valley. It is made up of ten cables, a direct attempt to reuse the skills of COMILOG workers in setting up the park. On every drive buffalo and antelope are spotted. Wednesday is fishing day, when visitors can see vast nets of muddy fish being emptied into barrels for sorting.

The hotel can arrange overnight stays for up to four people, including the guide, in the largest of the three electricity pylons in the park, followed by an early-morning walk in the forest (20,000CFA per person, or 30,000CFA with supper). It's very cosy at just 5m², but there are windows on each side with magnificent views of the surrounding forest. After dark, it's possible to see the lights of Moanda to the north. In the morning the forest is covered in mist and reverberates to the sound of monkeys and birds. The pylon was erected in the far-northwest corner of the park, which is the best part for walks in the forest, when lucky visitors will see gorillas or chimps. For the same reason a tented satellite camp is planned in the same part of the park. It should be ready for use by the dry season of 2003.

A nice short walk is to the falls just outside the southeastern corner of Module 3. The descent is very steep, but a cable banister has been rigged up to help prevent skidding, especially likely in the rainy season. Guests can easily visit the Poubara Falls (see pages 169–70) on their way to or from Mvengué airport.

The tiny, tiled building across from the main church is the **Maison des Artisanats**, where they sell some pottery and baskets. Follow the little road downhill from here and on the right are a potter's workshop and a man weaving with raffia.

The hotel also offers a tour of the various SODEPAL activities taking place in the vicinity of the hotel, namely the vivarium, the mushroom project, the breeding of cane rats and the small museum. The museum is in the former control room of the cable car. There are pictures of the cable car, bits of pottery found in the area and a couple of charts.

When to visit

The park can be visited at any time, but the best time is probably December, January and February. In the heart of the long dry season the grass is drier and animals tend to take cover in the forest. What's more, large groups of school children come for visits of up to three weeks in July and August, funded by Elf, Shell and CAMILOG.

THE BATEKÉ PLATEAU

Tucked away in the far southeastern corner of Gabon is a landscape different from any other that the country has to offer. The change occurs not long after leaving **Bongoville**, which lies at the mid-point between Franceville and Léconi. Bongoville, originally known as Lewai, was renamed to honour President Omar Bongo, who was born here in 1935. This small roadside village has benefited from the presidential connection with better-quality housing than neighbouring villages, a large stadium and a quality hotel, the Motel de Bongoville, which has rooms for 15,000CFA.

From this point on, the road cuts through endless, gently undulating plains of open grassland. The most remarkable feature of this new landscape is the almost total absence of trees. On the left, at a point with fabulous views in both directions, is Bongoville's cemetery. The Bateké highlands are the source of the River Ogooué, and are home to an impressive number of birds, some of which are not found elsewhere in Gabon. Before reaching Léconi, the road passes through **Souba**. This tiny village has a state-of-the-art conference centre (used for a single conference many years ago) and about 100 residents. **Lake Souba** – almost 20km (12.5 miles) down the small left turn before the Souba antenna – is famous for its amazing blue colour. It's possible to camp and fish here, but a 4WD is absolutely essential.

The small town of **Léconi** is the other side of the River Léconi. There is a hotel, a market, a bakery, a petrol station, a post office and two bars (Oxygène and Kataiaye). It is also the location of Andza, Gabon's only mineral-water company. Mostly, though, it is a base from which to visit the Léconi canyons and Léconi Park (see below). Léconi is the last place of tourist interest before the border with Congo.

The southern uninhabited part of the plateau has been designated the **Bateké Plateau National Park** because of its beautiful rolling savannah landscape and its exceptional bird diversity (some species are not to be found anywhere else in Gabon). A rough ride south in a 4WD across sand, followed by a 3-hour *pirogue* trip, leads to the **Projet Protection des Gorilles.** This is a private project covering an area of about 2,590km² (1,000 square miles) on the border with Congo. It was established by Howletts charitable trust to cater for gorillas reared in captivity at Howletts Wild Animal Park in southern England to be returned to the wild. At present, the camp is strictly out of bounds to visitors, but an airstrip and tourist lodge may figure in future plans.

The Léconi Canyons

There are about four canyons in the area, but the prettiest and most visited lie 10km (6 miles) beyond Léconi town. Like Lake Souba, they can only be reached in a 4WD. Even if you have your own car, it is best to take a guide, as the route is not always obvious (during the rainy season sections of it are flooded). The road emerges at the lip of a cliff without warning, and you'll find yourself looking down into twin canyons, the larger 'male' canyon and the smaller 'female' one behind. Strictly speaking these are not canyons, but semi-circular craters in the rock, with knobbly fingers of rock poking up from the crater floor, and clumps of tall trees interspersed between them. At sunset the rocks glow red and gold. The lake beyond is the **Lac aux Caïmans** (Caiman Lake), which should probably be named Crocodile Lake. Either way, hunters have ensured that there's very little here anymore.

Léconi Park

Popularly referred to as Léconi Park, the park's official name is **Société d'Exploration des Plateaux Bateké** (SDB). This is a private park founded in 1997. The park circumference is nearly 70km (43.5 miles), and the park area is 28,000 hectares (69,188 acres), of which 70% is grass savannah and 30% patches of rainforest. By the year 2007, sports hunting – of local and imported breeds, such as at the Lékédi Park (see pages 172–6) – will be on offer here. But for the moment, the park is a quiet place to relax and reflect. For many visitors, the scenery is its greatest attraction, even though in a single afternoon you are almost guaranteed to see eland (type of deer), great kudu, impala and springboks (all imported from Namibia). The zebras (also Namibian), jackals, civets and bush pigs are more difficult to spot. A couple of days spent camping in the park is the best way to profit from the beautiful landscape and serenity. The *pistes*, or tracks, are colour-coded to make driving around easier. The park management is also experimenting with growing pineapples, mangos and avocados for sale.

Getting there and away

Léconi is 100km (62 miles) from Franceville, despite what some of the road signs say. The road deteriorates dramatically after Kélé and there are many

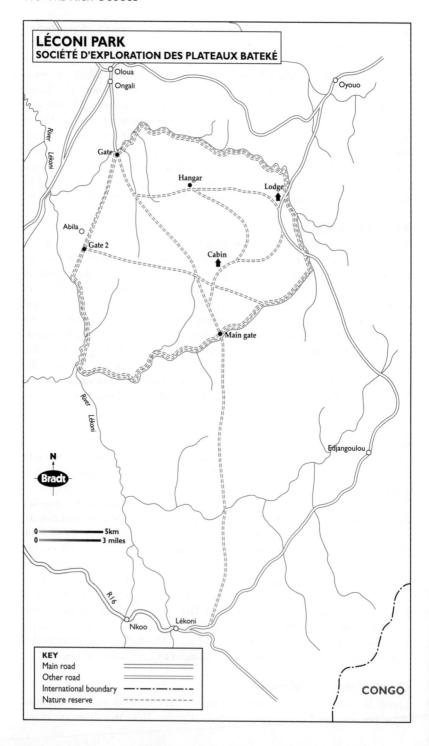

LÉCONI PARK
SOCIÉTÉ D'EXPLORATION DES PLATEAUX BATEKÉ

accidents. *Taxis-brousse* run between Franceville and Léconi daily, leaving Léconi from the big tree on the main road by the turn-off to the Léconi Hotel. If you don't have your own transport, you could contact the Léconi Park to see if a lift would be possible from Franceville or Moanda (they can also arrange special transfers). For a day trip to Léconi and the plateau, including lunch at the Léconi Hotel, contact Patrick Mennesson at the Pharmacie Moderne in Franceville (tel: 67 70 71).

How to visit

If you are not camping in the park (or at another location of your choice), then your only accommodation option is the **Hotel de Léconi** (tel: 69 90 03) in Léconi town. Fortunately the hotel is friendly, inviting and good value. Rooms are 15,200CFA, or 13,000CFA without TV. A set three-course meal in the restaurant costs 6,500CFA. The Senegalese hotel manager, Mr. Ndiaye, is an enthusiast of the region and will happily arrange excursions to the Léconi canyon, or a car and chauffeur to visit the area more generally (about 25,000CFA for 4 hours).

Visitors to the park can use their own car, with or without a park driver. The sandy roads must be taken slowly. The entry charge per person is 5,000CFA (children under 12 years are free). To hire a car and driver costs 15,000CFA, to be paid in addition to the entrance for each person. Drivers should be tipped at the end. To **camp** in the park costs 5,000CFA per tent, plus 5,000CFA per car. The park has an open-sided *cabane traditionelle* (cabin) made of bamboo and lianas, which makes an excellent picnic spot. There is also a small, rustic lodge on the white *piste* equipped with a barbecue (wood supplied), basic cooking utensils, and pineapples and mango trees in the garden. The cost is 15,000CFA per night. Take a sleeping bag and all provisions – bear in mind that food shopping is best done before arriving in Léconi.

To book excursions or the lodge in Léconi Park, contact the park manager Vincent Deschaumes (tel: 27 97 18; email: vdeschaumes@caramail.com), or Mme Tarteret at COMILOG (tel: 66 10 33). It is also possible to rent a park vehicle with driver/guide (or if you have a car then a guide only) to visit the Léconi canyon (10,000CFA). A good time to visit is June, when the new grass is shooting through the charred ground left by the annual savannah fires, and the animals are out. From October to January the orchids are in flower on the plateau.

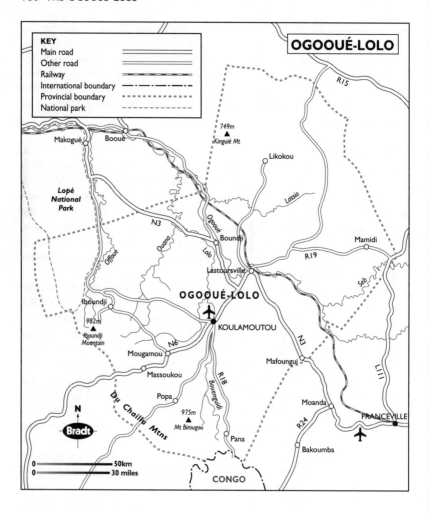

KEY
Main road
Other road
Railway
International boundary
Provincial boundary
National park

OGOOUÉ-LOLO

R15

749m
▲
Kinguié Mt

Makogué   Booué

Likokou

Lassio

Lopé
National
Park

N3

Ogooué

Ouana

Lolo

Boundji

Mamidi

Offoué

R19

Seb

Lastoursville

Iboundji

OGOOUÉ-LOLO

982m
▲
Iboundji
Mountain

✈
KOULAMOUTOU

N3

L111

N6

Mougamou

Massoukou

Mafoungui

Du Chaillu Mtns

Popa

Bouenguidi

R18

975m
▲
Mt Birougou

Moanda

FRANCEVILLE

Bradt

N

R24

✈

Pana

Bakoumba

0 ———— 50km
0 ———— 30 miles

CONGO

Above Explore tour bus to Porto Alegre, São Tomé (PM)

Below Roca Bombain, São Tomé, is one of the few plantations to have diversified into tourism, providing simple accommodation in the grand old plantation owner's house. (PM)

Left Banana Beach, Príncipe – the setting for a Bacardi advert (PM)

Above Street stall, Santo Antonio, Príncipe (PM)

Below Príncipe coast, with Jockey Cap Island in the distance (PM)

The Ogooué-Lolo

The Ogooué-Lolo is crossed by the Ogooué and its tributary the River Lolo, hence its name. A third important river, the Ofooué, marks the natural border between this region and the Ngounié region. In terms of landscape these two regions are remarkably similar, both being green and mountainous. The dense forest has long attracted forestry companies, and more recently scientists and conservationists. The du Chaillu mountains are rich in endemic species – just how rich is not yet known – and excursions on foot guarantee encounters with numerous monkeys and birds (see also *Birougou National Park* in *Chapter 8: The Ngounié*). Climbing Mount Iboundji represents the biggest challenge, but there are other, less-strenuous alternatives. The road directly south of the region's capital, Koulamoutou, leads to the Congo border via Pana.

KOULAMOUTOU

The regional capital since 1960, Koulamoutou, is a small town of about 10,000 residents, built at the confluence of the River Lolo and its tributary the River Bouenguidi. The town is divided in two by the River Bouenguidi, which is crossed by two bridges. On the Rive Droite (Right Bank) are the airport and the *gare routière*, while on the Rive Gauche (Left Bank) are the administrative buildings and the market. All the streets are surfaced and there are hotels on both sides. In spite of all this construction, Koulamoutou feels refreshingly green, no doubt the result of its fresh climate and the comparative lack of biting insects.

The town has been shaped significantly by the efforts and money of the current Minister of Tourism, who was born in the nearby village of Popa. He is very keen to promote Koulamoutou as a state-of-the-art urban centre not to be missed. Ever. Not only does he own all the hotels and taxis in town, but he has been the creative impetus behind all new projects. His insatiable 21st-century vision of the city includes a massive hypermarket, which will be well out of the reach of most of the town's residents. Koulamoutou is one of two cities chosen to host the Independence Day celebrations in August 2003, so it will be interesting to see what further improvements are made to the town in preparation for President Bongo's fleeting visit.

Getting there and away

There are regular flights to and from Libreville and *taxis-brousse* heading in both directions along the RN6, to Lastoursville and to Ndendé. At present there is no car-hire agency in town, but no doubt it's just a matter of time. That said, it is possible to hire a car with a compulsory chauffeur for use within town (daily rate about 55,000CFA). This can be arranged through any of the upper-end hotels.

Where to stay and eat

Given that the vast majority, if not all, of the hotels are owned by the current Minister of Tourism, this explains why there is a general hotel number (tel: 65 52 65). The **Hotel Bouenguidi** is the largest hotel (40 rooms) and the clientele are mostly business travellers. This is a luxury establishment with a pool, restaurant and bar. Room rates range from 24,000CFA to 64,000CFA, and there are bungalows at 100,000CFA a night. The riverside **Residence-Hotelier Bishi** is where the president and his ministers stay. This is the last word in luxury. It has a cobbled drive, two swimming pools, two bars, a large restaurant and rooms at 200,000CFA in little towers and even on an island reached by a short liana bridge.

A new hotel, **Hotel Biki**, is being built near the market, a conveniently central location. The hotel should be open at some point in 2003, with rooms priced at around 20,000CFA. **Chez Jaqueline** is a restaurant-bar serving good *grillades*. There are also rooms for about 16,000CFA. The **Catholic Mission** (tel: 65 51 59) is a popular place to stay for those on a budget, but it is often booked up. Even so, it is worth a look, not just for its striking red-brick church and tower, but for the magnificent view from its elevated position. In the same price range is **Hotel Le Pacifique**, which has rooms with fan for 7,000CFA.

What to see and do

Koulamoutou is very well catered for in terms of urban entertainment. There is a cinema and a **museum** dedicated to traditional crafts, including masks and musical instruments. There are also plenty of shops, bars, clubs, discos, restaurants and hotels – enough for many more visitors than it currently receives – and it seems as if new places are springing up all the time. More importantly, the town makes a good base from which to explore the **du Chaillu mountains**. The climate is noticeably fresher and cooler in the mountains, so come prepared.

Much to the Minister of Tourism's excitement, a succession of waterfalls, the **Mbougou falls**, has been discovered about 40km (25 miles) out of town on the Popa road, near the village of Mambouete. While not quite in the same league as the Mingouli falls (see page 161), they were pounced on as the perfect opportunity for attracting tourists. Work began immediately to construct an access road through the forest, erect shelters with rustic tables and chairs, and build a bridge over the River Siby. Having crossed the newly built bridge, it's a short walk to the falls along the River Bouenguidi. By the time this guidebook has been published, the works should be finished and organised trips will be on offer from Koulamoutou.

Not taking the turn-off towards the falls will bring you instead to the mountain village of **Popa**, about 90km (56 miles) to the southwest of Koulamoutou. Popa is a traditional centre of *Bwiti* and the site of a peak 975m (3,199 feet) high. Ask for a guide to take you to the summit. The climb is short (about an hour) but tough, but the reward is the magnificent views of the surrounding lush countryside. There is a decent hotel in the village, with rooms for around 15,000CFA.

A more demanding mountain climb is **Mount Iboundji** (982m), a steep-sided plateau overlooking the surrounding forest. Iboundji has been proposed as a biodiversity sanctuary. If this status is granted then work would be done developing footpaths. At present, the climbs are probably best left to experienced walkers. To reach the village at the foot of the mountain requires a 4WD. Leave Koulamoutou on the Mimongo road and turn right at Mougamou. Ask for a guide at the village (4,000–5,000CFA per day) who can take you either to the 100m (328ft) high waterfall round the back of the mountain (3 hours), or to the summit (5 hours). Both routes are very forested, steep, rocky and slippery. With the appropriate camping gear, it would be possible to camp on the mountain and then make the descent the next day.

LASTOURSVILLE

Lastoursville stretches along the River Ogooué, surrounded by dense forest. There are several small islands in the section of river that flows through town, one of which is known as *L'Île Fétiche*, apparently once a depot for slaves to be transported to Lambaréné. This site was to become the town called Mandji. The name Mandji lasted until 1883, when Savorgnan de Brazza founded a post here and replaced it with Maadiville, or 'oil town' (a reference to the concentration of oil palms). Its current name was decided upon in 1886, a year after a young French engineer, François Rigail de Lastours, died here from a severe bout of malaria. His tomb lies with those of other Frenchman in a bamboo grove not far from the Hotel Ngoombi.

The Adouma people did not exactly welcome the exacting Europeans and their demands. About 5km (3 miles) out of town on the Koulamoutou road is the **Catholic Mission of Saint-Pierre-Claver**, a complex of buildings with a beautiful towered church. The mission's first attempt to make a home here in the 1880s was aborted after attacks by the Adouma people, and the mission was only finally reinstated in the 1940s. The French administration's reception was equally hostile. They were driven off in 1896, but reinstated their post in 1909. Despite the fact that the rebellions continued, Lastoursville operated as the leading town of the Ogooué-Lolo.

Lastoursville is known for its *grottes*, or **caves**, carved into a cliff side at the edge of the forest above town. The caves should ideally be visited in the dry season, and always with a guide. To find one, ask for advice at the mission of the Hotel Ngoombi. Wear boots with a good grip, preferably waterproof, and take a good torch, also waterproof.

There are several rapids in the area, which accounts for the navigational skill of the Adouma. It should not be too difficult to negotiate with one of the *piroguiers* to visit the **Doumé rapids**, which lie 30km (19 miles) upriver. These rapids can also be reached by driving to the village of Doumé, but the trip by river is both more relaxing and more fun.

Getting there and away

There are *taxis-brousse* from Lastoursville to Koulamoutou and Moanda leaving at random times. Libreville is less than 600km (373 miles) away by road – starting with the RN3, then the RN2 and the RN1 – but passengers might have to change at Ndjolé. An alternative way to break up the journey would be to stop off at the Lopé Reserve. Lastoursville is also linked to Libreville and Franceville by the express-train line.

Where to stay and eat

At the top end is the **Mulundu Hotel** (tel: 73 31 56), which has a swimming pool, restaurant, and en-suite rooms with air conditioning. Next is the **Hotel Ngoombi** (tel: 64 00 61), which has air-conditioned rooms, a restaurant and a nightclub. The cheapest place to stay is the Catholic mission.

Part Three

São Tomé and Príncipe

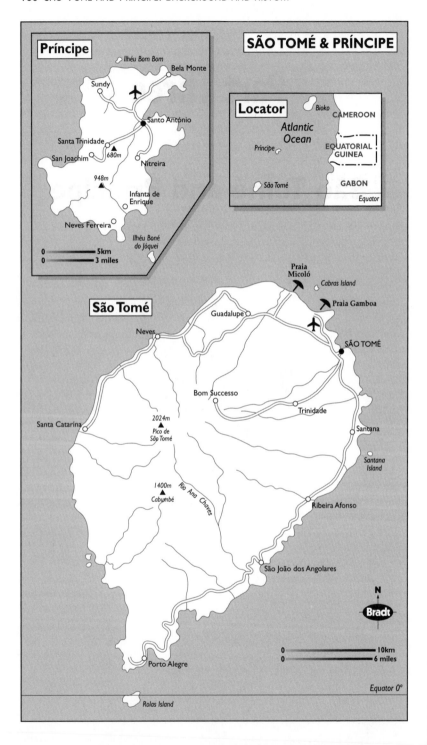

Background and History

FACTS AND FIGURES
Location
The Democratic Republic of São Tomé and Príncipe comprises the two main islands of São Tomé and Príncipe (set 150km (94 miles) apart), and a dozen tiny islets. The archipelago is scattered some 300km (180 miles) off the west coast of Gabon in the Gulf of Guinea. The islet of Rolas actually straddles the Equator.

Size
The total area of the islands is 1,001km² (386 square miles), of which 854km² (330 square miles) is São Tomé and 136km² (52.5 square miles) Príncipe. São Tomé and Príncipe is one of the smallest countries in the world, and is the second smallest in Africa, after the Seychelles.

Population
The estimated population is 165,000, making a population density of 165 people per km², 96% of whom live on São Tomé island. According to the Portuguese, the islands were uninhabited when they were colonised in 1470, which means that the entire population is of immigrant descent. Today's inhabitants can be divided into *Angolares*, the descendants of Angolan slaves; *Forros* or *Filhos da Terra*, descendants of the first Portuguese settlers and freed slaves; *Serviais*, contract labourers from Cape Verde, Angola and Mozambique; *Tongas*, the descendants of the *Serviais* born on the islands; and Europeans (primarily Portuguese).

SÃO TOMÉ AND PRÍNCIPE AT A GLANCE
Geography Two main islands (150km apart), and a dozen tiny islets
Location The archipelago is scattered some 300km off the west coast of Gabon in the Gulf of Guinea
Size São Tomé 854km², Príncipe 136km²
Population 165,000
Language Portuguese
Religion Christian
Government Multi-party republic
Currency Sãotomese dobra (db)

LANGUAGES IN SÃO TOMÉ AND PRÍNCIPE
Tjerk Hagemeijer

São Tomé and Príncipe exhibit an unexpectedly rich linguistic diversity. Apart from the official language, Portuguese, spoken by almost all of the inhabitants of both islands, three local Creole languages are spoken.

Santome or *forro** is the main Creole on São Tomé and is widely spoken and/or understood on both islands. Angolar or Ngola is the Creole language spoken by the Angolares, a closed community of the descendants of 16th-century runaway slaves with significant nuclei of speakers in the southern part of São Tomé, especially around the city of San João dos Angolares and at the other end of the island, in Neves. The fishing tradition of male Angolares resulted in the spread of the community to other coastal areas of São Tomé and its dispersion as a group. As a result of the contact between Portuguese and Santome, Ngola is threatened with language death, although there are still several thousand speakers.

On the island of Príncipe, a small community still speaks Lung'iye, a language even more acutely threatened with language death than Ngola, perhaps within a few generations. Unlike Santome and Ngola, it is nowadays hard to find people actually speaking Lung'iye.

These three Creole languages and Fa d'Ambô (literally 'speech of Annobón'), the Creole spoken on the small island of Annobón, a Portuguese possession until 1777, descend from a common root. This root was a contact language that must have arisen on São Tomé at the end of the 15th century and during the first half of the 16th century, when the island was permanently settled by the Portuguese. The birth of this language was the result of contact between the Portuguese and slaves from the African mainland, who were first imported from the Niger delta area (Nigeria), and above all the old kingdom of Benin (in Nigeria), while a few decades later slaves from Bantu areas, especially the Congo and Angola, became dominant.

Despite the fact that most lexicons of the Creoles has its roots in (old) Portuguese – although strongly modified by the phonologic rules of African languages – there is also a substantial number of words in the Creoles that can be traced back to the African continent, and particularly the regions indicated above. It comes as no surprise that Lung'iye – the first Creole to become isolated from the proto-Creole, when most slaves still came from Nigeria – exhibits more features of Nigerian languages and less from Bantu. Compare this to Angolar – originally the language of a runaway community that later absorbed a large number of Bantu speakers who were fleeing from the rough labour conditions at the sugarcane plantations after 1520 – which still exhibits a strong impact of Bantu lexicon. Despite this lexical particularity, the three Creole languages on São Tomé and Príncipe, as well as Fa d'Ambô, are structurally similar and all reflect the impact of Nigerian rather than Bantu languages. The three Creole languages, however, are not mutually intelligible, although people are conscious that they have many common features.

In addition to the local Creole languages, it should not be forgotten that there is a large number of people speaking varieties of Cape Verdean Creole in São Tomé. This was originally spoken on the Cape Verde islands, and is unrelated to the three Creoles mentioned. It was Cape Verdean contract labourers in the 20th century who introduced their own Creole language, which still constitutes a means of affirmation for the Cape Verdean community in São Tomé and Príncipe. (The large majority of Príncipe's inhabitants are of Cape Verdean descent.)

So-called Tonga Portuguese is another language variety still spoken, for example at Monte Café and Agostinho Neto, both plantations where mostly Umbundu-speaking contract labourers from Angola developed a new linguistic code based upon Portuguese. Because of the impact of Portuguese, through education, media, etc, this variety is bound to disappear gradually.

Unlike in some other Creole societies, for example in the Caribbean, none of the Creoles spoken on STP has the status of official language; they do not have an official orthography yet and do not take part in the educational system. Portuguese is the language of formal relations, whereas the Creoles are mostly spoken in informal environments. For example, most local bands, such as Sangasuza, Untwe's or África Negra, sing in Santome and typical dishes are Creole dishes, for example *kalulu*, *blabla*, *yogo* (Santome) or *zagwa* (Príncipe). It is common to find people switching between Creole and Portuguese.

Despite the lesser prestige of the Creole languages, there is a growing interest in their preservation, which resulted in the first International Colloquium on the National Languages, held in São Tomé, October 2001, and the need for an orthography is one of the government's concerns. Not only will research on and promotion of these languages result in the valorisation of the island's cultural patrimony, it will also greatly benefit education, since there is no doubt that Portuguese spoken in São Tomé is adopting Creole features at all levels of its grammar. On the other hand, it can also be observed that Portuguese impacts on the Creoles, especially at a lexical level; the latter is often called 'decreolisation'. As expected, the impact of Portuguese is especially prominent in and around the city of São Tomé and among younger speakers. Therefore the degree of proficiency in Creole (Santome) will greatly vary from speaker to speaker.

The first examples of writings in Creole (Santome) can be traced back to the second half of the 19th century, whereas the first serious study, *The Creole of São Tomé*, was delivered by Luis Ivens Ferraz in 1979. Ngola is the first of the Creoles to have its own descriptive grammar, *L'Angolar: un Créole Afro-Portugaise parlé à São Tomé*, by Philippe Maurer, published in 1995. Maurer is also working on a grammar of Lung'iye and, together with myself, on a grammar of Santome.

* The word *forro* is historically derived from (*carta de*) *alforria*, 'letter of manumission', a document granting freedom to slaves.

Languages

The official language is Portuguese, which is spoken by 95% of the population. There are also at least three Creole dialects. Spanish and Italian are quite often understood, if not actually spoken. A small number of people speak French, an even smaller number English (basically only well-connected businessmen and politicians).

Religion

An estimated 90% of the population is Roman Catholic, with the remainder following other Christian religions.

Government

Since the Constitution of 1990, São Tomé and Príncipe has been a multi-party republic. The head of state is the President of the Republic, who rules with the assistance of a Council of Ministers, headed by the prime minister. A National Assembly, elected by popular vote, holds legislative power. The presidential term is five years long, but any one president can be elected for a maximum of two successive terms. In the 2001 presidential elections Fradique de Menezes was brought to power. Following the 2002 legislative elections a coalition government was formed, between the Movimento da Libertacao do São Tomé e Príncipe/Partido Social Democrata (MLSTP-PSD) and the Movimento Democratica Forcas das Mudancas/Partido da Convergencia Democratica (MDFM-PCD). The MLSTP-PSD is the country's former Marxist party, while the MDFM-PCD is a coalition party established by the president. In April 1995, Príncipe was granted autonomous status in political and administrative matters. Ultimately, however, the island's seven-member regional assembly and five-member regional government remain accountable to the government of São Tomé.

Economy

Given the highly fertile soil, it's hardly surprising that the country's economic base has traditionally been agriculture. First sugar, then coffee and finally cocoa have dominated the farming industry. In the late 1970s cocoa was providing about 90% of export earnings. The rest of agricultural production has been palm oil, pepper and coffee. The fall in the price of cocoa in the 1980s, coupled with struggling economic reforms, meant years of an unstable economy and massive inflation. Debt was a massive issue. São Tomé and Príncipe had external debts of around US$300 million, making the debt burden per capita one of the highest in the world. Relations with the IMF and the World Bank are very good and in 2000 a deal was negotiated wiping clean most of the debt. São Tomé and Príncipe is one of Africa's biggest recipients of external assistance. The estimated 'gross domestic product' of US$50 million is in actual fact mostly foreign aid (US$45 million). The rest is cocoa. The average annual income is US$270. President Fradique de Menezes has said he is committed to developing new and existing economic avenues, including privatisation and selective tourism. Like most other Sãotomeans, however, he seems to think that future oil revenues will be the real solution to the country's economic problems and is energetically courting Nigerian and Angolan oil companies. The United Nations Development Programme (UNDP) has put together a comprehensive plan for tourism development, including guidelines on dealing with overseas investors wanting to restore plantation houses for use by tourists. But in all likelihood, developing tourism will not actively feature on the agenda for as long as excitement over oil eclipses everything else.

Currency

The currency is the Sãotomese dobra (db), which is divided into 100 centimos. In June 2003 US$1 equalled 9,090 dobra, UK£1 equalled 15,255 dobra, and € 1 equalled 10,630 dobra.

Topography

The islands lie at the southern end of a 2,000km (1,243-mile) chain of dormant volcanoes that includes Mount Cameroon in the north, and the islands of Bioko (Equatorial Guinea), Príncipe and São Tomé in the Gulf of Guinea. Contrary to what people tend to assume, geologists are agreed that of these islands only Bioko ever formed part of the African continent, as a peninsula. Príncipe and São Tomé were always separate, created by a series of volcanic eruptions. The volcanoes have now been dormant for thousands of years.

Each of the islands has a heavily forested and mountainous interior, characterised by sugarloaf peaks and giant needles of rock. There is a traditional saying in São Tomé and Príncipe that there are as many waterways as there are days in the year. Certainly the impression is that water is everywhere. The islands have a mixture of different coastal features, from idyllic palm-fringed beaches to volcanic rock, and where small rivers meet the sea there are sometimes mangroves. There is the occasional microclimate that confounds this general pattern, such as the dry grassy plains found in the north of São Tomé island.

Climate

The islands are hot and humid all year, with an average of 12 hours of light per day and an average temperature of 27°C (maximum temperature 43°C). Temperatures are cooler and fresher in the mountains where rainfall is much heavier. The mountains are often shrouded in mist and cloud. The short dry season, or *gravana*, runs from late December to January, and the long one from June to September. Skies are cloudier and temperatures more moderate during the *gravana*. The rainy seasons – from October to December and February to May – are very hot and very muggy. For many unbearably so – just getting from the bedroom to the beach brings out a sweat. Characteristically there are heavy downpours that will cut short a day on the beach. On the upside these downpours leave clear, blue skies. Heavy rain makes trekking difficult, if not dangerous. That said, be prepared to get wet even during the so-called dry seasons, especially in the forests at altitude and in the southwest of both islands. There is a dramatic difference in annual rainfall between the northwest (2,000mm) and the southwest (6,000mm) of the islands, due to the combination of mountainous terrain and southwesterly ocean winds.

NATURAL HISTORY AND CONSERVATION

Long before the arrival of humans, the virgin islands of São Tomé and Príncipe were colonised by flora and fauna. Since the islands never formed part of the continent, these 'colonisers' would have been brought here by birds, the breeze and the ocean currents. A plant or animal would become established if it found the conditions favourable and the competition manageable. Many species did – so many in fact that one scientist claims to have 'discovered' 25 different shades of green among the archipelago's flora and fauna. Each of the islands in São Tomé and Príncipe has endemic species, which have adapted as a result of being in a particular environment over a long period of time. A number of animal groups, such as large mammals, are not represented at all on the islands.

Of all the Gulf of Guinea islands, São Tomé has the greatest biological diversity and the highest number of endemic species. This is because volcanic activity here stopped before that of the other islands, meaning that the forest and living creatures are more established. So, of the seven endemic species of amphibian found in the country, five are endemic to São Tomé alone. Some 800 plant species have been recorded on São Tomé, of which 120 are endemic, including a giant begonia that grows to over 3m (10ft) and numerous orchids. Of the 55 species of bird that call the island home, 15 are endemic and some of the others are very rare.

Taking the country as a whole, there are 26 endemic bird species, including the short-tail, the shrike and the grosbeak. A slow walk almost anywhere on Príncipe is rewarded by sightings of endemic birds, such as the delicate Príncipe spierops, the colourful Príncipe golden weaver and the busy Príncipe sunbird. If you're lucky, you might spot the rare green ibis, a very rare and difficult bird to see. The islets off Príncipe are teeming with sea birds – including the brown booby, the sooty tern, and brown and black noddies – plus Jockey Cap Island boasts its own subspecies of seedeater, even though it lies only a few kilometres from Príncipe. Ornithological interest has peaked in recent years, but there is much research still to be done. For more information, see page 30.

By the time the Portuguese landed in the 15th century, the islands would have been entirely covered in forest. Their arrival had important and sometimes threatening consequences for the existing biological equilibrium. Over the next five centuries forest was extensively cleared for cultivation at altitudes below 800m (2,625ft), and new species of flora and fauna were introduced, either intentionally or inadvertently. Apart from human beings, there were numerous new animals, from dogs and goats to chickens and rats. Plants were brought to farm, including sugarcane, coffee, cocoa, vanilla, sweet

THE TURTLE IN FOLKTALES

The turtle is probably the most popular and important character to appear in traditional tales from both São Tomé and Príncipe (in all of the languages) and Gabon. He is a crafty and clever animal who always wins through in the end, by finding an ingenious solution to seemingly insurmountable problems. The turtle is also a bit of a cheeky rascal, the kind of character who enjoys a joke at the expense of his friends. Other characters with whom the turtle often appears are the king, his daughter (who is a bit rebellious and is to be married) and the soldier. The tales often tackle themes in everyday life, such as love, perseverance and solidarity. Here are two examples:

A tale from **Pedro Nobre** (see page 198): Once upon a time there was a king who was looking for a worthy husband for his daughter. One day the turtle came to him with a proposal. 'If I beat the fast monkey in a race then I will marry your daughter,' he said. The king agreed. The night before the race the turtle put large bunches of the monkey's favourite bananas on the track. The next morning the monkey sped off in a cloud of dust and the turtle set of at a slow, steady pace. While the monkey kept stopping to munch bananas, the turtle just plodded on. On the final stretch the monkey was clutching his sides and groaning. The turtle crossed the finishing line first and won his bride.

A tale from **Jean-Pierre Bayé** (see page 131): Once upon a time in the dry season the turtle and his friends were suffering from thirst. One hot morning the turtle had an idea, and gathered together his friends. 'Let's dig a well in the forest!' she said. The animals agreed. The elephants used all their strength to pound the dry earth but were unable to dig a hole. Then the hippos tried, and the gorillas, and finally the monkeys, all to no avail. Then it was the turn of the turtles. The turtles formed a circle and started to scratch and scrape at the ground with their small legs. The going was slow but eventually water gushed out from the well. All the animals cheered and leapt into the air with joy.

potatoes, papaya and manioc. Other plants were introduced for decorative reasons or, as with the acacia tree, for the purpose of shading the delicate cocoa and coffee crops from the direct sun. The new pressures meant certain vulnerable species were now endangered, but most species have demonstrated an incredible ability to survive despite the forest clearing, hunting and new competitors. In 1975, when many plantations were abandoned, lush forests, known locally as *capoeiras*, were quick to grow back.

Today an estimated 74% of the country is covered by rainforest, the boundaries of which more or less correspond to those of Obo National Park. Obo covers 300km² (116 square miles) through both the islands, protecting parts of all the country's different habitats: lowland and montane forest, mangroves and savannah. The driving force behind the establishment of this extensive protected area in 1999 was the environmental organisation ECOFAC (see box on page 31). ECOFAC is also training forest guards, teaching about soil conservation and looking into reafforestation initiatives. ECOFAC's areas of conservation also include the marine environment, specifically turtles. Through a combination of increased awareness, training and financial incentives (ie: ecotourism), local communities are being encouraged to protect instead of hunt turtles.

HISTORY

Our knowledge of the history of São Tomé and Príncipe dates from the arrival of the Portuguese. The islands, apparently uninhabited, were 'discovered' by Portuguese navigators on December 21 1470. This was Saint Thomas's day, hence the island's name. They settled here, and immediately began cultivating. It is impossible to divorce the islands' history from the history of slavery. The location of the islands made them a crucial shipment point for slave traders supplying American plantations. The Portuguese, who had met with little success in their attempts to grow sugarcane on the Cape Verde islands, quickly turned São Tomé into Africa's leading producer of sugarcane.

The end of the 16th century was marked by slave unrest. According to oral tradition an Angolan from Praia Grande, called **Roy Amador**, commanded a slave revolt in the capital and proclaimed himself king. Captured, he was hung by the Portuguese in 1596. Amador has become an important national symbol, and the myth of the slave-king lives on as he is commemorated on dobra bank notes.

From the second half of the 16th century to the beginning of the 19th century São Tomé's sugar production declined – the humid climate produced a poorer-quality sugar than that from South America – and the economy was sustained by the slave trade. The introduction of coffee at the beginning of the 19th century, followed by that of cocoa not long after, gave the economy a great boost. At its peak in 1870, Sãotomean coffee accounted for more than 10% of world production, and as coffee production declined in the years that followed, cocoa was more than ready to take its place. By the beginning of the 20th century São Tomé and Príncipe was the number-one cocoa producer in the world.

Portugal finally abolished **slavery** in 1875. Despite this, conditions did not improve much. Freed slaves simply became *contratados* (contract labourers) under the new system. Very few freed slaves returned to their home countries, and more people continued to be shipped in from the African mainland to work on the coffee and cocoa plantations in conditions not far removed from slavery. Contracts were supposedly for four years, after which the employer was supposed to pay the worker's return voyage – more often than not a reason was found not to. These poor working conditions were brought to international attention by a British journalist, Henry William Nevinson, in his book *Modern Slavery*. The British government joined forces with the chocolate makers, most prominently Sir William Cadbury himself, to implement an international boycott of the islands in 1909. The depth of their indignation on behalf of their fellow man in Africa was exacerbated by the fact that cocoa had recently been introduced to the British possessions in Africa.

Slowly, improvements were made. Each plantation acquired a hospital, a school and a chapel, but these changes were mostly cosmetic. It was just a matter of time before a stand was made against the Portuguese oppressors. In 1953 – eight decades after slavery was officially abolished – the *forros* marched with whistles and machetes from Batepà to Trinidade, where they were showered with machine-gun bullets. In total, the Portuguese militia massacred more than 1,000 plantation workers, and in so doing gave birth to the country's nationalist political party, the Movimento de Libertação de São Tomé e Príncipe (MLSTP).

Independence came 22 years later, in 1975, when the Portuguese government eventually succumbed to the demands of the MLSTP. The Portuguese plantation owners upped and fled, and the Marxist government seized the plantations. Before independence a mere 28 private *roças* accounted for 80% of the cultivated land, with the remaining 20% shared between 11,000 smallholders. After independence the *roças* were nationalised and regrouped into 15 state enterprises concentrating on cocoa production. During the years of the single-party state, the West was shut out and the country was little more than a Soviet satellite with clear ideological ties with Cuba, China and nearby Angola, who even stationed 1,000 troops in São Tomé from 1978. The bitter irony of independence was a floundering economy. The Portuguese had withdrawn their money and experience and cocoa production fell massively from 10,000 tonnes in 1974 to 3,200 tonnes in 1990. The force of this blow was further exacerbated by the collapse of the cocoa market. Without its major export earners, the island was sliding into a subsistence economy shored up by international aid and debt relief. By the early 1990s President Manuel Pinto da Costa had concluded his flirtation with Marxism and begun re-privatising the plantations.

The keystone of the president's democratic reforms was the **new 1990 constitution**, whereby the country became less isolationist, opposition parties were legalised and presidents were restricted to two five-year terms. Under this constitution the system of government is semi-presidential, meaning there is a relatively good balance of power between the president and the government. The president is supposed to rule through a cabinet chosen by the prime minister, who is supposed to be the choice of the majority party in government.

In the presidential elections of 1991 victory passed to **Miguel Trovoada**, the prime minister since 1975. He was re-elected in 1996 (narrowly beating the former president). In the latest presidential elections in 2001, power passed to **Fradique de Menezes**, born to a Portuguese father and Sãotomean mother. De Menezes had dual citizenship before forsaking his Portuguese citizenship so that he could stand as a presidential candidate. He is a successful businessman and reputedly the richest man on the island, having made his wealth by exporting cocoa and importing cement. He has declared his commitment to improving roads, schools, hospitals, electricity and running water. Because of all this, and because people believe he gives smallholders a good price for their cocoa, he is very popular. Even so, the Sãotomeans seem to alternate between being hopeful and cynical about what he can achieve. Some believe the good times are coming regardless, putting their faith squarely in the recent oil discoveries offshore to turn around the country's stagnant economy. De Menezes has already formed a Joint Development Zone (JDZ) with Nigeria, and predicts oil platforms will be up and running by 2007. In 2001 the JDZ apparently provided the economy with US$12 million, which subsequently could not be traced. There is also talk that with the JDZ, the Nigerians are going to fund the construction of a new port. In some quarters there are fears of the Nigerians taking over.

Politics in São Tomé and Príncipe is very complex and, some say, highly personal. For evidence of this one need look no further than the legislative elections of 2002, most of which I was in the country for. The run-up to the elections was a time dominated by confusing political manoeuvres, equally confusing speculation and daily allegations of corruption. Apparently votes were being 'bought' with cash, TVs, wood for houses or boats. One neighbourhood, **Folha Fede**, actually boycotted the elections, demanding that their very basic living conditions be improved first. They were complaining that they had received an insufficient *bagno*, 'bath' or bribe. The president immediately set about fixing their road and his party was rewarded with a clear majority from that small community.

At the final count, however, it was the islands' oldest and traditionally most popular party, the **MLSTP-PSD**, which came through with 24 of the national assembly's 55 seats. The president's party, the MDFM-PCD, took 23 seats. This was a blow to De Menezes, who had hoped to form his own government and who has gone on record as saying he wants to 'work with people I can work with'. (His rivals say this proves he has dictatorial aspirations.) The remaining eight seats were taken by Ue-Kedadji, a coalition party backed by former president Miguel Trovoada and his son, Patrice Trovoada. This was a painful result for the Trovoadas, especially since they had spent US$12,500 on chicken, sandwiches and beer, prepared by the Hotel Miramar, to keep the voters happy on election day. Trovoada Junior – whose name is sometimes linked to drug smuggling – used to be foreign minister in De Menezes' government, until there was a major falling out. Despite this bust-up, just two weeks before the elections the MDFM-PCD and Ue-Kedadji almost formed a coalition in a last desperate attempt to ensure the MLSTP would not win. The coalition apparently collapsed the day after a contract was signed because they could not decide who would be prime minister if they won.

Speculation and rumour aside, 20 foreign observers monitored the elections and said they were free and fair. The bottom line is that the MLSTP-PSD eventually formed a coalition government with the MDFM-PCD, and that President De Menezes has made a lot of promises. Only time will tell whether he is willing or able to keep them.

USEFUL INFORMATION
Tourist information and travel agencies
There is a tourist office next to the post office on the waterfront in São Tomé town, but don't expect to be overwhelmed with information (Avenida 12 de Julho, Sâo Tomé town; tel: 21542; fax: 22970; web: www.saotome.st). Work

has begun on the official country website, but only certain sections are up-and-running at the moment. For general questions and information about excursions on São Tomé or to any of the other islands, you're better off walking in to one of two travel agencies in town. They currently also receive a lot of general enquiries from prospective visitors before they travel, which they hope will now be answered by this guide!

Navetur-Equatour CP 147 and 277, São Tomé; tel: 21748, 21309, 23781, 71953; fax: 21748, 21093, 22122; email: navequatur@cstome.net; web (in English): www.navetur-equatour.st. Navetur is a travel agency run by a husband-and-wife team, Luis and Bibi (Equatour is the company's shipping arm, founded by Luis's father). They love the country and are fantastically helpful, doing that bit extra to make sure visitors have a great time. They can arrange walks in the forest, excursions to other parts of the island, or just about anything else you can think of, including hardcore birding trips to the remote southwest. They can also inform you about Tchiloli performances (see box on page 212). Bibi can speak several languages fluently, including English, French and Danish.

Mistral Voyages Avenida Yon Gato, CP 297, São Tomé; tel: 21246, 23344; fax: 22142. Also at the Miramar Hotel; tel/fax: 23865; email: mvoyages@cstome.net; web (in English): www.ecotourisme.gabon.com. This travel agency is affiliated to Mistral Voyages in Libreville and is very professional and well run. Their two offices offer day and half-day excursions around the island, by road or by boat, trips to Cabras or Rolas Island for lunch, and half-day guided tours of São Tomé town. Visitors can also do a half-day guided tour of Monte Café plantation, including lunch, for US$40.

Both agencies can arrange airport pick-ups, car rental, visas for Gabon, and packages to Bom Bom Island Resort on Príncipe. They will also book or confirm flights for you (Mistral Voyages is Air Gabon's representative on São Tomé). Alternatively, there are also airline offices for **TAP Air Portugal** and **TAAG Linhas Aéreas de Angola**. For more details on how to get to São Tomé see under *Getting there and away* in *Chapter 16*.

If it's boating excursions of any type that you're after, then a good person to contact is Noberto Vidal at **Flogatours** (av Marginal 12 Julho, PO Box 984; tel: 24394; fax: 22454; email: flogatours@cstome.net). Noberto really knows São Tomé's waters and its fish and will regale you with his tall stories. He can take you out snorkelling or fishing for the day to Cabras Island or Lagua Azul, or on boating-camping trips lasting several days. You'll need about a week if you want to circumnavigate São Tomé island in the traditional style of nomadic fishermen, camping at night on the beaches. Choose to fish using either the traditional frayed-rope method or a modern hook and line. He also claims to know the best places to find turtles, whales and dolphins, and sometimes takes birdwatching groups for trips of several days into the remote southwest. Aside from Portuguese, Noberto speaks French, English and Italian.

The environmental organisation **ECOFAC** (see box on page 31) is wholly responsible for developing the tourist trails in São Tomé and Príncipe's forests, and for founding turtle-protection projects on its beaches. It is

ECOFAC (tel: 23284) who supplies the guides for Mistral Voyages and Navetur. Walkers with their own transport who turn up at ECOFAC's Bom Successo base will more often than not find someone willing to guide them to Lagua Amelia for a small fee, but to be sure ring in advance. The most experienced guide on São Tomé is **Luis Mario Almeida** (tel: 71063, or try via the ECOFAC office), who has spent years walking and camping in the forest. With unflagging enthusiasm he points out birds and explains the medicinal and nutritional nature of forest plants. He is the best person to ask about the different routes up the Pico de São Tomé and along the Xufe Xufe River in the southwest. Luis Mario speaks Portuguese, French and Spanish, but little English. The country's only English-speaking guide is **Pedro Nobre**, who works for ECOFAC in Príncipe and can be contacted through the office there (tel: 51073).

For those visitors who would rather have everything booked and organised for them right from the start, the tour operator **Explore Worldwide** escorts small groups of 12 or fewer to São Tomé between October and March. Tours last for a week, during which time visitors get to experience a combination of trekking and beach life. There is an option to spend a week in Gabon before the São Tomé leg begins. A second possibility is to join the specialist birdwatching tour organised by **Birdquest Ltd**. This 24-day tour concentrates on Gabon, with the final week spent walking in both São Tomé and Príncipe. See under *Tour operators* in *Chapter 3*, pages 38–40, for contact details of both companies.

If you want an additional **map** to those in the guidebook, most of the hotels and travel agencies sell one of two simple, fold-out maps for US$5. The two maps that are currently available, however, are out of date in terms of which roads are surfaced or no longer passable, and what's where in São Tomé town and Santo Antonio. The Mistral Voyages office at the Miramar Hotel also doubles as a bookshop. There's not much published about São Tomé and Príncipe, but they make an effort to stock what there is (see *Appendix 2, Further Reading*).

Entry requirements
All visitors must have a valid passport and a return ticket. An International Certificate of Vaccination against Yellow Fever is also a necessity for those travelling from an infected area. Visas are also required by all arrivals, except passengers in transit who are not leaving the airport. If your home country has a Sãotomean embassy, you should obtain your visa before you travel as this is cheaper and more efficient. The cost varies between US$30 and US$50 (visas are free for children under two years). Visas can be issued while you wait at some embassies, or you can apply by post, sending a cheque for the required amount, a valid passport, a passport photo, proof of return air ticket and an SAE (for registered post). Depending, you may need up to a month for your visa to be issued by post, or perhaps as little as a week if you pay extra for the 'urgent' service. The visa will expire if you do not travel within three months of its issue.

If you do not buy your visa in advance, you can do so at the airport. If you have come from a country where there is an embassy you will have to pay US$60. Passengers from countries without embassies are charged US$50. You will need to leave your passport at the airport overnight and pick it up the following day. Visas are valid for one month, but extensions should be obtainable in about a day without problem if you go to São Tomé's Immigration Department. The cost of extensions tends to vary, but should be about US$5.

Diplomatic representation abroad

Below are the contact details of the embassies and consulates you are most likely to need.

Angola Rua Eng, Armindo de Andrade, 173 Mira-Mar, Luanda; tel: 34 56 77; fax: 34 30 02

Belgium 175 Av Tervurun, 1150 Bruxelles; tel: 734 89 66; fax: 734 8815

Canada Av Beaconsfield 4068, Montreal H4A2H3, Quebec; tel: (514) 484 27 06; fax: (514) 484 29 09

France 42 Cours Pierre Puget, 13006 Marseille; tel : 04 91 33 96 69; fax : 04 91 54 11 26

Gabon PO Box 489, Libreville; tel: 72 15 27; fax: 72 15 28

Portugal Av Almirante Gago Coutinho 26, 1000 Lisbon; tel: (21) 846 19 17, 846 19 18, 846 19 06; fax: (21) 846 18 95

United States 400 Park Av, 7th floor, New York, NY 10022; tel: (212) 3170533; fax: (212) 3170580

Airport taxes

Tourists are required to pay an airport tax of US$20 when they leave (children under two years are exempt). Visitors are expected to pay in US dollars, not dobras. Have the exact money as it's unlikely change will be available.

Customs

It is permitted to import or export any amount of local or foreign currency as long as it is declared. You are allowed to carry a reasonable amount (there is no precise limit – one or two cartons of ten packs of cigarettes is fine) of tobacco, and perfume in opened bottles.

Time zone

São Tomé and Príncipe is on the same time as GMT.

Business hours

As a general rule all businesses in São Tomé and Príncipe – including shops, the post office, travel agencies and banks – have a long midday break, sometimes shutting as early as 12.00 or 12.30, and not reopening before 15.00 or 15.30. The norm is to close on Saturday afternoons and all day Sunday. The same is not true for the markets and local food stores, which tend to stay open from 06.00–00.00.

Communications

The post office is on the waterfront (Monday–Friday, 07.00–12.00 and 13.00–15.00). Airmail post to Europe takes 2–3 weeks.

International direct dialling is in theory available from São Tomé and Príncipe, although in practice you often need to go through the operator. It's possible to phone or fax abroad from any of the upper-range hotels. You can also make international and local calls using phonecards at the CST office opposite the cathedral. There is no mobile-phone coverage, although this is planned for 2003. To telephone in to the country from anywhere in the world, the code is +239 12. The country's only internet café, or more accurately internet bar, is the **Tropicana Club**, near the police station (tel: 25301). Downstairs is the small bar, which has two cyber terminals and a couple of televisions, and upstairs is a long room with 16 cyber terminals. The upstairs room is open every day from 10.00–13.00. Internet use costs 10,000 dobra per 15 minutes, and between 11.00 and 13.00 it's half price. The connection is generally reliable and not excessively slow.

Money

Travellers on a serious budget can survive on about US$30 a day. This will cover the basics – the cheapest accommodation, food and transport. You can easily spend well over five times that at the other end of the scale. It's a curious fact that no matter how fledgling a tourist infrastructure may be, there will always be the option of at least a couple of luxurious hotels where you can spend over US$100 on a room for the night. Of course, the idea is not just to sleep and eat, but actually to experience the islands as well. Extras such as car hire, trekking, diving and big-game fishing probably won't feature daily in anyone's itinerary and should be budgeted for separately. See the *Getting around* and *What to see and do* sections in the following chapters for an idea of costings.

Foreign exchange

In the past most hotels and taxis would only accept payment in US dollars, but since the dobra has stabilised there is no longer the same reluctance to use it. That said, many prices are still given in dollars, so it can be easier to carry money in both currencies. Restaurants and local shops prefer the dobra. In theory travellers' cheques in dollars can be cashed without problem at the Banco Internacional de São Tomé e Príncipe (BISTP) on the Praça de Independência in São Tomé town. Here money can also be withdrawn on your visa, although as the authorisation is all done by fax the whole process can take a couple of days or more. Very few establishments accept payment by credit card, except major hotels and travel agents, certainly no shops. Money can be changed commission-free at banks. Changing US dollars, euros and to a lesser degree pounds sterling into dobra is not a problem. I would recommend bringing dollars, which you can use if necessary to pay taxis or buy goods, although you are more likely to be overcharged. I would resist immediately changing all your dollars into dobra. Dobra cannot be exchanged outside the country and even before leaving it can be difficult and time-consuming to change dobra into dollars. Bear in mind that you will need dollars for your departure tax and any flights you want to book. Dollars can in theory be bought with commission from the BISTP, but in reality they are not always available. It may save you some time to go straight to the black-market moneychangers who hang around Avenida Conceição and Rua do Municipio. Be very clear about the agreed rate of exchange. There is a bank in Santo Antonio that can give you dobra in exchange for dollars.

Medical facilities and health
There is one large and reliable hospital in São Tomé town, where they can do x-rays and other emergency treatments. The hospital has a great view over the bay. The most common medical problem amongst travellers is malaria. The Clinica Sao Pedro on Boa Morte Road, off Santana Road, charges 5,000 dobra for a malaria test. Give a simple name (even if it's false) and make it clear that one test is sufficient – they have been known to do two tests for foreigners thereby charging twice. They can give you the result in 30 minutes. If you think you need a malaria test when you are on Príncipe, go to the Posto Sanitario, or medical clinic (tel: 51084), next to the New Apostolic Church in Santo Antonio. You can wait for the results. There is also a hospital (tel: 51005) between the port and the airport. The nearest decompression chamber is in Libreville. Tap water on the islands should be boiled or sterilised before drinking.

Electricity
The electricity supply is not always reliable for the people, but hotels of quality have generators to ensure their guests need never know when there are power cuts. Plugs are two-pin. Adapters are not sold on the island.

Security
São Tomé and Príncipe is a very safe place to travel. Travellers should employ the same care and attention as they would in any new place, particularly if it's crowded, but personal security is genuinely not a worrying issue here. Security forces are barely visible and there's no need to carry any identification. It is a very peaceful country. Strangers may approach you on the street to chat, but their attitude is invariably courteous and friendly. There's no need to bribe or tip people to get by.

Public holidays
In addition to the main Christian holidays and New Year's Day, several other holidays are celebrated:

February 3	Martyrs' Day
May 1	Labour Day
July 12	Independence Day
September 6	Armed Forces' Day
September 30	Agricultural Reform Day
December 21	São Tomé Day

Bargaining

It is normal to bargain for unpriced items in the markets and to try to make a deal in a hotel – no matter how up-market – if you are going to be staying several nights. The pleasanter you are and the longer you are staying, the better your chances of success.

Tipping

Leaving a tip of 10% in tourist restaurants is accepted as the norm, but tipping willy-nilly in hotels and elsewhere is not expected. Although tipping of guides elsewhere in the world is often crucial to their earnings, there is a general intention in São Tomé and Príncipe's embryonic tourist industry that this will not be the way here. For example, the Navetur travel agency claims they pay their guides a decent enough wage so that they are not forced to rely on tips. The theory is that tourists can therefore give tips as they were once intended, as a voluntary gift for good service.

What to bring

The same suggestions for what to take to Gabon can be applied here. See under the relevant section in *Chapter 3*.

When to go

What you are hoping to see or do will determine the best time of year for you to travel. Broadly speaking the best time to go if you want to be in the forest a lot is either of the two dry seasons. December and January are the best months to climb the mountains, as there is least rain. Birdwatchers may favour the short dry season (December–January), which is the mating season. At this time a number of forest birds become more vocal, and can therefore be found more easily. By contrast the rainy season is generally a better time for photographers in search of bright-blue skies. The seas are often not as rough either. See under *Climate* earlier in this chapter for a breakdown of the weather at different times of the year.

Each year between mid November and early February the country's beaches are visited by turtles, who come to lay their eggs when the winds and tides are right. Tourists may be able to witness this, or to see the hatched baby turtles heading for the sea 45 days later. Humpback whales, killer whales and dolphins can be spotted off the northeast coast from August to October. The big-game fishing season at the Bom Bom Island Resort in Príncipe is from July to December.

Suggested itineraries

3 days A day in São Tomé town, a day's trek in Obo National Park and a day spent exploring the east or north coast.

1 week From São Tomé town don your walking boots to trek between plantation houses in the island interior. In your last couple of days make time for Lagõa Azul and Agostinho Neto.

2 weeks Spend the first 7–8 days in São Tomé town, Lagõa Azul and Agostinho Neto, as well as trekking between plantation houses in the island interior. In the remaining time, relax in Santana and/or Príncipe, where you could also do some more trekking.

THE ULTIMATE TRAVEL MAGAZINE

Launched in 1993, *Wanderlust* is an inspirational magazine dedicated to free-spirited travel. It has become the essential companion for independent-minded travellers of all ages and interests, with readers in over 100 countries.

A one-year, 6-issue subscription carries a money-back guarantee – for further details:

Tel.+44 (0)1753 620426
Fax. +44 (0)1753 620474

or check the *Wanderlust* website, which has

details of the latest issue, and where

you can subscribe on-line:

www.wanderlust.co.uk

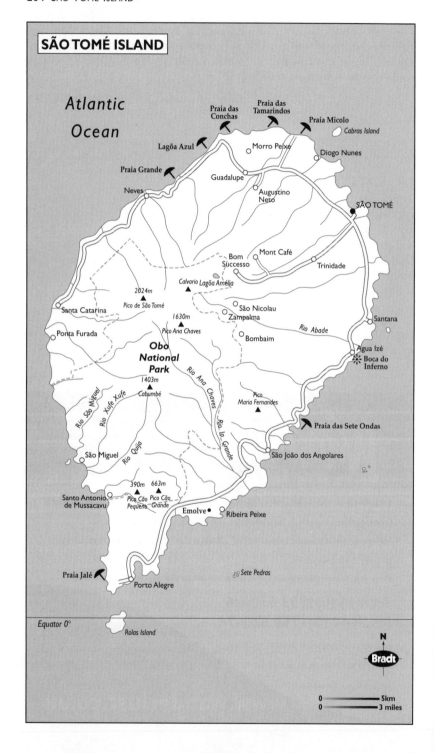

SÃO TOMÉ ISLAND

Atlantic
Ocean

Praia das
Conchas
Praia das
Tamarindos
Praia Micolo
Cabras Island

Lagõa Azul
Morro Peixe
Diogo Nunes

Praia Grande
Guadalupe

Neves
Augustino
Neto
SÃO TOMÉ

Bom
Successo
Mont Café
Trinidade

Calvario Lagõa Amélia

2024m
Pico de São Tomé
São Nicolau
Zampalma
Santana

Santa Catarina
1630m
Pico Ana Chaves
Rio Abade

Ponta Furada
Bombaim
Agua Izé
Boca do
Inferno

Obo
National
Park
1403m
Cabumbé

Rio Ana Chaves

Pico
Maria Fernandes

Rio São Miguel
Rio Xufe Xufe
Rio Ió Grande
Praia das Sete Ondas

São Miguel
Rio Quijá
São João dos Angolares

390m 663m
Santo Antonio Pico Cão Pico Cão
de Mussacavu Pequeno Grande
Emolve
Ribeira Peixe

Praia Jalé
Sete Pedras

Porto Alegre

Equator 0°
Rolas Island

N

Bradt

0 ———— 5km
0 ———— 3 miles

São Tomé Island

ORIENTATION

Tourism is not an established part of life on São Tomé and Príncipe at the moment. Fewer than 5,000 visitors from Europe came here in the year 2000, and of these hardly any were tourists. Currently, the country's tourist 'industry' caters primarily for expats from Gabon or Angola who are looking for a weekend escape or need to renew their visas. To describe the islands as 'unspoilt' and 'off the beaten track' are not the sort of overblown travel-guide claims that need to be taken with a spoonful of salt. This is what the islands are really like – honest!

The arrival point for travellers is São Tomé town, on the island's northeastern coast. It is a town that oozes decrepit charm and merits a couple of days' aimless strolling. To access the island's real charms, however, visitors must leave civilisation behind and head for the beach or the forest. Some of the trails in Obo National Park follow overgrown roads or railroads that were once used to transport coffee and cocoa from now-abandoned plantations to the coast for export. The speed at which these remains of human activity are being swallowed back into the forest is a tribute to the regenerative powers of nature.

GETTING THERE AND AWAY

One of the main obstacles to tourism in São Tomé is the difficulty and cost of actually getting there. The only direct flight from outside Africa is from Lisbon with **TAP-Air Portugal** (Avenida 12 de Julho; tel: 22307; fax: 21528; email: genitap@cstome.net). It's cheaper to fly to Libreville with Air France or Air Gabon and then get a connecting flight to São Tomé with Air Gabon for about US$200 return. There are at least two flights a week. This is the obvious solution for those combining a trip to the islands with a trip to Gabon (see under *Getting there* in *Chapter 3* for more details). There are also flights to São Tomé with **TAAG-Linhas Aéreas de Angola** (Avenida Giovanni; tel: 22593, 23947; fax: 21823; email: taagstp@cstome.net) from Luanda in Angola, from where you can make flight connections to many other African and European countries.

Flight bookings can also be made at either of the two travel agencies in São Tomé. See under *Tourist information and travel agencies* in *Chapter 15* for their contact details. There are at present no passenger boats running between Libreville and São Tomé.

GETTING AROUND

The road network in São Tomé is concentrated on the surfaced coastal road that runs from the northwest right down to Porto Alegre in the south. Once you leave this main artery, the roads tend to peter out into dirt tracks requiring a 4WD, or *pajero*. Most of the *roças* and beaches are only accessible by *pajero*. Mistral Voyages and Navetur can arrange car and jeep rental for you. The cost starts at about US$35 a day for a car, US$60 for a *pajero* and US$90 for a minibus seating eight people (fuel not included). For an extra US$10 you will be supplied with a driver. There are few cars so driving is not much of a problem, but although distances don't look far on the map the going can be slow. Expect to spend a good two-and-a-half hours driving from São Tomé town to São João dos Angolares.

Otherwise there's an irregular local bus service that will take you from São Tomé town to the main points of the island for between 2,500 and 5,000 dobra. Buses leave from the open-air market near the Conceição Church.

The roads and pavements are in a bad state of repair in São Tomé town, but the town is small enough to walk around. Watch your step when walking at night as there are few street lights and a lot of pot-holes. There is a taxi rank just in front of the main market in São Tomé town. Negotiate the fare before setting off. To hire a taxi for the day should cost approximately US$35. Diners or clubbers needing a taxi at night should arrange both their outbound and return journeys before the sun goes down, as all the taxis have disappeared by about 19.00.

Cycling around the island is a fantastic, leisurely possibility in the dry season. Navetur can find you a bike for around US$5 a day.

SÃO TOMÉ TOWN

The Portuguese established São Tomé town in 1485. It quickly became a slave port, with slave ships rolling in daily to Ana Chaves Bay, which was named after the wife (and then the widow) of one of the governors in the 17th century. Five centuries on, the Portuguese are gone and the legacy of post-colonial hard times is everywhere you look. The streets are cracked and pot-holed, grass grows out of the pavements and the elegant, pastel-painted colonial townhouses are stained with mildew. This is a city whose heyday seems to belong inexorably in the past, and whose future is uncertain. Stray away from the hubbub of the markets or miss the fishermen bringing in their midday catch of red snapper, wahoo and marlin, and the town seems to have a rather forlorn, deserted atmosphere. At night you could walk the city-centre streets and not encounter another living soul.

Where to stay

Accommodation in São Tomé town is not cheap, but there is at least a certain amount of choice. The first three hotels listed can organise excursions around the island, as well as boating or fishing trips.

Hotel Miramar Av Marginal 12 Julho; tel: 22511, 22588, 22862; fax: 21087; email: hmiramar@cstome.net; web: www.miramar.st. This is São Tomé's oldest and

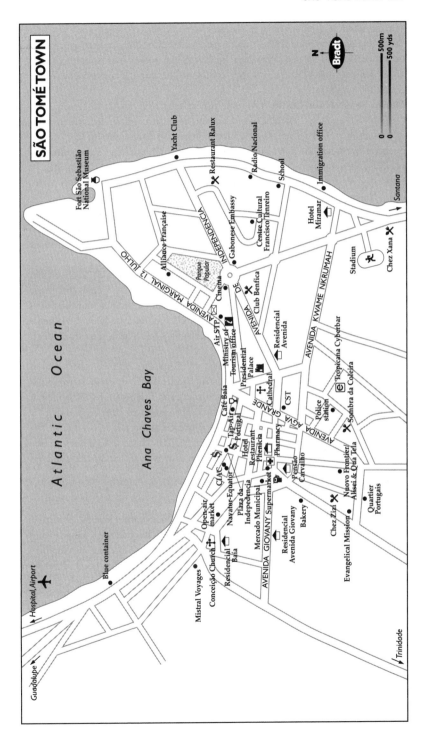

SÃO TOMÉ TOWN

N
Bradt

0 | 500m
0 | 500 yds

Atlantic Ocean

Ana Chaves Bay

Guadalupe →

Hospital, Airport ✈

Blue container ●

Mistral Voyages ●

Conceição Church ✝

Residencial Baía

Open-air market

CIAC

Navetur-Equator

Plaza da Independência

Mercado Municipal

AVENIDA GIOVANY Supermarket

Residencial Avenida Giovany

Bakery ●

Café Baía

Tap-Air Portugal

Hotel

Restaurant Phenicia

Pharmacy

Pensão Carvalho

Chez Zin ✗

Evangelical Mission ●

Quartier Portugais

Nuovo Frontier Alisei & Otá Tela

AVENIDA MARGINAL 12 JULHO

Fort São Sebastião National Museum

Alliance Française

Parque Popular

Cinema

Air STP

Ministry of Tourism office

Presidential Palace

Cathedral ✝

GRANDE

CST

AVENIDA ÁGUA

Police station

Sombra da Coleira ✗

Tropicana Cyberbar e

Residencial Avenida

AVENIDA DE

Club Benfica

INDEPENDÊNCIA

Gabonese Embassy

Centre Cultural Francisco Tenreiro

Rádio Nacional ●

School ●

Hotel Miramar

Immigration office ●

AVENIDA KWAME NKRUMAH

Yacht Club ●

Restaurant Ralux ✗

Stadium ✈

Chez Xana ✗

Santana →

Trinidade ↓

grandest hotel. Its facilities include a conference room for 100 people and a 600m²
swimming pool surrounded by a tropical garden. All the rooms have refrigerator,
telephone, satellite TV and safety deposit boxes. Single rooms start from US$90 a
night, doubles from US$130, including continental breakfast. The Presidential Suite
is US$300 a night.

Marlin Beach Hotel On the way to the airport; tel: 22350; fax: 21814; email:
marlinbh@cstome.net. There is a pool, a tennis court and well-tended gardens dotted
with bungalows, but the airport-style furnishings in the rooms are a bit of a
disappointment and the hotel is separated from the beach by a road. Room rates start
at US$50 for a standard single, and US$80/120 for single/double mini-suite, plus
US$5 for breakfast. This hotel and the Bom Bom Resort on Príncipe are owned by
Chris Hellinger, a renowned German-born South African said to have made his
money mining diamonds in Angola. He apparently started up these hotels at the
invitation of the Sãotomean government, which was keen to generate money from
tourism after their flirtation with Marxism left the country broke. Speculation about
his other business interests is a national pastime.

La Provence On the airport road close to the airport; tel: 21038; fax: 22335; email:
laprovence@cstome.net. This is a rambling, homely hotel run by French couple and
former dance partners, Christine and Richard. There is a swimming pool and garden.
Nightly rates start from US$55 for a double and US$110 for a studio with kitchen.
There are special discounts for guests of more than a week. This is the sort of hotel
that guests get very loyal about.

Residencial Avenida Av da Independencia; tel: 22368; fax: 21333; email:
ravenida@cstome.net. This charming mid-range hotel has 17 air-conditioned rooms
with en-suite bathrooms, plus telephone and television. Rooms are US$50/65 for a
single/double, or US$65/95 for half-board rate. The patches of greenery and the
open-air bamboo bar give the hotel an inviting tropical ambiance.

Residencial Baía Av Concaição; tel: 21155; fax: 22921. This is a clean hotel without
an ounce of atmosphere. However, rooms are en suite with air conditioning and, in
some cases, fridges. Rates are US$40/60 a single/double with breakfast. Suites are
US$50/70.

Hotel Phenicia Rue Angola; tel: 24203; fax: 24206; email: phenicia@cstome.net.
From the outside this hotel right in the city centre looks rather shabby, but inside
there is wood everywhere, which is rather attractive. It has recently changed hands
and been refurbished. Rooms are small, but clean, with en-suite facilities, double-
glazed windows and relatively quiet air conditioning. It is the first hotel I have seen
in Africa in this price bracket to have a fire escape (although admittedly it only
reaches the first floor). A room costs US$50, and breakfast is an extra US$5 per
person.

Residencial Avenida Giovany Av Giovany; tel: 23929; fax: 21709. A little bit out of
the way, this hotel is a clean, no-frills establishment. A street-side room with shared
bathroom costs US$10/15 a single/double. An en-suite room with mod cons costs
US$35/50.

Pensão Carvalho Rua de Mocambique; tel: 22952. This little place has six rooms
with shared bathroom for 120,000 dobra per room. It's a friendly little street – the
punters in the bar next door and the French butcher opposite are equally chatty.

Where to eat and drink

There are good restaurants in some of the hotels listed above. The **Hotel Phenicia** has a lovely wood-panelled restaurant and bar with an extensive menu. It's an excellent choice for vegetarians as there are Lebanese meze dishes and pizzas, in addition to the usual fish and meat. The food at the restaurant of the **Residencial Avenida** is reliable but dull, and service is slow. Much better to enjoy a drink at the popular bar and then eat elsewhere. The smart restaurant at the **Residencial Baía** has a nice-looking menu but it is *always* empty. The **Marlin Beach Hotel** has an acceptable restaurant, which does a buffet lunch on Sundays. Expats come down to the bar on Thursday evenings for happy hour (18.30–19.30) and things liven up considerably. There is a pricey restaurant and a separate bar at the **Miramar Hotel**, but you eat much better for your money at **La Provence**. There is always a good choice of typically French *plats du jour*, which might include old favourites such as steak-frites, cassoulet and crème caramel.

A justifiably popular restaurant for its delicious dishes using local produce is the **Filomar** (tel: 21908), which is on the coast near the airport. The restaurant has a lovely, breezy terrace overlooking the water. It does excellent grilled fish with rice or plantain fritters, salad and salsa, and also has some Cape Verdian specialities. **Club Benfica** (tel: 24069) is a Portuguese bar-restaurant through and through: Portuguese dishes, Portuguese beer and Portuguese old soaks propping up the bar. The food is actually very good, but ordering in advance is recommended as the chef can be temperamental and has been known to flounce out in the middle of a shift. At weekends the Portuguese soaks bring their families and the atmosphere is more relaxed. Another venue serving Portuguese dishes, with an appealing décor of wood and blue-and-white tiles, is **6 Septembre** (take the road to the left before the Marlin Beach Hotel; tel: 24154). Prices are reasonable and portions are generous. A more central and intimate Portuguese place is **Restaurant Ralux** (tel: 22108).

The new bar-restaurant **Bigodes**, meaning 'moustache', has a large wooden terrace overhanging the water and looking back to town (tel: 23944). Its proximity to the airport and the fact that the manager (who is the one with the moustache) works for Air São Tomé means that it sometimes functions as a departure lounge. Check in at the airport, then come here for a farewell drink, asking the bar staff if they will inform you when the plane is about to leave. It's a relaxed place serving barbecued meats, omelettes, salads, hamburgers and ice creams. There is a small play area for young children.

There are a few informal establishments serving typical Sãotomean food at budget prices. **Chez Zizi** is a small eatery where you can eat a tasty and filling meal for about 15,000 dobra. **Chez Xana** is a similar place on the waterfront. They will happily move a table outside for you if you want to enjoy the ocean view. **Sombra da Coleira** (tel: 21836) is a relaxed open-air place popular with Sãotomeans. They come to enjoy the barbecued meat or just to have a drink with friends. On the pavement opposite the Protestant Mission there are usually women selling fried fish in the evenings.

TRADITIONAL DISHES

Fish is an important source of protein in the Sãotomean diet, including red snapper, tuna, barracuda, marlin, flying fish and wahoo. It's eaten freshly fried, or is smoked or dried for use later. Smoked fish has been cut open and smoked on a barbecue. It keeps for about two weeks, but the process can be repeated to prolong conservation. Dried fish is lightly salted fish that has been left to dry in the sun until hard. It can be kept for up to six months. This smoked or dried fish is then cooked slowly, along with plenty of local vegetables and spices. *Calulu* is a popular example. It is usually made with different types of smoked fish, prawns, palm oil, aubergine, tomato, onion, bay leaves, and plenty of spices. *Cachupa* – originally a Cape Verdian dish – is another fish dish, this time cooked up with corn, green beans and broad beans. *Muzengué* is made with smoked fish, breadfruit, cabbage, palm oil, onion and spices. Chicken is sometimes substituted for fish in these dishes. As in any society, food plays an important social role. The fertile soil means even the poorest families have enough to eat, although the diet may not be very varied or well balanced. *Vitamina* is a colloquial name for a white man, used in the sense of someone who is very well fed.

As far as carbohydrates are concerned, there's certainly no shortage of choice. In addition to yams, breadfruit, plantains, sweet potatoes, and tarrow, there are several different varieties of banana, which can either be boiled or simply peeled and eaten. Leftover rice can be used to make *arroz doce*, a sweet rice perfect for breakfast made with coconut oil, milk and

Funnily enough, there is not an extensive choice of daytime snack places. One favourite of mine is **Café Baía,** a friendly, local café where you can buy an excellent coffee and a filled roll for 15,000 dobra. Another favourite, although a bit more expensive, is the **Passante Café** adjoined to the Miramar Hotel. This is *the* place to enjoy a coffee overlooking the Atlantic, and they do great toasted sandwiches and pizzas. The **Blue Container** – an old cargo container – is an informal food stand serving grilled fish and cold drinks. Its seafront position makes it a good place from where to watch the fishermen come ashore with their catch. The little café-restaurant, **Sabor da Ilha,** at the entrance to the Parque Populaire, can be a pleasant place to have a refreshing drink and a snack while soaking up the atmosphere (but be wary of the dodgy ice creams!).

There is a handful of nightclubs on the island, but the best is **Club 35** in Trinidade. The entrance fee is 30,000 dobra, and you'll need to pre-arrange for a taxi to pick you up and take you back to São Tomé town.

Where to shop

There's very little shopping to be done on any of the islands. São Tomé town gives the impression that there are more closed-down shops with empty windows than bustling places open for business. As far as souvenirs go there are sometimes CDs of local bands on sale in the main hotels, and the Hotel sugar. The choice of fruits on the islands is mouth-watering – jackfruit, pawpaw, pineapple, mangosteen, custard apple, mango and casamangas.

Alongside these locally grown ingredients are certain commonplace European imports. São Tomé receives regular aid shipments of powdered milk, wheat flour, sunflower oil, spaghetti and biscuits. The quality may be questionable, but prices for the consumer are low. Ironically, imported wheat flour (complete with weevils) is a third of the price of locally produced manioc flour. There are NGOs trying to change this reliance on imported goods and stimulate local production of quality foodstuffs, usually by joining several small agricultures together to form co-operatives. The members of these co-operatives are then given training, equipment and assistance with transporting and selling their produce. For example, there are now small co-operatives using fruits to make jam, vinegar, wine, dried fruits, fruit juices and the local firewater, *aguadente*. These products are not traditional staples, and sadly many co-operatives are struggling due to insufficient demand. The success of these new economic initiatives may well lie in exporting, and new markets in Gabon and elsewhere are being investigated. See under *Where to shop* below for where you can buy most of these items in São Tomé town.

In the rural areas you'll often see palm trees being tapped. A tree can be good for 5 litres of palm wine a day for many years. Strong palm wine is an acquired taste, and is at its best in the morning when it is less potent. An alternative local brew is Rosema beer, which is sold in large 0.5 litre bottles.

Miramar shop has the odd T-shirt or book for sale. The **CIAC** is a former beer warehouse turned gallery, which holds temporary exhibitions of paintings and sculptures, often by local artists. Pop in to buy or just to look.

To buy delicious locally made produce – such as honey, jams, dried bananas, roasted coffee beans, breadfruit chips and breadfruit flour – follow the sign for the Italian NGO Nuovo Frontier/Alisei. To the left as you go through the large wooden gates there is a little shop founded by an associated local NGO called **Qua Telo** (Monday–Saturday 08.00–13.00). Prices are reasonable and sales give valuable encouragement to struggling private enterprises.

Visitors needing to supplement their wardrobe can buy clothes and flip-flops very cheaply at the **open-air market** on the way to the Conceiçao Church. For fruit and vegetables go to the **Mercado Municipal**. Other foodstuffs – cheese, cereals, yoghurts, pasta – can be found at the supermarket across the road. There's a bakery selling soft Portuguese bread rolls on the right-hand side of the road heading out of town.

What to see and do

Visitors can see most of São Tomé town in one day of unhurried strolling. The commercial heart of the city is the lively market area, but the historical heart is to the east, around the **cathedral**. This Portuguese whitewashed structure

TCHILOLI

Tchiloli has been performed as a theatre piece in São Tomé since the 16th century. Like the Auto da Floripes (see pages 232–3), it draws heavily on Portuguese text and Portuguese traditions. Unlike the Auto da Floripes, *Tchiloli* performances are not confined to once a year. Most public holidays, religious or civil, will feature a performance. The basic story is always the same. The son of Emperor Charlemagne has treacherously killed his best friend in order to snatch his wife, but his dastardly deed is discovered. The Emperor must decide whether to condemn to death or spare his heir. The murderer aside, the characters fall into three camps: victims (the victim, his wife and his family), witnesses and authority figures (the Emperor, his wife and his confidante). The Emperor's dilemma – reason of state versus justice – can be interpreted as a message about the colonial situation.

dates from the 16th century. There are services Monday–Saturday at 06.00 and 17.30, and on Sundays at 06.00, 10.00 and 17.30.

To one side of the cathedral is the dusky pink **Presidential Palace**, set in lush gardens with fan palms, banana trees and African roses. Try to take photos of the palace and the presidential guards at the gates may wave their AK47s in your direction. Don't be tempted to photograph the floodlit palace by night, either. It may look as if the guards have gone home but really they've just moved into the shadows in the garden.

Continue down Avenida de Independencia – past the **Parque Populaire** – and at the waterfront turn left. Looking out to sea protecting the town is the **Fort São Sebastião**, built in 1575 and now used as the **National Museum**. In front of the fort are statues of the first Portuguese sailors to arrive on the island – João de Santarém, Pero Escobar and João da Paiva. The museum smells of mothballs and there are leaks during heavy rains, but it is definitely worth a look. The guide will take the entrance fee (sometimes US$1, sometimes US$2), then accompany you through the museum. Among the first exhibits are 17th- and 18th-century religious figurines from the various churches on the island and furniture taken from the Roça de Augustino Neto (see page 213). In the colonial room upstairs Portuguese governors adorn the walls, their medals displayed in glass cases below. In a separate case is a silver plate presented to '*Senhor Governnador de São Tomé e Príncipe*', Governor Carlos de Sousa Gorgulho, in thanks for the islands' commercial success. It is dated 1952, a year before this same governor ordered the Batepa massacre in which 1,000 *forros* plantation workers were killed. The most disturbing exhibits are the photographs of some of the bloated bodies of the massacre victims and the weapons used against them. Rooms 11 and 12 contrast a plantation owner's bedroom with the quarters of one of his slaves. From the fort's roof there is a great view of the bay.

At the western end of the waterfront is a small, pink, oddly shaped building. This is the **Fisherman's Church**, where fishermen traditionally pray before going out in their boats. A great out-of-town trip is to take a boat to **Cabras Island**, which also gives visitors a chance to see the town from the water. Cabras Island was apparently once used as a stone quarry for houses and roads on São Tomé. The only activity visitors may see nowadays is the occasional fisherman out in his dugout. The islet has a delicious beach for swimming, and for just ten sweaty minutes of effort you are rewarded with far-reaching views from the lighthouse. There are travel agencies offering half-day or full-day trips to Cabras Island from US$80 for a boat carrying up to eight people. See under *Tourist information and travel agencies* in *Chapter 15* for their contact details.

There is a **cinema** with 1,000 seats near the Parque Populaire. It was restored after independence, but somehow never got up and running. It is named after the Sãotomean poet Marcelo da Veiga.

THE NORTH

It is possible to head north out of São Tomé town and keep driving to just beyond Santa Catarina, about one-third of the way down the west coast. The north of the island can be explored in a day if you have your own transport (a 4WD is necessary for digressions off the main road). It is the driest part of the island, and behind the beaches there are grassy savannah areas dotted with tamarind and baobab trees, most famously around Lagua Azul. These open areas are excellent zones in which to spot the island's savannah birds, such as the francolin, the laughing dove and savannah weavers. These birds can be spotted on the half-day coastal trail between **Diogo Nunes** and **Praia das Conchas**, from where it is possible to rejoin the main road to get a taxi or a lift back to the capital. If possible, stop at the small town of **Guadalupe** to pop into the church to see the gilded, wooden statue of the virgin and child.

São Tomé is known for having beaches of many different kinds. Along the north coast are some of the best beaches in the country, including Praia Micolo (yellow sand), Praia dos Tamarindos (white sand), Lagôa Azul (stoney) and Praia Grande (black sand). **Praia Micolo** is a long sandy stretch of coastline with coconut trees and a shady picnic area. ECOFAC runs a turtle project here; any sticks in the sand surrounded by netting mark where turtles have laid their eggs. **Lagôa Azul** (Blue Lagoon) has beautifully clear, calm waters, which make it a popular spot for swimming and snorkelling. Some of the corals here are very rare.

A must-see is **Augustino Neto**, a large cocoa plantation best reached by hire car or taxi. Take the left-hand turn just after the turn-off to Praia Micolo and about 100m before reaching Guadalupe. The plantation was traditionally worked by Angolans, which explains why its original name, Rio do Ouro (Golden River), was changed after the death of Augustino Neto (a powerful nationalist poet and the first Angolan president) in 1979. His painting is half-way up the impressive driveway leading up to the hospital. The plantation's most impressive building is the hospital, which just a matter of years ago was the second most important one on the island. Now it no longer functions and is falling into decay. The windows are smashed, and goats and chickens play on the hospital steps. An Angolan businessman is said to have bought the hospital but as yet there are no indications of what he intends to do with it.

Continuing west along the coastal road will bring you to **Neves** – historically the most industrial town on the island by virtue of its deep-water port – beyond which lies the village of **Santa Catarina**.

THE ISLAND'S INTERIOR

A short drive of 10km (6 miles) from São Tomé town into the island's interior brings you to the small town of **Trinidade**. Most visitors just pass straight through this sleepy, dusty place on their way to Obo National Park. The spectacular hills beyond town are the location of the state enterprise **Monte Café**, where it's possible to take a tour of the premises. You can book a half-day tour with lunch via a travel agency, or turn up independently and ask someone to show you around. Since independence, coffee production here has reduced, although according to Sãotomeans, and many others as well, Monte Café coffee is still the best in the world. In its heyday this plantation was farming 1,400 hectares of coffee. Today fewer than 1,000 hectares are still farmed, producing 40 tonnes of quality coffee a year. The majority of this is exported, but some is sold at the small on-site shop.

Further along the main road lies **Bom Successo**. This is an ECOFAC site with toilets, large-scale maps of the park, a herbarium and a botanical garden. Visitors can ask to be shown around the garden and told the success stories of the aphrodisiac and quinine trees, before making the short and easy walk to the **São Nicolau** waterfall. The waterfall is about 30m (98ft) high; you'll know you're getting close when you hear the crashing water. Otherwise, take the uphill path to **Obo National Park**. This protected area incorporates *capoeiras* (post-agricultural forest) that has sprung up in abandoned plantations. There is also pristine, ancient forest at higher altitudes. The path takes you through small food plantations and abandoned coffee plantations before reaching the wooden archway that signifies the official entrance to the park. For about an hour, the path climbs uphill through the forest to a covered wooden shelter surrounded by massive trees, from where there is a steep path leading down to **Lagoa Amelia**. This old crater-lake in an extinct volcano is 150m (492ft) in diameter and 65m (212ft) deep. I was told that it was named after a Portuguese woman who slipped and died here; the descent is certainly rather precarious. The vegetation surrounding the swampy clearing, with its different mosses, grasses, lianas and giant tree ferns, has an almost mystical quality.

Returning to the main path, trekkers have a choice of either taking the path up the **Pico de São Tomé** (2,024m) or following the route south to Bombain. It's a full day's walk up to the summit of the Pico de São Tomé, and the going can be really tricky if there's a lot of rain, particularly in the final section. Calvario is at an altitude of about 1,600m and is normally the next resting place after the turn-off to Lagoa Amelia. After that it's Estação Sousa, notable for its orchids. The path then narrows dramatically as far as the base of the peak, which trekkers normally reach by the end of the afternoon. For the most part the going is very steep, and tree roots and lianas serve as essential handholds.

For the final ascent to the summit there are aid ropes attached to the trees. If the sky is clear there are wonderful views over the forest. Early and energetic trekkers may continue for another six hours to descend the mountain. Otherwise it's a case of camping overnight in the forest and awakening to the dawn chorus. Rather than backtracking, it's more usual to descend towards Neves in the northwest and then return to São Tomé town via the coastal road.

The less-strenuous option is to head for **Bombain**, where the day's trek can be rounded off nicely with a generous hot meal and a bed, or at least a mattress, at the *roça* Bombain (your only other option is to camp). It's a lovely route through the forest, taking in abandoned plantations and waterfalls, and crossing and re-crossing old plantation roads, railtracks, streams and the Abade river. As well as the usual birds, keep an ear and eye out for bats, snails, monkeys and black cobras. The usual lunch spot is Nova Ceilão, or your guides may speedily erect a shelter of bamboo and palm fronds elsewhere. The last two hours of this six-hour walk is in open country, past the Zampalma farming settlement and a couple of little villages, where you may be offered a taste of the local hooch, palm wine.

In the final stretch the track takes you gently downhill, until all of a sudden exhausted trekkers find themselves in a grassy clearing surrounded by misty sugarloaf mountains, the most impressive of which is Pico Formosa Grande. At one side of the clearing is the beautiful old house of *roça* Bombain, and opposite – so that the plantation owner could keep an eye on them – are the now dilapidated cottages of the workers. Most of the workers' houses have collapsed roofs and rotten doors and the handful of families that stayed to make a subsistence living for themselves have relocated to the stables. When the plantation was founded in the 1940s it grew cocoa, coffee, vanilla and plantain. Like all the other plantations, Bombain was seized by the government at independence, but as part of the new policy of re-privatisation Bombain ironically now has a Portuguese owner once again. The new owner has new ideas – pimentos, oranges, mangoosteens, bananas and ecotourism. Before or after a day's hiking, ecotourists can birdwatch or take photographs of the scenery from the *roça*'s bougainvillea-clad balcony.

From Bombain to São João dos Angolares is a steady nine-hour hike, or a good couple of hours in a 4WD. The hiking route first skirts the Pico Formosa Grande before continuing through a succession of valleys and ridges. There are amazing views of the volcanic peaks of Cabumbé (the island's second highest at 1,403m), the phallic 663m Cão Grande (big dog) and the more ladylike Maria Fernandes. Overall this is a tougher walk than that of the day before – clearly marked paths dotted with endemic giant begonias and towering bamboo alternate with hair-raisingly steep sections of loose rocks and gloopy mud. Somewhere along the way the park is actually left behind. Trekkers finally emerge into the open at Vale de Carmo, for the climactic spectacular 360° views of mountains and forest. It's another 5km (3 miles) along a cobbled plantation road to *roça* **São João dos Angolares**, and even further to the village, unless you have managed to arrange for a 4WD to be waiting for you here.

The rambling *roça* São João dos Angolares was built in about 1913. The building directly in front of the main house is the former hospital and the row of houses to the left are for the workers. The breezy veranda overlooking the Atlantic is the perfect place to relax with a beer or a book, but if that sounds too self-indulgent then there are several short walks to be done. It's an easy downhill stroll of less than 30 minutes to the village and the beach (see under *The east coast* later in this chapter). If you follow the track to the right of the old hospital you might find plantation workers crushing palm nuts to make palm oil, and further on there is a little waterfall from where there is an interrupted view out to sea. If you want to go in search of the Dwarf Olive Ibis then ask Amilcar, the young manager of the *roça*, to find you a reliable guide.

How to visit Obo National Park

Bom Successo can be reached in just 30 minutes from São Tomé in a 4WD, and vehicles can safely be left here while trekkers go walking for the day. It is usually possible to pick up a guide for the day at Bom Successo, but ring ECOFAC in advance to be sure (tel: 71034). The round-trip to Lagoa Amelia is the shortest existing trail and can be done in a half-day. For longer walks, trekkers are advised to arrange their transport, guide and accommodation (for non-campers) in advance. Non-campers are faced with limited alternatives for accommodation and food in the interior, and none at all if you are in the **remote southwest**. Unless the Pico de São Tomé is ascended in one very long and tiring day (and I wouldn't recommend this), then a night's camping is unavoidable. For a two-day trip organised by a travel agency covering guides, transfers, tents and food, it will cost about US$75 per person for two people, less if there are more.

Camping trips of several days to the southwest are very physically demanding and uncomfortable, and have only ever been undertaken by passionately committed birdwatchers. See the box *On foot in the forest* (pages 156–7) for some helpful tips. The southwest is the best place to see the island's endemic birds and to find undisturbed turtle beaches. There are a few possibilities. Trekkers can walk along the coast from Ponta Furada to Porta Alegre. Alternatively they can take a dugout from Santa Catarina to São Miguel, and from here walk up the River Xufe Xufe, or instead head for the ancient forest of the upper River São Miguel. For where to find advice and assistance in organising any of these trips, or to discuss other possibilities, see under *Tourist information and travel agencies* in *Chapter 15*.

I would suggest that a two-day, two-night trip from Bom Successo to *roça* **Bombain** and then from Bombain to *roça* **São João dos Angolares** is the 'softest' way to trek in the interior. Either of the travel agencies in São Tomé town can arrange the whole package for you (guides, accommodation, meals, transport to and from São Tomé town). Alternatively, hire a car and drive to either *roça* (note that Bombain can only be reached by 4WD or on foot, while São João dos Angolares is accessible by ordinary car). A night at either *roça* costs around US$25 for dinner, bed, breakfast and US$18 without dinner. Booking in advance can be done through a travel agency (even if you are not booking a

whole package), and is advisable to ensure they have supplies in. The *roça* São João dos Angolares can also be visited just for lunch or dinner if you phone ahead (tel: 61140).

The food at both *roças* relies on what is grown at the plantation. Dinners might include some sort of stew, breadfruit, tarrow, sweet potatoes, rice and fruit, and breakfast might be salty omelettes or sweet and spicy rice puddings. Both *roças* are hugely atmospheric – candlelight, creaking floorboards, patterned tiles – but fairly basic. Water and electricity are erratic and guests may end up sleeping dormitory-style on mattresses on the floor.

There is a second plantation in São João dos Angolares, the **Fraternidade**, which has a building prepared for tourists, although I don't know of anyone having actually stayed here. The plantation is on the top of a hill and there are impressive views of the mountains. It is accessible by 4WD. The guest building is right in the midst of the drying sheds and the workers' quarters. At the moment there are three double rooms for US$10 a night with shared showers and toilets. To book in person on arriving in town, go and see the plantation owner Fernando who lives in the blue house on the right-hand side of the road heading south out of town. To reserve in advance call between 06.00 and 18.00 and be prepared to speak Portuguese (tel: 61159). There are no cooking facilities at the Fraternidade so guests must either picnic, arrange something with one of the workers' families, or go into town to eat. There's very little in the way of eating establishments in the town. Basic foodstuffs are sold at the daily market and the surrounding kiosks, and there are a couple of little bars near the town square.

Apart from the food at the *roça* São João dos Angolares, the one really delicious eating establishment in town is **Chez Nezo** (opposite Fernando's blue house), where Nezo's mother will cook you up a generous meal to be eaten on her terrace. You will need to order your food a few hours in advance (tel: 61149). Nezo is a talented artist and musician. His group *Grupo Tempo* can be booked to play for a couple of hours on the veranda of the *roça* São João dos Angolares if they are given enough advance notice.

The east coast

Follow the coast south from São Tomé town and the first place you'll come to is the friendly town of Santana. Santana is known for three things: its beautiful church, its quality hotel and its views of the picturesque **Ilhéu Santana** (Santana Island). The Club Santana hotel (tel: 22023; fax: 21664; email: santana@cstome.net) is right on the beach and has a very good French restaurant.

Continuing south brings you to the magnificent blow-holes known as **Boca de Inferno** (Hell's Mouth). Turn off the main road to reach the blow-holes. The built-up area with its (empty) information kiosk and (usually empty) picnic tables seems rather out of place. This place is probably the country's oldest tourist attraction. Even in colonial times it was visited as a place with magical powers. It was said that when the founder of the nearby plantation Izé wanted to return to Portugal, he would leap into the Boca de Inferno on his horse and be catapulted there.

Of the beautiful bays that follow, visitors may want to pause at the one known as the **Praia das Sete Ondas** (Beach of the Seven Waves), whose defining characteristic is a peculiar sandbank.

The next point of interest is **São João dos Angolares**, a lively place to stop over for an afternoon or a couple of days for forest walks and swimming. There is a wide black-sand bay lined with coconut palms and fishermen's dugouts. A couple of rivers coming down from Obo National Park meet the sea here. When the tide is out you'll find mudskippers and aspiring footballers on the beach, above which is a sprawling village made up of wooden houses on stilts. This area is inhabited by the *Angolares*, the descendants of some 200 Angolan slaves washed ashore when a slave ship was shipwrecked on the **Sete Pedras** (Seven Rocks) in the 16th century. The ragged chain of black rocks can be seen piercing the water's surface out at sea. Another school of thought says the *Angolares* were already settled on the island when the Portuguese 'discovered' it in the 1470s. For information about places to stay or eat in São João dos Angolares, see under *How to visit Obo National Park* earlier in this chapter.

There are good views to be had of the Cão Grande not long after leaving São João dos Angolares, although more often than not the pinnacle is shrouded in mist. A good place to stretch your legs is at the Ribeira Peixe waterfall, a broad chute of water that is best seen after heavy rain. To reach the falls, turn off the main road and after 200 yards take the track off to the left either in a 4WD or on foot, and then follow the narrow footpath for five minutes until you reach the falls. A few minutes beyond Ribeira Peixe on the main road is the rutted road that leads to Emolve, a government-owned plantation that has received funds to make palm-oil soap. You can ask to be shown around if it is open, although unfortunately the palm-oil soap is not actually sold here.

The southernmost inhabited point of the island is the sleepy fishing village of **Porto Alegre**, a total of 37km (23 miles) south of São Tomé town. The road south of São João dos Angolares was until recently impassable to anything except a 4WD, but in the year 2000 the whole coastal road was surfaced and, although not perfect, can now be happily tackled in an ordinary car or by mountain bike. There is no obvious reason for visitors to come here unless they intend to stock up on dried fish or continue their journey to Rolas Island. Those with time to kill could wander through the village to the abandoned plantation on the peninsula (the towering chimney belongs to an old drying shed). Beyond Porto Alegre there is little apart from forest. ECOFAC is investigating the possibility of setting up a rustic campsite on **Praia Jalé** in conjunction with the local community, to enable tourists to view turtles.

ROLAS ISLAND

Ilhéu das Rolas (Rolas Island) is a tiny islet dissected by the Equator, a short boat-ride from Porto Alegre. It can be visited for the day, but to really relax or go scuba diving, a weekend is better. The only place to stay or eat is the **Rolas Island Beach Resort** (tel: 261196; fax: 261195; email: rolas@cstome.net). Prices are steep and getting steeper, a clear indication that its Portuguese owners are targeting the luxury end of the market. Rates start at around US$125/215 bed and breakfast for a single/double. Lunch *or* dinner is an additional US$22 per person, and lunch *and* dinner an additional US$40, but fortunately the food is very good and the staff very friendly. The resort has the potential to be a successful luxury haven, but stories of how the villagers were forcibly moved away from their homes on the beach to make way for it does leave a sour taste in the mouth.

At the water's edge is a fantastic landscaped pool, complete with wooden walkways, bridges and a bar. Behind the pool are two rows of bungalows, which unfortunately align directly with one another so that only the front row has an ocean view. Each bungalow has two rooms with a private balcony. The décor is all wood and natural fabrics, with wicker lampshades and tasteful paintings on the walls. Unfortunately in recent times the beach directly in front of the hotel has had a lot of brown algae washed up on to it, which the village women are employed to scoop out by the basket load. Unaffected, and just a few minutes' walk from the resort, is **Praia Café**, the best beach on the island. Here the water is at its clearest and calmest. There is a resident scuba-diving instructor here, but at present the resort only has enough equipment for eight divers. If they do manage to find booties that fit or a boat that works then divers can go diving up to three times a day. The first two dives with all equipment included cost US$40 each; dives three and four cost US$35; dives

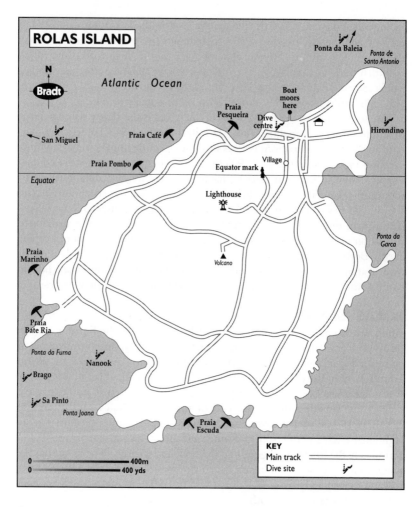

five to eight US$30. For most of the year the water averages at a warm 26–28°C. The following are some of the most popular dive sites:

Hirondino is perfect for inexperienced divers and night dives. Most of the dive will be spent at a depth of 14–17m. Expect to see octopus, rays, barracuda and parrotfish.
Nanook and **Sa Pinto** are both sites where divers hope to see sand sharks, while at **San Miguel** (a 40-minute boat ride away) hammerhead sharks are sometimes seen.
Braga is a dive site with a lot of hard coral. It is the best place to see fish, including red snappers, rays of almost 1m diameter, and moray eels.
Ponta da Baleia is a site suitable for experienced divers. There is a good possibility of seeing turtles here.

The island is criss-crossed by numerous trails. It's a leisurely two-hour walk under shady palm trees to circumnavigate the island. There are intermittent views of the water crashing against the shore and occasional blow-holes reaching up to 15ft high. The loose and mossy volcanic rocks make walking boots a better option than flip-flops. Wear insect repellent and keep an eye out for falling coconuts. To climb up to the Equator marker, turn left after the dive centre and go past the village. At the crossroads, turn right. The track then splits into two; veer to the right for the **Equator**. The Equator mark itself is nothing remarkable – as you approach it your right foot is in the northern hemisphere, your left in the southern – but there is a nice view. For an even better view over the whole island return to the main track and take the next right to the **lighthouse**. Almost immediately after turning, keep a keen eye out for a tiny track off to the left, which winds uphill for about 10 minutes. The keeper, who has lived here with his family for about 30 years, will take you up the lighthouse. If you get lost anywhere on the island, just keep walking – before too long you will reach the water's edge and can then follow the coast round to the resort.

Getting there and away

The Ilhuas Rolas Beach Resort runs a free transfer between the island and Porto Allegre. Boats leave Porto Allegre for the island at 09.00, 11.00 and 15.30, and leave the island for Porto Allegre at 10.00, 14.30 and 16.30. The transfer time is about 20 minutes, and the views in both directions are worth a photograph.

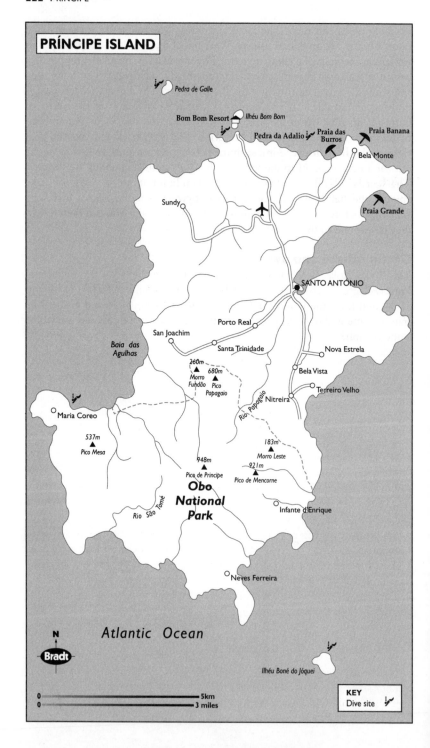

PRÍNCIPE ISLAND

Pedra de Galle

Bom Bom Resort — Ilhéu Bom Bom

Pedra da Adalio — Praia das Burros — Praia Banana

Bela Monte

Sundy

Praia Grande

SANTO ANTÓNIO

Porto Real

San Joachim

Santa Trinidade

Nova Estrela

Baia das Agulhas

260m ▲ Morro Fundão

680m ▲ Pico Papagaio

Bela Vista

Terreiro Velho

Rio Papagaio

Nitreira

Maria Coreo

537m ▲ Pico Mesa

183m ▲ Morro Leste

948m ▲ Pico de Principe

921m ▲ Pico de Mencorne

Obo National Park

Infante d'Enrique

Rio São Tomé

Neves Ferreira

Atlantic Ocean

N

Bradt

Ilhéu Boné do Jóquei

0 ——————— 5km
0 ——————— 3 miles

KEY
Dive site

Príncipe

ORIENTATION

Príncipe island is 19km (12 miles) long by 15km (9 miles) wide. It's crumbling capital, Santo Antonio, is thought to be the smallest settlement in the world to have the status of a town. Next to it, São Tomé town feels positively sparkling and full of life. The population of the whole island is about 5,000, of which seven are expats. More than 1,500 people live in Santo Antonio and along the roads leading into town. The airport is in the northeastern part of the island, a short drive to the north of Santo Antonio. Continuing north along the airport road soon brings you to the northern coast and the luxury Bom Bom Island Resort. Seen from the aeroplane, the resort looks impressive, a defiant human outpost isolated by the Atlantic Ocean on one side and thick forest on the other.

Príncipe has not yet been extensively explored by ornithologists or scientists, let alone tourists. Forest covers most of the island, starting less than 5km (3 miles) outside Santo Antonio. The forest is mostly ancient in the south, with blocks of post-agricultural forest in the central and northern parts of the island. When the Portuguese abandoned the island in 1975 people turned to a subsistence existence and for the most part large-scale cultivation has stopped. The plantations, plantation houses and the roads that led to them were left to be gradually reclaimed by the forest. Even with a 4WD there are now only a few roads that can still be used. The southern part of the island is unreachable except by water and uninhabited except for the odd fisherman on the coast.

The southern interior is characterised by distinctive phallus-shaped mountains, although the island is less mountainous than São Tomé. The highest peak is the Pico de Príncipe, which at 948m (3,110 feet) is less than half the height of the Pico de São Tomé. However, the interior is just as rich in flora and fauna as its larger neighbour. Its wildlife include mona monkeys, African grey parrots, and numerous varieties of orchids and begonias. There are also six bird species that are endemic to Príncipe and even a subspecies that is endemic to tiny Ilhéu Boné do Jóquei (Jockey Cap Island). Because of lack of demand and lack of resources, the trails in Príncipe's forest are not maintained as they are on São Tomé. Nevertheless, if you do want to go trekking it's fairly straightforward to organise guides and transport.

Only a handful of the visitors that São Tomé receives ever come to Príncipe. This is more a result of the cost of flights coupled with the fact that they just don't know anything about it than a reflection of what Príncipe has, or hasn't, got to offer. What it has got is wild, unspoilt beauty; what it hasn't got is an advanced tourist infrastructure. Those that do actually make it here fall roughly into two camps: fishermen who come to compete in the big-game championships held at the Bom Bom Resort, and naturalists and birdwatchers who are keen to see something of Príncipe's biodiversity.

GETTING THERE AND AWAY

The quickest and most reliable way to get to Príncipe is by aeroplane from São Tomé with, unsurprisingly, Air São Tomé e Príncipe. Flights aren't cheap, however. The plane used by Air São Tomé e Príncipe is a Twin Otter, which carries 17 passengers and 2 crew. Flights are usually full so you should aim to book at least a couple of days before you hope to travel. The flight takes 50 minutes. As you come in to land the plane swoops over the northern part of the island (try to sit on the right-hand side of the plane). To book, head to the Air São Tomé office, or use one of the travel agencies. The price is the same (US$130 return) and non-residents *must* pay the fare in US dollars, so if you only have dobras you will have to change them first. If there is a problem with the aircraft, passengers are sometimes transported (minus their baggage) in a Portuguese military aircraft, and if the problem is very extended then Air São Tomé e Príncipe might charter an aircraft from Gabon or Angola.

As a much cheaper alternative there are ships bringing supplies and a limited number of passengers from São Tomé to Príncipe two or three times a week. Nobody has a good word to say about these ships – they are dirty, uncomfortable and unreliable. There is no adhered-to timetable, and it is difficult to find out when boats are leaving, or once they have left when they will arrive. In theory, the journey should take about eight hours, but boats can break down or lose direction, in which case the Portuguese military will eventually send out a search plane and the boat might return to São Tomé after up to four days at sea. If that hasn't put you off and you actually find your way on to a boat, you should take enough food and water for several meals. To make enquiries in São Tomé, ask someone to show you to the Somagol office (Bairro Riboque; tel: 24262). In Santo Antonio head to the pink, double-storey Port Authority building next to the police station. Tickets cost about US$10 each way.

It is also possible to book a package to Príncipe's Bom Bom Resort with a travel agent in São Tomé or in Libreville. For those intending to stay there anyway, this works out cheaper than booking your flights, accommodation and meals all separately.

GETTING AROUND

Out-of-date maps show roads snaking to most parts of the island, but these maps should not be believed. Once it was possible to reach Maria Coreo on the southwestern coast by road; today a 4WD can grunt and groan its way as far as San Joaquim, now the west coast's most southerly settlement. In colonial times a road linked Santo Antonio to Neves Ferreira in the far south, via

Infante d'Enrique. This road too is broken up, overgrown and impassable. Today there are an estimated 12km (7.5 miles) of useable roads on the whole island. Using Santo Antonio as the starting point, the main ones are: to Sundy in the northwest, Bom Bom in the north, Bela Monte in the northeast, and Nova Estrela and Nitreira in the southeast. The best-maintained road is the one from Santo Antonio to the airport and on to Bom Bom.

At the last count there were 29 vehicles on the island, so the possibilities for hiring your own means of transport are not extensive (friends of mine once hired a tractor in desperation). For the most part the locals walk everywhere, so if you do end up with a car, no doubt you'll also end up picking up and depositing a steady stream of friendly hitchhikers. It's a great way to meet people. The Romar Hotel has two cars, and the Palhota also has a car. You will need to specify whatever journey or journeys you wish to make, but the daily rate for the car plus driver (and you can't rent the car without one) is approximately US$40–50.

There is also a limited public-transport system – a bus seating 30 people – which runs between various stops on the island that can be reached without a 4WD. The cost is 5,000 dobra a journey. The bus waits outside the Mercado Municipal with a sign indicating its next destination and it doesn't leave until a good number of the seats are taken. If you want to charter the bus you must pay for every seat. If you want to get to Bom Bom, the easiest way is to cadge a lift on the staff truck that leaves the Mercado Municipal at 06.00.

A lift into town from the airport will cost 5,000 dobra per person. If you have booked to stay at the Bom Bom Resort, someone from the hotel will be waiting for you with a refreshing drink when you get off the plane. At some point in the future the Bom Bom Resort is intending to rent out bicycles and 50cc scrambler bikes.

WHERE TO STAY AND EAT

The accommodation options on Príncipe are limited, but this is integral to the island's charm. The island's beaches are unsullied by aggressive tourist hotels that have forced out the locals, and let's hope it remains that way. There is one basic and one mid-range hotel in Santo Antonio, plus the Bom Bom Resort on the north coast. The choice for mid-range travellers is set to broaden soon, however, in what sounds as if it will be a controlled, environmental manner. If the plans of certain European plantation owners come to fruition, visitors will soon be able to stay at **Terreiro Velho**, a working cocoa plantation with sea and mountain views, and **Bela Monte**, another working plantation overlooking Praia Banana. The set-up in both will probably be quite simple, and guests will be able to see a plantation at work (and take part if they wish!). ECOFAC is also looking into establishing a basic camp for turtle watching, possibly at **Praia Grande**. The owner of the Tropicana internet bar in São Tomé town also has plans to open a tourist hotel with six rooms in Santo Antonio.

Leaving aside future accommodation possibilities, here is a breakdown of what actually exists at the moment:

Bom Bom Island Resort Príncipe; tel: 12 51114; fax: 12 51120; email: bombom@cstome.net; web: www.bom-bom.com. This is the most luxurious hotel in the whole of São Tomé and Príncipe (it is classes above its sister hotel the Marlin Beach in São Tomé town). The resort is made up of two parts: 25 spacious bungalows on Príncipe and a bar and restaurant on Ilhéu Bom Bom (Bom Bom Island). The two islands are linked by a 230m (755ft) wooden walkway. Some of the bungalows open out straight on to the beach; others are built into rocky outcrops overlooking the beach and the water, and the family bungalows (parents plus up to 5 young kids) surround the swimming pool. The food is very good – lots of fresh fish and calorific cakes and tarts. In the bar is a blackjack table (it's the only licenced gambling table in Príncipe) and the beaks and fins of dozens of blue marlin that were caught by resort guests. The massive sailfish hanging from the ceiling is a fibreglass replica of a catch weighed at 50kg (110lb). See under *Big-game fishing* and *scuba diving* later in this chapter for more details of these activities. There is also a gym. Unless you're here to go big-game fishing, the best time to visit is outside the season, when you may well have the place all to yourselves (at present the average occupancy is less than 10%). Prices for full-board are US$175 per person per night, or US$250 July–August.

Pensão Residential Palhota Tel: 51060, 51160. This mid-range hotel has 10 rooms with en-suite bathrooms at US$50, including breakfast. There's air conditioning, a TV and even a fridge in some of the rooms – when the town has electricity that is.

Pensão Romar Miguel Bombarda Street; tel: 51124. This basic hotel has 5 rooms with fan at US$10 each. The rooms don't have private bathrooms, and the water in the shared bathrooms is a bit temperamental. A small balcony overlooking the street doubles as the restaurant. The food at the hotel is reliable, the service less so. A good tip is to order your breakfast or supper for a time half-an-hour earlier than you actually want it. That way you shouldn't eat too late. Underneath the hotel is a small bar.

Arca de Noe Just down from the Roman Catholic church, on the right. This is a boarding house rather than a hotel and rooms are usually let on a long-term basis.

There is a handful of small restaurants in town, all of which require advance warning so that they can buy and prepare your fish or meat. Worth a stop is the **Cantinho Alegre**, a little place set back from the road near the Mercado Municipal. The usual price for a meal of octopus or fried fish with rice or plantains is 15,000 dobras. Two venues that feature in Santo Antonio's nightlife are the Bar Santo Antonio (sweaty disco complete with flashing lights and sparkly balls) and the less-lively Bar Barbosa.

SANTO ANTONIO

It doesn't take long to find your way around this pretty town surrounded by mountains and water. This is a small place with a slow, relaxed atmosphere. The country's maxim *leve leve* (slowly, slowly or gently, gently) might have originated here. It's the sort of place where it's difficult to imagine that anything much ever happens or happens very fast – except for its demise that is. (Unfortunately, the rumours that the Portuguese plan to restore the town and win it UNESCO World Heritage Status have so far come to nothing.)

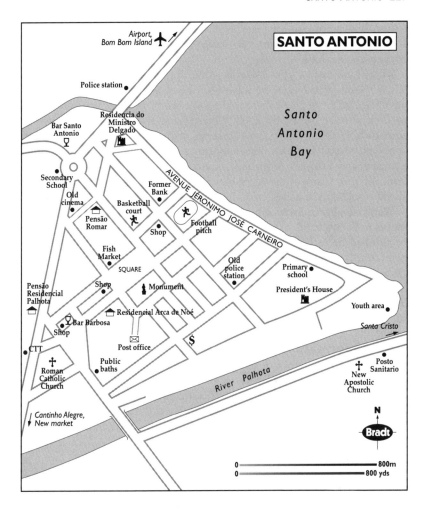

Santo Antonio seems to be falling apart beneath one's eyes. Pause in the overgrown square or study the dilapidated seafront buildings and you might think the town had been bombed. In reality its enemy is the corrosive salty air that makes such quick work of disintegrating the old colonial buildings. Some, such as the former bank, are no more than ruins taken over by plants, while others have crumbling façades in faded pastel green or pink. Wandering around, it's difficult to believe that this town was the country's capital between 1753 and 1852 (the capital was transferred from São Tomé town because Santo Antonio was considered more stable).

There are lots of churches in Santo Antonio, but the largest and most important is the Roman Catholic church. The current building was erected in 1947 on the site of the previous church. It's worth looking for two beautiful statues inside. One is a Portuguese wooden statue of St Anthony, the town's patron saint, whose feast day is June 13. The second is a life-size figure of

Christ. Both are at least 250 years old. Padre Elia, an Austrian polyglot who has lived here for over eight years, can regale you a few stories of island life if you happen to meet him.

There's no need to put aside any time for shopping in Santo Antonio. There's nothing to buy in the way of souvenirs, and very little in the way of anything else. A couple of shops in the town centre sell basic provisions, such as milk powder, sugar, palm oil, batteries and soap. If you need to buy foodstuffs to take trekking, your best bet is the Mercado Municipal. From about 06.00 you can buy tinned tomatoes, chillies, herbs, onions, butter, plantains and bananas. Availability is erratic and prices are steep (by local standards) for many of the vegetables, which are imported from São Tomé. Bread is sold opposite the Pensão Romar.

Water supplies in Santo Antonio are not always reliable and water from the taps is not considered safe to drink. A dam is being built and is scheduled to be finished by early 2003. Under this project water purified at a treatment plant near Porto Real will be pumped into Santo Antonio and beyond town as far as the hospital. Let's hope this dam functions better than the one built by the Portuguese some years ago, which ground to a halt after just 30 minutes. The electricity supply in Santo Antonio is not to be trusted either. Sometimes the petrol runs out and the generators don't run for days.

Useful information
There is no tourist office or travel agency on Príncipe – there just isn't the demand, or the need. For advice or help organising a trek, ask either at the Bom Bom Resort or the ECOFAC office (tel: 51073). Almost all the staff at the Bom Bom speak English, and Pedro Nobre at the ECOFAC office is the only walking guide on either of the islands to be fluent in English.

The bank is open Monday–Friday 07.30–12.00 and 14.05–15.15. The post office is open Monday–Friday 07.00–12.00 and 14.00–17.00. There are four policemen on Príncipe. The police station is the blue building on the left-hand side of the road as you leave town towards the airport. Personal safety is not a cause for concern. Sunday services are held at the Roman Catholic church at 08.30, 10.00 and 18.30. In addition to these, there are also services by Padre Elia on other parts of the island. For information about medical facilities, see the relevant section under *Useful information* in *Chapter 15*.

WHAT TO SEE AND DO
If you are staying at the Bom Bom Resort anything and everything can be readily organised by a walk to reception. Even if you are not staying at Bom Bom, any big-game fishing and scuba-diving trips must be organised through the resort. If you want to go trekking ask the ECOFAC office to find you a guide (roughly 60,000 dobra per day). As an alternative to organising a boating excursion through Bom Bom, ask around the port for a fisherman willing to take you out in a big dugout canoe or *karioky*. The journey will be longer but cheaper, and because the boats can get closer to shore than the Bom Bom's large motorboats, there's the added advantage of a dry landing. It's gentler on

the wallet too. A round-trip to Jockey Cap Island by *karioky*, for example, will set you back about 250,000 dobra, whereas hiring a 10m (32ft) motorboat from the Bom Bom costs US$125 per hour.

Trekking and birdwatching

It doesn't take long to find birds on Príncipe. Despite the large-scale forest clearance wreaked here during colonial times, many of Príncipe's birds have adapted well to new habitats, whether they be abandoned plantations or roadsides. Even walking slowly along the road that snakes through the forest south of Bom Bom virtually guarantees you sightings of most of the island's six endemic species. Keep an eye out for monkeys swinging in the trees. Climbing any of Príncipe's heavily forested peaks is more of a fitness challenge and should not be attempted without a reliable guide. At present only the Pico de Papagaio has trails prepared by ECOFAC with tourists in mind, and ECOFAC's next project will probably be **Morro Fundão** (260m) from where there are views of all of Príncipe's other peaks. There are of course other possible trekking routes, but expect the going to be tough, and even dangerous, in parts. Below is some information about the most obvious possibilities.

The round-trip up **Pico de Papagaio** can easily be completed in a day. There are great views and a concrete structure at the summit, complete with a grating under which local teenagers leave love notes. Near the summit the trail becomes very narrow, steep and slippery.

The highest peak at 948m is the **Pico de Príncipe**. This mountain has only been climbed a few times, most recently by a team of three botanists and two guides in 1999. The time before that was in 1958. At some point ECOFAC intends to explore possible tourist routes up the *pico*, and only then will they recommend it as a possible trek. If you decide to attempt it anyway, you must take an experienced guide and allow two days, camping overnight near the summit. Get dropped off at San Joachim and arrange for your return lift before you set off. As well as birds, look out for giant snails, frogs, lizards and even crabs. At the summit is a cement structure that was built in 1929.

Even more effort is required to visit the ancient, lowland forests in the south of the island. Like the **Pico de Príncipe** this is an excellent place to

AFRICAN GREY PARROTS

This noisy parrot, with its short, red tail and grey plumage, is found all over Príncipe and in the north of São Tomé. Home for many of the parrots on Príncipe is Pico Papagaio (Parrot Peak), but they can be spotted looking for fruit in other parts of the island during the day. Serious parrot hunters catch about 40–50 young parrots a year and transport them out of the country, where they can make about US$40 for each bird. ECOFAC is trying to stop this trade, by raiding boats leaving the island and releasing the parrots back into the jungle once their flight feathers have grown back.

find the endemic subspecies of the Príncipe Thrush – remains of snail shells are a good clue that a thrush has recently been feeding. The southern part of the island can only be reached by water. Take a boat and a guide to the former port of Neves Ferreira, from where it is possible to hike along an old stone path to the atmospheric ruins of the **Infante Dom Henrique** plantation. To visit the southwest of the island, probably the best option is to take a dugout along the **River São Tomé**, which is sometimes trawled by parrot catchers.

Another wonderful birding area is around **Maria Correia**, once again no longer accessible by road but the bay is quite popular with fishermen. If you want to come here you will need to organise a boat and a guide for the day, which is enough time to poke around the abandoned plantation house of Maria Correia and perhaps climb the **Pico Mesa** (Table Mountain) to the southeast. This is a beautiful and easy walk, apart from the last section where you need to climb a waterfall – the dry season is recommended! The top of the mountain is flat and apparently once served as a refuge for escaped slaves.

A good target by boat for birdwatchers are the **Tinhosa Islets**, two rocky outcrops that serve as a seabird colony located about 22km (14 miles) south of Príncipe. Closer to Príncipe is **Jockey Cap Island**, or Ilhéu Boné do Jóquei (otherwise known as Caroço Island), a tiny island just 6.5km (4 miles) by 9km (5.5 miles). If you disembark to climb up for the view, take care moving around as the large volcanic rocks shift about. Jockey Cap Island and the Tinhosa Islets were probably once part of Príncipe.

Beaches

Beaches are an important part of island life and Príncipe is no exception. The two beaches at Bom Bom are good for swimming or jogging. The hotel has snorkelling gear and intends to supply sun-loungers and hammocks before too long. In popular opinion, however, the most beautiful beach is **Praia Banana**, a curve of silky smooth sand the shape and colour of a giant banana. This beach was made famous by a Bacardi rum advert. If you access the beach by land you may be charged an exorbitant US$10 by the owner of the Bela Monte plantation, whose land you have to cross to get down to the beach. As a result of this levy (or the threat of it) you're very unlikely to bump into anybody here, least of all an impoverished resident. The beach can also be reached by boat, of course, which avoids the levy issue altogether.

West of Bom Bom there are a couple of fisherman's villages on beaches, accessible only by boat. One of these, **Praia das Burros**, was reputedly first settled by escaped slaves and referred to as Stupid Beach by the Portuguese, who were convinced they would never survive. The villages rarely see visitors and are very friendly. Take enough money to treat a few people to drinks if you want to take photographs of the wooden huts, the fisherman repairing their boats and the rows of fish laid out to dry. Continuing further along the coastline brings you to **Praia Grande**, known for turtles and rolling surf.

The **Bay das Agulhas** is considered by some to be the most stunning on the whole island. Nowadays it can only be reached by boat. There is a beach east of Santo Antonio that is popular with local residents. Take the road out of town past the New Apostolic Church and the medical centre and at the junction follow the road round to the left. On New Year's Day the whole town heads there to party.

Big-game fishing and scuba-diving

In terms of watersports, Príncipe far outshines São Tomé. The Bom Bom Resort has all the necessary gear for big-game fishing, including a fleet of equipped boats (a 28ft Blackfin, a 28ft Bertram and three 32ft Blackfins) and a certified championship scale. In fishing circles the resort has made a name for itself as being the holder of seven listed world records for various line classes. The waters seem to be teeming with Atlantic sailfish, wahoo, dorado and red snapper. The season for blue marlin is July to September, and for Atlantic sailfish it is September to December. Even for the uninitiated, fishing for one's supper is exciting stuff. A full day's fishing for six on a 32ft Blackfin costs US$800, lunch included.

Scuba diving also has to be organised at the Bom Bom Island Resort, where the resident instructor runs an organised dive centre. Being a volcanic island, there's a lot of volcanic rock and hard coral, so the colours are not as bright or varied as those found in the Red Sea, for example. There are a lot of fish though and the water is a nice 25°C average all year round. Most of the dives are relaxing drift dives off a boat. Boat dives cost US$45–65, all equipment included, and become cheaper if you book a package of five or ten dives. The cost is greatly reduced if you have your own equipment. Night dives are possible for divers who have their own torches. If you're not a qualified diver you could do a 'resort course', where you're introduced to all the gear, given a practice session in the pool and then taken on a shallow shore dive (less than 10m). Alternatively, stick to snorkelling.

Below is a breakdown of Príncipe's most popular dive sites.

Bom Bom Resort has a set shore dive for beginner divers where they dive through a large arch. Expect to see snapper, octopus, angelfish and maybe the aeroplane fuselages scuppered by the resort owner for your underwater entertainment.

Pedra de Adalio is a reef dive to the west of Bom Bom, reached by boat. Look for octopus and eel, groupers and sturgeons.

Pedra de Galle is a challenging deep dive to 30m (98ft) along a sheer rock face teeming with trigger fish, snapper and barracuda.

Maria Coreo is another deep dive to 30m (98ft), only suitable for advanced divers. There are all kinds of reef fish, as well as moray eels, turtles and nurse sharks.

Jockey Cap Island has a dive of about 24m (79ft). There are normally large schools of small fish here, and there's a good chance of sighting barracuda, parrot fish, trigger fish and even turtles.

Shark dive about 1 hour by boat south of Príncipe is a dive site where you have a chance of sighting reef sharks and hammerheads.

PLANTATION HOUSES

In colonial times there were seven plantations on Príncipe, of which the most important were Sundy, Porto Real and Belo Monte. Like all the country's plantations, these three passed to the government at independence, but some have since been privatised. Porto Real is partly owned by the government and partly privatised in lots as small as 2 hectares (5 acres). Sundy is government owned but offers are welcome, and **Bela Monte** is once more European property. Many of these plantations have abandoned buildings that are still very impressive, despite being in such a sad state of repair. The large, former hospital at **Porto Real** was once better stocked than the hospital in Santo Antonio, and, until recently, one of the rooms in Porto Real's tumbledown *roça* had piles of damp documents left by the former Portuguese owners. There's talk of the Portuguese making Porto Real into a museum, or maybe a hotel, but at the moment it's just talk.

The grandest *roça* of them all must be **Sundy**, even though it too is falling apart. The first thing you see is the large former hospital, which indicates that this was once a plantation of considerable size and standing. This impression is reinforced by the castle-like walls and the imposing gates. It's a decrepit grandeur that strikes you when you enter the gates – the grass in the rectangular courtyard is scrubby, the roofs of some of the buildings are subsiding and many windows are broken. A lot of the buildings are empty, but some are occupied as homes for the families still living here. The families survive by subsistence farming, making a few extra dollars each month by selling a bit of cocoa and honey.

The principal house is meant to be a summer retreat for the president. It's in a better state than the rest, but even so no president has put in an appearance in recent years. It's possible to look around the house if you get a letter from the Residencia do Ministro Delgado (local governor's office) in Santo Antonio, which you show to the caretaker when you arrive. If you are going with the Bom Bom Resort they will organise this for you. The caretaker will discreetly trail you around, and try to answer any questions you may have. The three bedrooms upstairs are all identically furnished except for their colour schemes. Apparently the president's room was the green one, closest to the bathroom and furthest away from possible intruders. The blue and red rooms were for his bodyguards. All these rooms have a spectacular view over flame trees to the sea.

The plaque in the grass – to the left as you enter the gates – commemorates the British astronomer Sir Arthur Eddington. He successfully tested Einstein's theory of relativity here in 1919, choosing the site because of its proximity to the Equator. During a total eclipse, Sir Eddington proved that gravity would bend the path of light when a massive star passes it.

Theatre

The **Auto da Floripes** is the island's definitive theatre piece. It has been performed in Príncipe for generations, and perfectly typifies the island's mixture of European and African influences. Like *Tchiloli* (see box on page

212), the Auto da Floripes draws on an episode in Charlemagne's life. The show lasts all day until nightfall. To catch the Auto da Floripes, you will need to be in Santo Antonio around the time of St Laurent's day (August 10). Only in exceptional circumstances can it be performed at other times of the year.

The show includes a bit of everything – dancing, singing, jokes, mimes – and is performed in two parts. In the first part the two groups, the Moors in red and the Christians in blue and white, file through Santo Antonio. To avoid colliding they call to one another with a horn. In the second part, the Christians gather near the church, the Moors about 200m (656ft) away on the waterfront. The battle is then acted out, with long interruptions when someone will attempt to convince his adversary to change allegiance. Oliveiros (the Christian) wounds Ferrabras (the Moor) and is then taken prisoner. He is saved by Floripes, a young Muslim girl, who is converted to Christianity by her love for him. She helps him escape and flees with him to Charlemagne's camp. Thus peace is made and order restored.

234

Hot on Africa!

Just some of our destinations for serious explorers...

*Bradt Guides are available from all good bookshops,
or by post, phone or internet direct from*

Bradt Travel Guides Ltd

Tel: +44 (0)1753 893444

www.bradtguides.com

Appendix 1

LANGUAGE

French is the official language in Gabon and English is not widely spoken at all. Don't rely on finding English or French speakers in São Tomé and Príncipe, where you'll need basic Portuguese to get by.

English	French	Portuguese
good morning	*bonjour*	*bom dia*
good evening	*bonsoir*	*boa tarde*
good night	*bon nuit*	*boa noite*
goodbye	*au revoir*	*adeus*
how are you?	*comment allez-vous?*	*como est?*
I'm fine	*très bien*	*bem, obrigado*
yes	*oui*	*sim*
no	*non*	*não*
please	*s'il vous plaît*	*por favor*
thank you	*merci*	*obrigado* (man speaking)/ *obrigada* (woman speaking)
you're welcome	*de rien*	*de nada*
I would like…	*je voudrais…*	*queria…*
is it very far?	*c'est très loin?*	*é muito longe?*
there	*là*	*la*
here	*ici*	*aqui*
stop	*arrêtez*	*stop!/pare*
help!	*au secours!*	*socorro!*
how much is it?	*c'est combien?*	*quanto custa?*
it is too much!	*c'est trop cher!*	*é demasiado caro!/é muito caro!*
do you speak English?	*parlez-vous anglais?*	*fala inglês?*
I don't understand	*Je ne comprends pas*	*não compreendo*
I don't speak French/ Portuguese	*Je ne parle pas français*	*Não falo português*
where is…?	*oú est…?*	*onde é…?*
toilet	*la toilette, le WC*	*a casa de banho, sanitarios, lavabos, WC*
chemist	*la pharmacie*	*a farmacia*
doctor	*le médecin*	*o médico*
the hospital	*l'hôpital*	*o hospital*

English	French	Portuguese
police	*la police*	*a polícia*
market	*le marché*	*o mercado*
supermarket	*le supermarché*	*o supermercado*
hotel	*l'hôtel*	*o hotel*
bus station	*la gare routière*	*a estação dos autocarros?*
post office	*la poste*	*os correios*
telephone	*le téléphone*	*o telefone*
drinking water	*l'eau potable*	*água pot·vel*
some food	*de la nourriture/*	*comida/um bocado de comida*
	quelques chose à manger?	

World Travel Starts at Stanfords
Maps and Guides for all corners of the World

Stanfords Flagship Store
12–14 Long Acre, Covent Garden, London, WC2

Other Stanfords Stores:
Stanfords at The Britain Visitor Centre: 1 Regent Street, SW1
(Maps and Books of the UK and Ireland only)
Stanfords at the Scottish Tourist Board: 19 Cockspur Street, SW1
(Maps and Books of Scotland only)
Stanfords in Bristol: 29 Corn Street, Bristol, BS1

International Mail Order Department
Tel: 020 7836 1321 Fax: 020 7836 0189

www.stanfords.co.uk

Appendix 2

FURTHER READING
General Africa reading
There are some really excellent general biographies of the African continent. Gabon is rarely focused on, although this omission is a tribute to its stability and prosperity relative to many of its neighbours. George Alagiah's *A Passage to Africa* (Little Brown, 2001) is a portrait of a handful of Africa's most troublespots. As someone who spent his formative years in a newly independent Ghana and went on to become the BBC's Africa correspondent, Alagiah's understanding of Africa's problems and solutions is as personal as it is well-informed. Equally interesting is American journalist Blaine Harden's *Africa: Dispatches from a Fragile Continent* (Harper Collins, 1993). Other good general books include John Reader's *Africa: History of a Continent* and David Robbins's *Aspects of Africa* (Penguin, 1996).

Historical interest
Mary Kingsley wrote several works about Africa (see box on pages 10–11) but the best one to start with is her *Travels in West Africa* (Phoenix, 2001), which is fascinating and often funny. Of Paul B du Chaillu's writings, the most accessible is *Explorations and Adventures in Equatorial Africa* (London, 1861), a personal account of his explorations from 1856–59. As far as I know there is no Pierre Savorgnan de Brazza in English translation. His first journey, 1875–77, is described in *Au Coeur de l'Afrique* (Paris, 1992). There is no shortage of works by Albert Schweitzer, of which the best one to start with is probably *From My African Notebook* (Bradford and Dickens, 1938). This book gives a valuable insight into the running of the hospital at Lambaréné and this man's vision of Africa (see box on pages 110–11).

The following books are more academic, and mostly in French. There is a collection of transcripts from interviews with Omar Bongo by Christian Casteran in a book entitled *Omar Bongo: Confidences d'un Africain* (SA, 1994). Marc Aicardi de Saint-Paul's *Gabon: The Development of a Nation* (published in France 1987 and translated into English 1989, Routledge) gives some useful background information, if a little outdated now. André Raponda-Walker's *Rites et Croyances des Peuples du Gabon* (Paris, 1962) studies the beliefs of the different peoples of Gabon. This is just one of many publications by this prolific and greatly respected writer. He was born in 1871, the son of a Mpongwe woman and a British trader called Bruce Walker. (Bruce Walker set up the first trading posts in Gabon for the British firm Hatton and Cookson, including the one at Lambaréné.) André Raponda-Walker was to become the leading Gabonese historian of the last century. He was both a bishop in the

Catholic church and a scholar who strongly believed in the value of recording indigenous beliefs and the medicinal powers of the forest. He died in 1968. There is also Christian Dedet's *La Mémoire du fleuve: L'Afrique aventureuse de Jean Michonet* (Paris, 1985), which tells the story of Jean Michonet, who amongst other things is an initiate of *bwiti*. More recently, James W. Fernandez has written a comprehensive study of *bwiti* in a book entitled *Bwiti: An Ethnography of the Religious Imagination in Africa* (Princeton, 1982).

Natural history

ECOFAC produce an excellent series of books about the flora and fauna of both Gabon and São Tomé and Príncipe. You can find them at most of the Maison de la Presses in Libreville, or failing that at the ECOFAC office in Batterie IV (look for the ECOFAC logo next to the Gros Bouquet II school, open Monday–Friday 08.00–12.30 and 14.30–18.00, Wednesday open without interruption 08.00–17.00). To buy ECOFAC's books before arriving in Gabon, contact UK-based NHBS Mailorder Bookstore (tel: 01803 865913; fax: 01803 865280; email: sales@nhbs.co.uk; web: www.nhbs.co.uk).

Nik Borrow's *Birds of Western Africa: an identification guide* (C Helm, 2002) is the most comprehensive guide. Each colour plate is accompanied by essential extra information of the birds' biology and behaviour.

Ber Van Perlo's *Birds of Western and Central Africa* (Princeton University Press, 2002) and Ian Sinclair and Peter Ryan's *A Field Guide to the Birds of Africa, South of the Sahara* (Struik, Cape Town and New Holland, London, 2003) are alternative new guides.

Patrice Christy and William V Clarke's *Guide des oiseaux de la Reserve de la Lopé* (Ecofac, Libreville, 1994) is a colour-illustrated field guide published in French. Bird names in the body text at least are given in English and Latin as well. Where different names were used by William Serle and Gérard Morel in their *A Field Guide to the Birds of West Africa* (Harper Collins, 1977; translated into French in 1979), these have also been included.

Patrice Christy and William V Clarke's *Guide des oiseaux de Saõ Tomé et Príncipe* (Ecofac, Libreville, 1998) is published in French, but the introduction, with its invaluable information about habitats and bird-watching sites, is also translated into English and Portuguese. Throughout the names of birds are given in French, English, Latin and Portuguese, as well as their local names where applicable. There are indexes in English, French and Latin.

Jonathan Kingdon's *The Kingdon Field Guide to African Mammals* (Harcourt Publishers, 1997) is the definitive guide. There is also *A Field Guide to the Mammals of Africa* (Collins).

Lee White and Kate Abernethy's *Guide de la Végétation de la Réserve de la Lopé* Gabon (Ecofac, Libreville, 1996) is excellent, and relevant way beyond La Lopé.

André Raponda-Walker's *Les Plantes Utiles de Gabon* (Libreville-Paris, 1995) is this scholar's run-down on the different plants in Gabon and their properties.

Literature

Literature is one of the least advanced areas of the arts in Gabon. Compared to sculpture or music, the industry of Gabonese novels is very much in its infancy. Gabon's few seminal works, written in French, include Hubert Ndong Freddy's *Les Matitis* and

Laurent Owondo's *Au bout du silence*. Also of interest is André Raponda-Walker's *Contes Gabonais* (Paris, 1967), a collection of Gabonese fables. Gabon has never been a popular choice for foreign writers either. The vast majority of titles below do not relate exclusively, or even fleetingly, to Gabon. I've listed them because of their literary merit and related interest. More than one is on my to re-read list.

Chinua Achebe's *Things Fall Apart* (Heinemann, 1958) is set in a village in eastern Nigeria, but the tone and themes have a much wider resonance.

Caroline Alexander's *One Dry Season: In the Footsteps of Mary Kingsley* (Bloomsbury Publishing Ltd, 1989) tells of Alexander's determined and resourceful attempts to recreate Mary Kingsley's 1895 journey a century on.

Peter Biddlecombe's *French Lessons in West Africa* (Abacus, 2002) tells some tales of his extensive travels as a journalist in a number of West African countries. Gabon – or more accurately President Bongo's 'gold-plated Cadillac' – scrapes a cursory mention in the chapter on Benin.

Jan Brokken's *The Rainbird: A Central African Journey* (Lonely Planet Publications, 1997) is an entertaining and historically rich account of his travels through the jungles of Gabon, brought to life by anecdotes about the first explorers and missionaries, as well as the people he meets on the way.

Joseph Conrad's *Heart of Darkness* (London, 1902) paints a chilling portrait of the colonial white master, Mr Kurtz, who is driven to evil by a jungle 'so hopeless and so dark, so impenetrable to human thought, so pitiless to human weakness'.

Dian Fossey's *Gorillas in the Mist* (Boston, 1983) is part scientific report, part personal account of her remarkable thirteen-year study of four gorilla groups living in the Virunga mountains that span the former Zaire (DRC), Rwanda and Uganda. These mountain gorillas (*Gorilla gorilla beringei*) are a different subspecies to the lowland gorillas (*Gorilla gorilla gorilla*) found in Gabon, but Fossey's in-depth knowledge of gorilla behaviour makes it well worth the read.

Toby Green's *Meeting the Invisible Man* (Orion, 2001) is an engaging and fearless account of his travels looking for magic and mystery in West Africa.

Barbara Kingsolver's *The Poisonwood Bible* (Faber and Faber, 2000) is the compulsive story of an evangelical Baptist missionary and his family who head to the Belgian Congo (Zaire) in 1959.

Redmond O'Hanlon's *Congo Journey* (Hamish Hamilton, 1996) is hugely informative and at times side-splittingly funny. O'Hanlon's journey takes him from Brazzaville across the jungles of the Congo as far as fearsome Lake Télé, in search of the dinosaur spoken about by local pygmies. He travels like a 19th-century explorer (minus the prejudices), making extensive notes on everything, from his travelling companions to the power of fetishes. His unflagging curiosity and enthusiasm are inspirational.

Maps

There are two Gabon country maps that I know of. The first is a 1:1,000,000 Gabon map, with a 1:50,000 inset of Libreville, the work of IGN (136 bis rue de Grenelle, Paris, France). The second is a 1:980,000 map of Gabon and Equatorial Guinea produced by ITMB (www.itmb.com), but it is not available in Gabon. Both maps should be available to order through bookstores before you travel. The IGN map, as well as regional and city maps for Gabon, are also sold in Libreville (see under *Books and Maps* in *Chapter 6*).

São Tomé and Príncipe

Written material in the English language does not, to my knowledge, exist for São Tomé and Príncipe. Those who read French will find the following useful.

Lucienne Wilme's *São Tomé et Príncipe: balade sur deux jeunes iles du plus vieux continent* (ECOFAC, São Tomé, 2000) is a slim, paperback introduction to the country, primarily concerned with the islands' flora and fauna.

Dominique Gallet's *São Tomé et Príncipe: Les iles du milieu de monde* (Karthala, 2001) is a comprehensive portrayal of the islands' history and culture. There are some photographs and line drawings.

Patrice Christy and William V. Clarke's *Guide des oiseaux de São Tomé et Príncipe* (ECOFAC, São Tomé, 1998) has an introduction in French, English and Portuguese, and indexes of French, English and scientific names. The entries are in French only.

Michel Tournadie's *São Tomé et Príncipe* is a beautiful coffee-table book of photographs and snippets of information.

Travel magazines

Travel Africa magazine has consistently the best coverage of African destinations, with articles written by African specialists. *National Geographic Magazine* ran a series of pieces on Mike Fay's Megatransect (see page 33).

Travel guides

Le Gabon aujourd'hui (Jaguar, 2002) is a cross between a coffee-table book and a travel guide, with places covered alphabetically. It's written in French, and as far as I know has not been translated into English.

Websites

The web is not as yet a very reliable source for prospective travellers to Gabon or São Tomé and Príncipe. In theory these sites provide up-to-date general information:

Gabon

www.mbolo.com
www.assala.com

São Tomé

www.saotome.st

Index

Page numbers in bold indicate major entries, those in italics indicate maps.